Printed in the United States of America,

Author and Editor: Richard Harteis

Cover Art: "Dyavolski most" (Devil's Bridge) Mark Patnode

Cover Design: Suzanne Shelden (SheldenStudios.com)

Consultant work: www.WilliamMeredithFoundation.org

Bulk Discounts available: www.Poets-Choice.com

ISBN978-0-9909257-3-6

Poets's Choice Publishing
337 Kitemaug Road
Uncasville, Ct. 06382

WWW.POETS-CHOICE.COM
marathonfilm@gmail.com

Welcome address by H.E. Elena Poptodorova,
Ambassador of the Republic of Bulgaria to the United States of America
On the occasion of the Bridge of Light art exhibit

Slater Memorial Museum, June 21, 2015

Ladies and gentlemen,
Dear guests,

I am delighted to welcome you to the opening ceremony of a spectacular art showcase that, true to its title, creates a brilliant "bridge of light" connecting two nations' rich and distinct cultures. This one-of-a-kind exhibit displays nearly one hundred works from both American and Bulgarian artists. The cultural collaboration between these nations demonstrates that the power and beauty of art truly has the ability to transcend oceans. It is with sincere regret that I am not able to be in attendance to share this experience with you in person.

I would like to extend great thanks to the Slater Memorial Museum for hosting this ceremony and for displaying this exhibit for the next two months. The artists featured in this collection are part of an artistic exchange between the Griffis Arts Center here in Connecticut and the Orpheus Foundation in the Rhodope Mountains of Bulgaria, a partnership that has been in effect since 2002. I want to convey my support and appreciation for this strong and flourishing relationship that allows American and Bulgarian artists to be immersed in each other's vibrant and vivid cultures.

Also, I must express gratitude to the late William Meredith, without whom, this exhibit may not have been possible. His adoration and appreciation for art lives on today through his loved ones and through the William Meredith Foundation, which strives to honor his legacy of generosity and devotion to the arts.

During Meredith's time as United States Poet Laureate in the late 1970s, Bulgaria was still a communist nation experiencing heavy influence from its Soviet neighbor. Despite geographic and sociopolitical barriers, Meredith forged a camaraderie between the United States and Bulgaria through the exchange of art and literature. He supported the artistic renaissance that was occurring in my country at that time and actively advocated human rights and free artistic expression. For these reasons, in 1996, Meredith was granted honorary Bulgarian citizenship by the first democratically-elected president, Zhelyo Zhelev. It is because of Meredith's initiative to establish a friendly American-Bulgarian cultural exchange that this exhibit is here today.

The various styles in this showcase not only offer beauty and inspiration to audiences, but also an opportunity to learn about the history and culture of another nation. Timeless art, such as these pieces, reminds us that all humans—no matter what race, religion, or ethnicity—are connected by fundamental emotions such as joy, pain, fear, and hope. In today's increasingly radicalized world, it is important to promote acceptance and cooperation by focusing on such commonalities rather than differences, something that Meredith so wisely encouraged decades ago.

This afternoon you will find much to observe, including a concert honoring Meredith's poetry and the launching of the 2015 William Meredith Award for Poetry. Thank you for coming and expressing your interest and support for this unique transatlantic artistic partnership. I hope you enjoy!

Elena Poptodorova

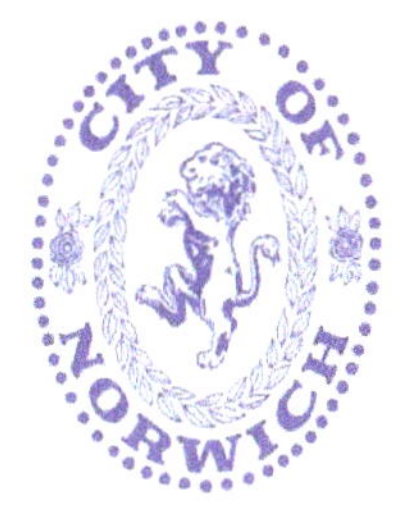

Office of the Mayor

Deberey A. Hinchey

June 21, 2015

Good Afternoon,

On behalf of the City of Norwich, I welcome you all to the Bridge of Light, Artistic Illumination from the Balkans exhibit here at our most wonderful museum, the Slater Museum. You will be part of a history making exhibit, witnessing the creativity of 100 works of art by Bulgarian and American artists.

Our world experiences so many disparities and conflicts, but through the medium of art, culture, creativity and dedication we flourish. We can stand together, listening and seeing in person, the binding foundation of art that is strengthening our commitment to each other. We each can feel the vibrancy and meaning to a piece of art in our own way. We come together in unison in recognizing the significance of the talent and the story of art.

You will experience these artists in a variety of venues. The music, poetry and awards tonight will demonstrate the lifelong passion of William Meredith to promote art and literature. His mission was one of equality, acceptance and his voice remains in the forefront of tonight's gathering. You will be part of the "Light" that will go forward to bring out this message of peace, honor, human rights and artistic expression.

It is with much regret that I am not able to be with you this afternoon. My thoughts are with you and I look forward to seeing the exhibit. Thank you to the William Meredith Foundation, the American and Bulgarian artists and all the individuals responsible for bringing this important world exhibit to Norwich. I am deeply honored.

Warm regards,

Deberey Hinchey

Mayor Deberey Hinchey
City of Norwich

City of Norwich Mayor's Office
100 Broadway, Room 330 • Norwich, CT 06360
Phone: (860) 823-3743 • Cell (860) 334-2549 • Fax: (860) 885-2914
dhinchey@cityofnorwich.org • www.norwichct.org

TABLE OF CONTENTS

140 Debi Pendell
145 Brian Stephens
149 Anne Seelbach
151 Catherine Doocy
154 Pola Ester
156 Ariel Mitchell
158 Brad Guarino
161 Ted Efremoff
163 Christopher Zhang
167 Greg Bowerman
169 Xingxin Zhang
170 Nancy Frankel

176 Sharon Griffis

188 Richard Harteis

190 William Meredith

By Janet Gezari

BRIDGE OF LIGHT

By Richard Harteis

Artistic Illumination from the Balkans

In the east is it said, "between one person and another, there is only light." BRIDGE OF LIGHT: Artistic Illumination from the Balkans traces the important artistic connection between the United States and Bulgaria William Meredith first established decades ago when he served as US Poet Laureate. This bridge has become an important part of his legacy as a teacher, poet and friend to artists. But the bridge continues as a vital cultural institution into the present and beyond. The luminescence which developed among Bulgarian artists and American colleagues continues to radiate years later in the many exchange residencies between the Griffis Arts Center in New London, and the Orpheus Foundation in Sofia, the many art exhibitions in both countries, from Seattle to Washington, from Sofia to Moscow as well as the numerous original publications and translations that have come to light over the years by Bulgarian and American writers.

BRIDGE OF LIGHT includes nearly 100 works of art by Bulgarian and American artists who have shared their talent over three decades in this retrospective at the Slater Memorial Museum in Norwich Connecticut. During the two-month long exhibit (June 21, 2015 – August 28, 2015), the Meredith Foundation will launch the 2015 William Meredith Award for Poetry given posthumously to Andrew Oerke, a poet who published in Bulgaria and traveled the country extensively with his wife and fellow writer, Anitra Thorhaug. As with other Meredith Awards, the publication of Oreke's book, THE WALL is made possible in part by the generous support of John and Lorraine Hracyk. Lorraine is an alumna of the Norwich Free Academy (class of '67) and their cousin, Kristie Leonard is the Director of the library, yet another dimension to the "family affair" nature of this exhibition.

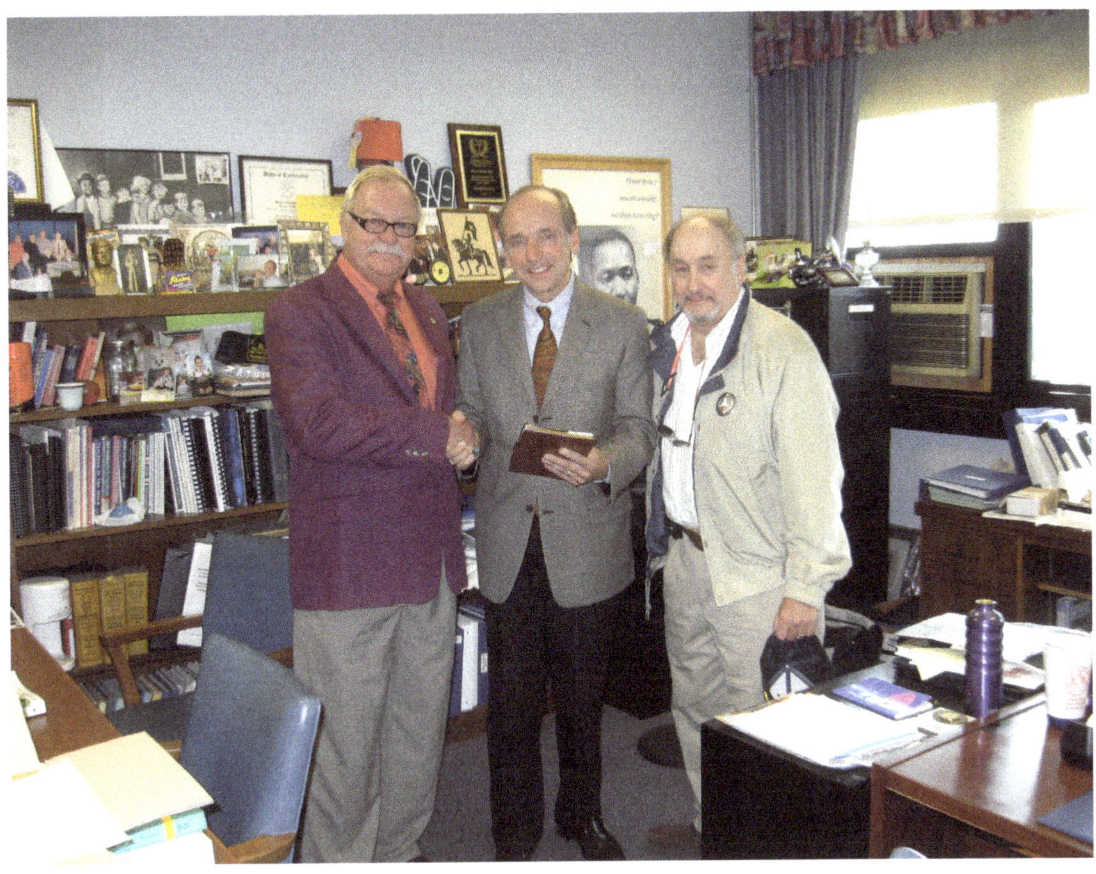

(Richard Harteis and Board Member, John Hracyk present student copies of the Mystic Seaport publication of Meredith's WRECK OF THE THRESHER to Donald Macrino, at that time Principal of the Waterford High School.)

BRIDGE OF LIGHT enables us to take stock of the important work that has been created over the years and serves as a fitting tribute to our beloved famous local son, William Meredith and the many friends who have crossed the bridge he first established between our two countries both coming and going. After his death in 2007 friends came together to establish a foundation to continue his legacy through educational and artistic programs such as this exhibition:

WWW.WilliamMeredithFoundation.org

First Lady Hillary Rodham Clinton wrote a letter joining Connecticut College in a celebration of William's 80th birthday in which she says, "The arts have always been a unifying force in our world, bringing people together across vast cultural, social, economic and geographical divisions. Through his work, William Meredith both enhances and strengthens the American spirit. As you honor Mr. Meredith, you celebrate the timeless power of poetry and poets as our American memory, our purveyors of insight and culture, and express the very heart of what connects us, plagues us, and makes us fully human."

The first point of light for this bridge ignited in the late 1970's when William Meredith took a sabbatical from his 35-year teaching career at Connecticut College to take up his post at the Library of Congress. In Washington, an ardent cultural attaché from the Bulgarian Embassy, Krassin Himmirski lobbied on behalf of Bulgarian artists and the renaissance that was occurring in his country at the time. Meredith was impressed with the poetry and invited five poets to visit the US and read their work at different venues around the country such as Berkeley and the Iowa Writer's workshop.

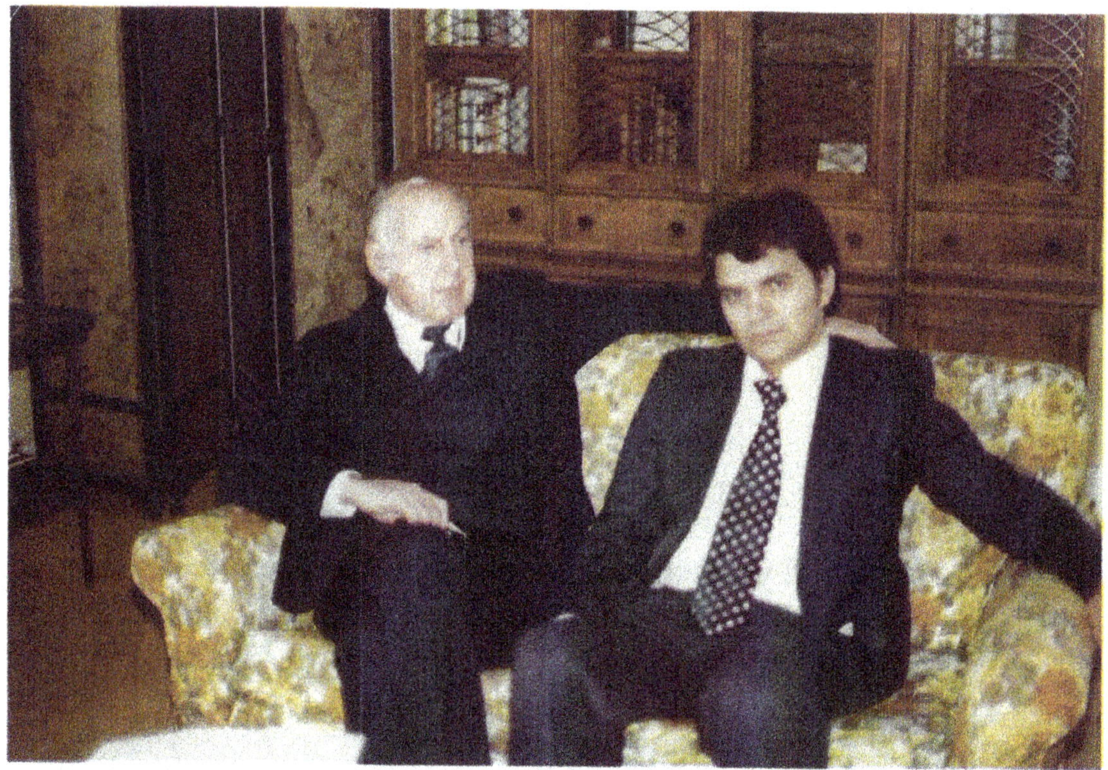

Krassin Himmirski, First Bulgarian contact when William served as US Poet Laureate at the Library of Congress, 1980

Lyubomir Levchev was among the visitors and the two men struck up a friendship that lasted a lifetime.

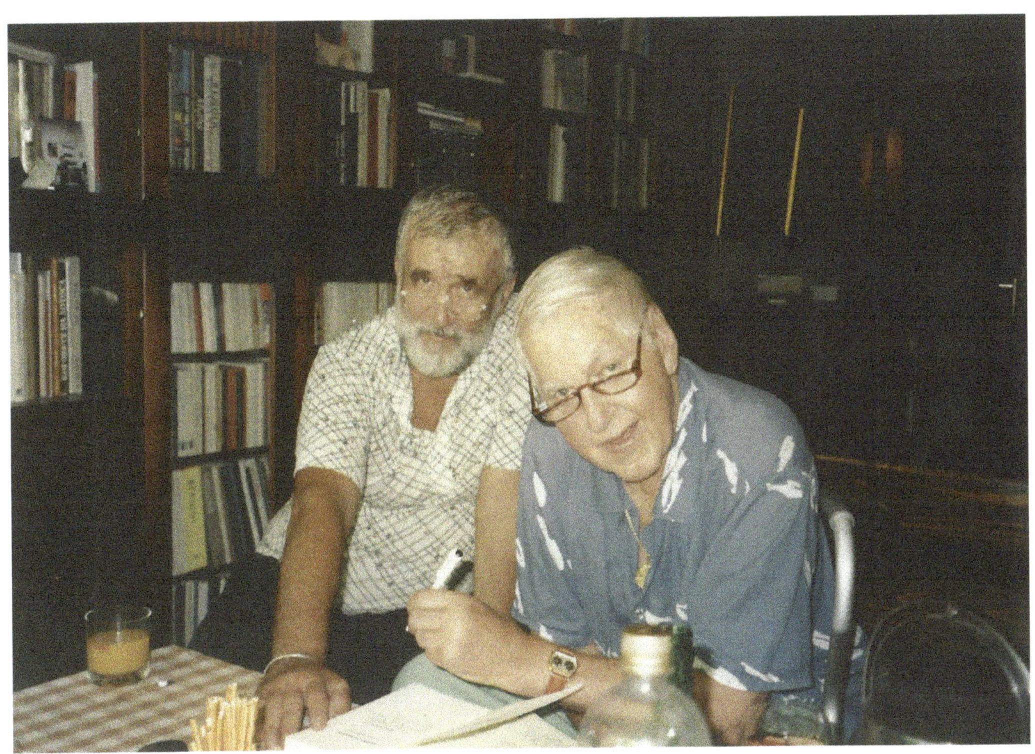

Lyubomir Levchev and William Meredith at Lyubo's home in Sofia

The Bulgarians were grateful for this window into American life and the prospect of English language publication. At the time, Levchev was a highly regarded national poet, serving as First Deputy Minister of Culture. And like the Minister of Culture, Ludmilla Zhivkova to whom he introduced Meredith, Lyubomir Levchev encouraged glasnost through international writers meetings and the celebration of Bulgaria's 1400-year history as a nation.

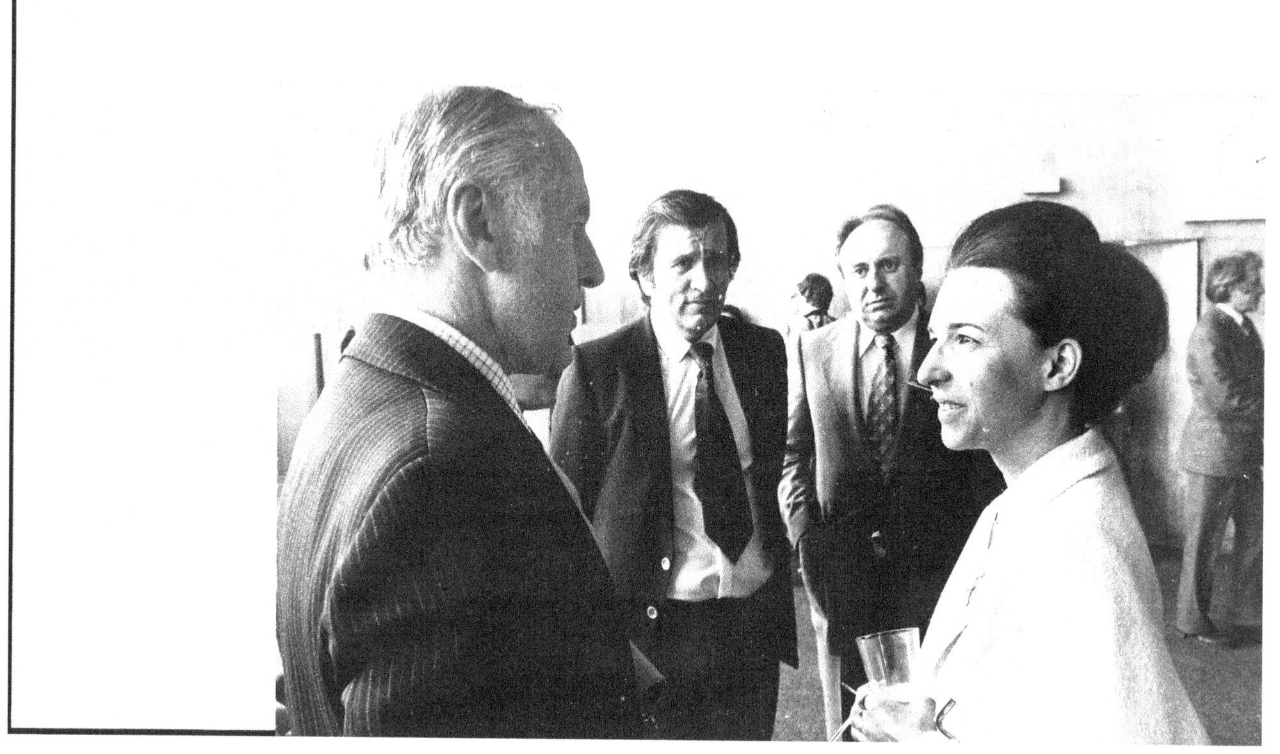

(William Meredith meets Lyudmilla Zhivkova, Minister of Culture in the early 1980's)

Meredith was routinely invited to these conferences as were John Cheever, Erskin Caldwell, Kurt Vonnegut, Maxine Kumin, and John Balaban among others. Bulgaria was firmly in the Russian camp under the dictatorship of Todor Zhivkov, but for better or worse, the American delegation defended democratic values against Cuban, Iranian, and Serbian rhetoric in heated and open discourse.

"You're all being duped," Robert Penn Warren's wife, Eleanor Clark proclaimed one spring at the Academy in New York – travel behind the iron curtain during the cold war wasn't universally appreciated among fellow writers. But, William felt that if poets couldn't have a dialog across political and cultural barriers, there seemed to be little hope for any understanding among peoples. At one point Bulgaria was engaged in a kind of ethnic cleansing whereby Muslims were forced to take Bulgarian names and were forbidden to dress in their native garb. William and I were able to speak out in support of human rights and artistic freedom for minorities and dissidents during our travels. In 1989, I carried a list of more than a hundred artists who had signed a letter to parliament "resigning" from the culture to our Ambassador Sol Polansky.

"Aren't you afraid to be seen with us," I asked the poet Blaga Dimitrova who had given me the letter and who later became the first Vice President of Bulgaria after "the change." "My husband has been interrogated for twelve hours now. They know where I live, they know what I think. We've had enough." And like the earlier political movement in Prague that spring, the courage of these artists eventually helped bring down the Communist government.

Years later, in 1996, after a Fulbright year at the American University in Blagoevgrad William and I were accorded citizenship by the Bulgarian Parliament and Bulgaria's first democratically-elected president, Zhelu Zhelev. Sadly, the father of his country died the very day we announced the 2015 William Meredith Award for Poetry at the Bulgarian embassy on January 30.

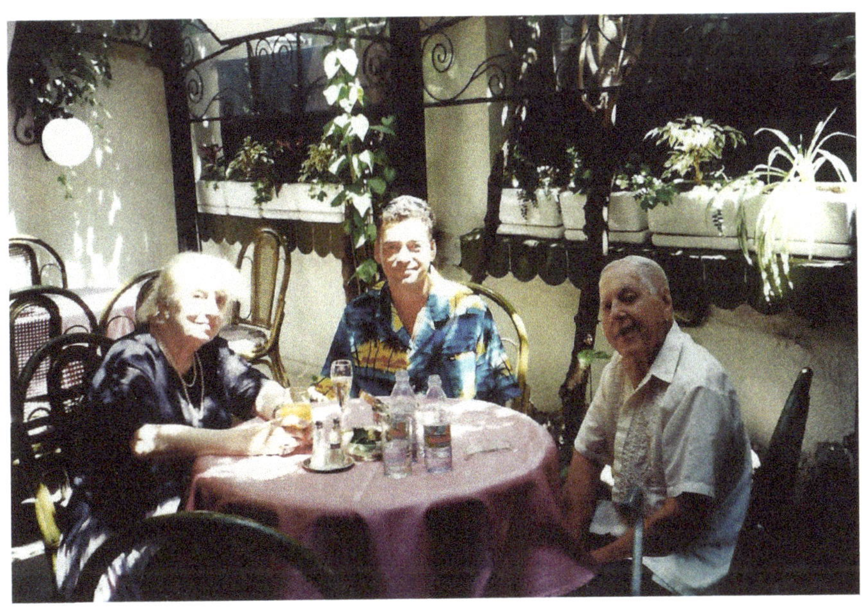

Poet Blaga Dimitrova, Nick Prodanov, and William after the change

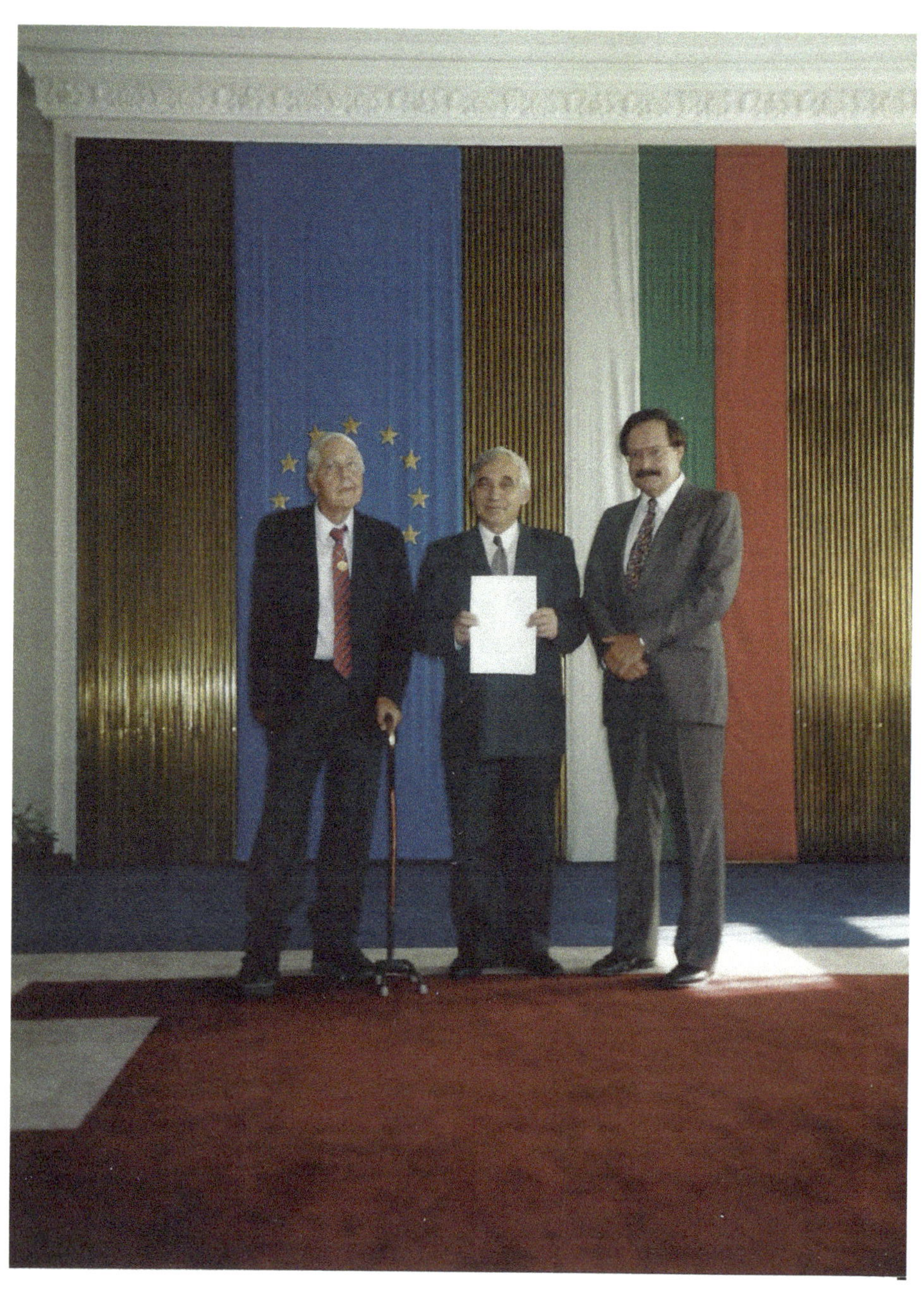

William Meredith, President Zhelu Zhelev,
and Richard Harteis presented citizenship, 1996

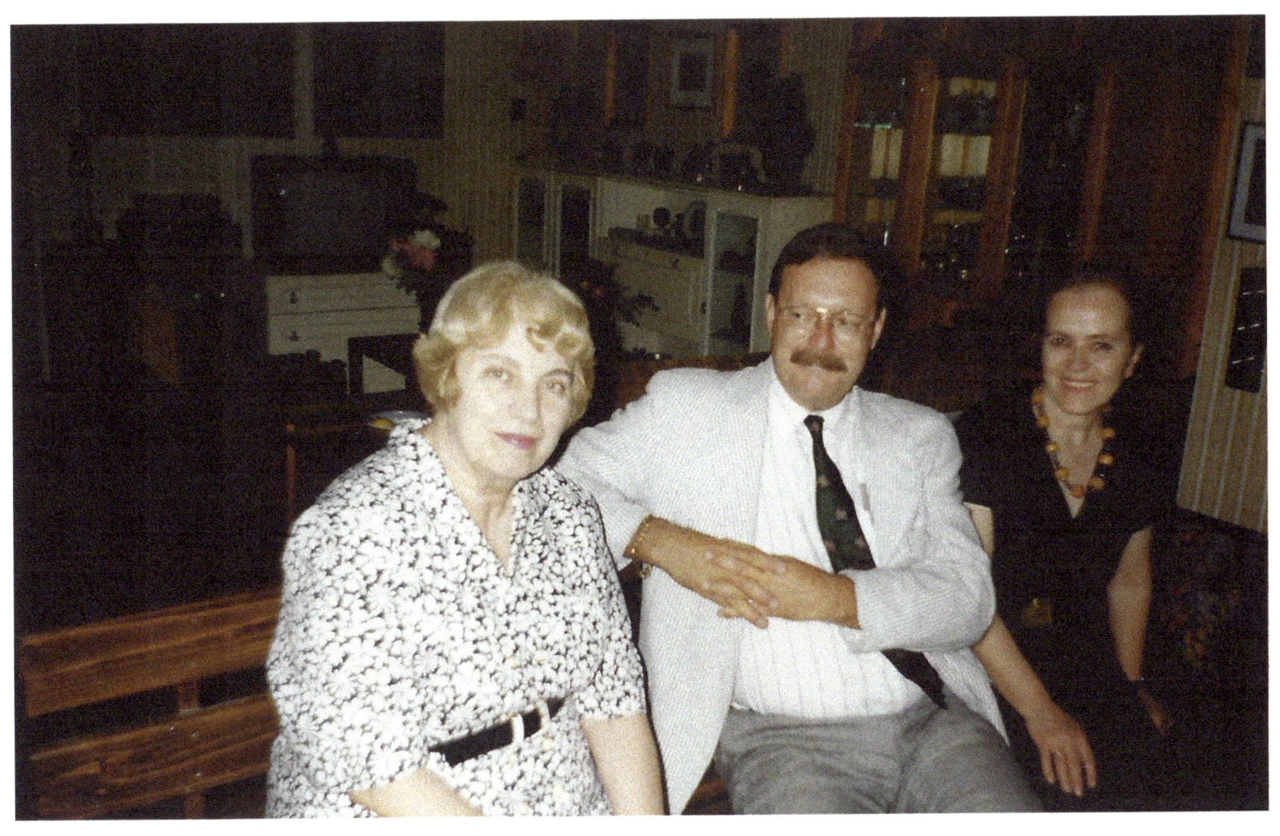

Blaga Dimitrova in Sofia with Dora Boneva
at home of Lyubomir Levchev

During the early days of our travel to Bulgaria, we were introduced to the master painter, Stoimen Stoilov. When his studio mysteriously burned down, he was permitted to use an old factory which became a center of lithographers in Varna, the "Atelier Vulcan." As official guests, we were invariably presented with gifts by the artists – a kind of barter used to pay the government rent, I gathered. But Stoimen and his remarkable sister and daughter, both fine artists in their own right became like family to me and William. Their generosity knows no bounds, and the gift of their art has graced the walls at Meredith Center as well as numerous book covers, illustrations, and broadsides.

One important project relied on the Disabled American Veterans and Dominion Power who commissioned a series of etchings "illustrating" the poem by Meredith memorializing the loss of 128 lives in the sinking of the nuclear submarine, SS Thresher in 1963. The poem and etching were sent to all surviving families of that disaster.

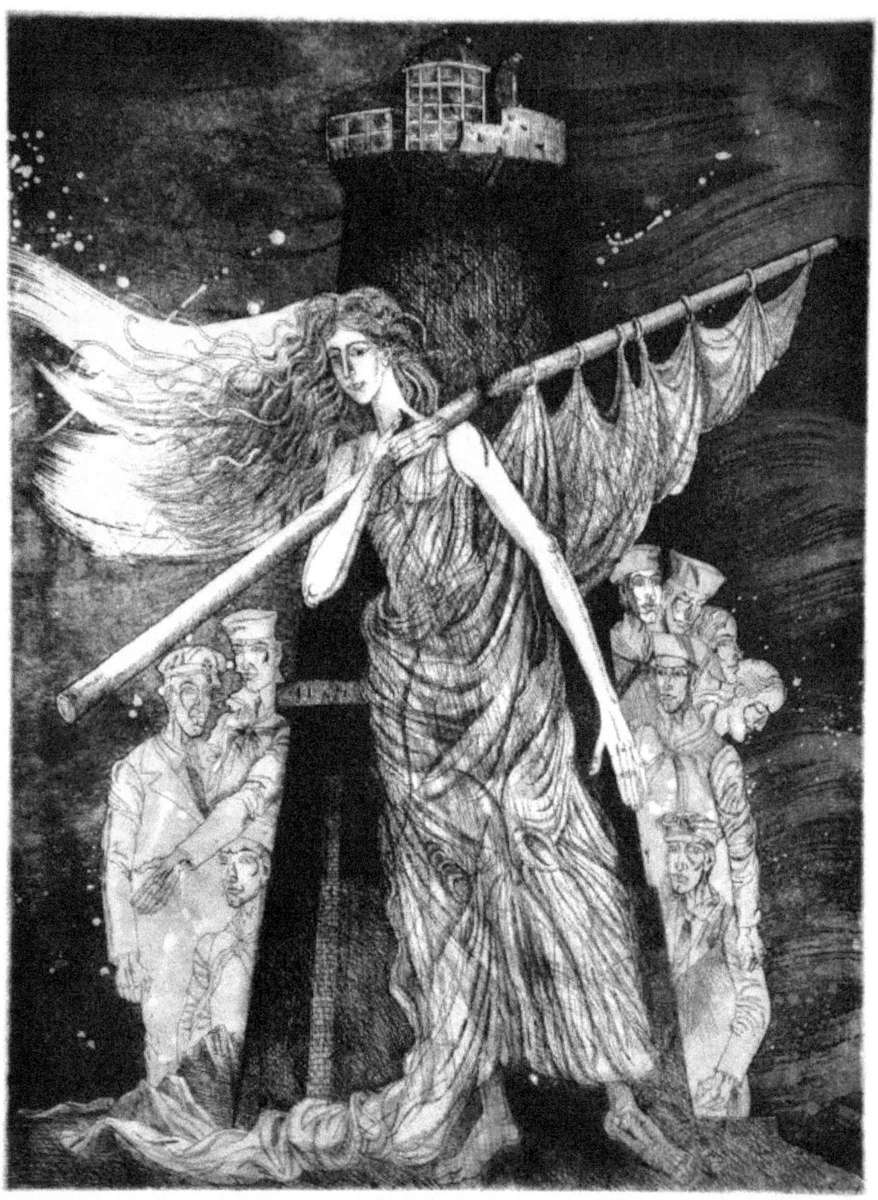

Stoimen Stoilov etching, "Sea Guardian"

On November 29, 2014 this project expanded into a permanent memorial for City Hall in New London for the brave sailors, many of whom came from our community. The following photo shows the New London High School Navy Junior Reserve Officer Training Corps Color Guard as it posts the colors during the Pledge of Allegiance at the start of the dedication ceremony:

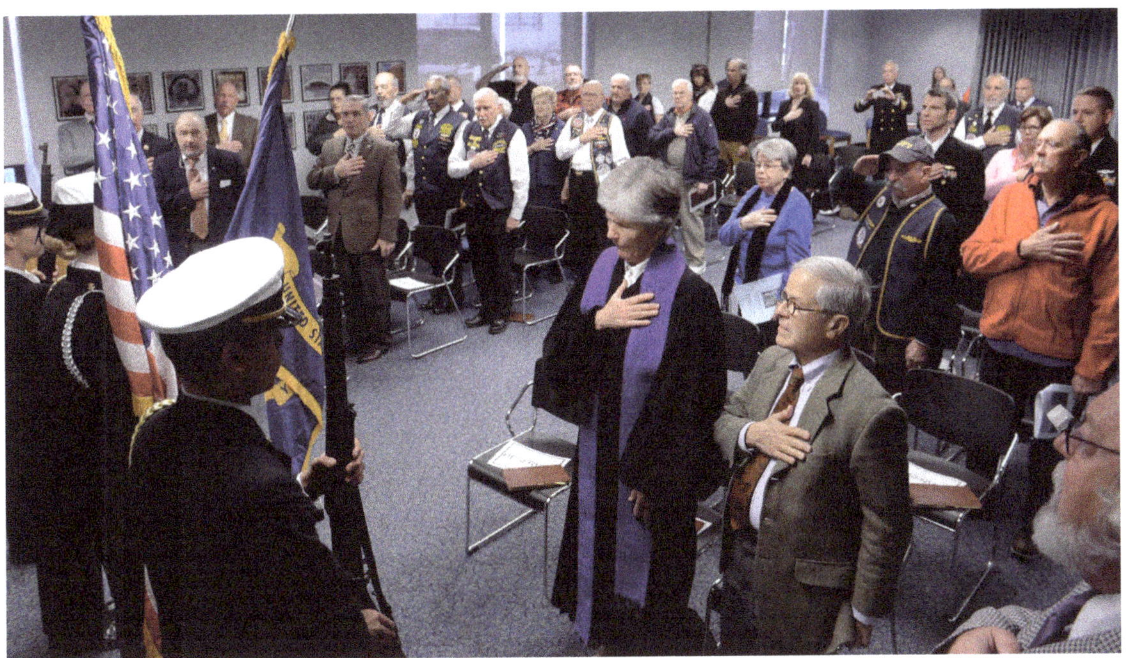

PHOTO CREDIT: TIM COOK/THE DAY

Another group of zany and talented artist friends became known as "The River People." One hot summer afternoon after too much rakia, trout, and white wine, I suggested that we all go home and shape up for the dinner to which the President of the American University had invited us. I opened our door at 6:00 and Lydia Assenova, Boiko Dimitrov, Niki Marinov and Lucien Dimitrov staggered into the living room as though they had just survived a plane crash. Instead of going home to rest and shower, they had gone to the river, put their feet into the water and continued drinking. "Golden days, in the sunshine of our flowered youth," or some such romantic palaver. But these guys had a talent for more than painting and sculpture.

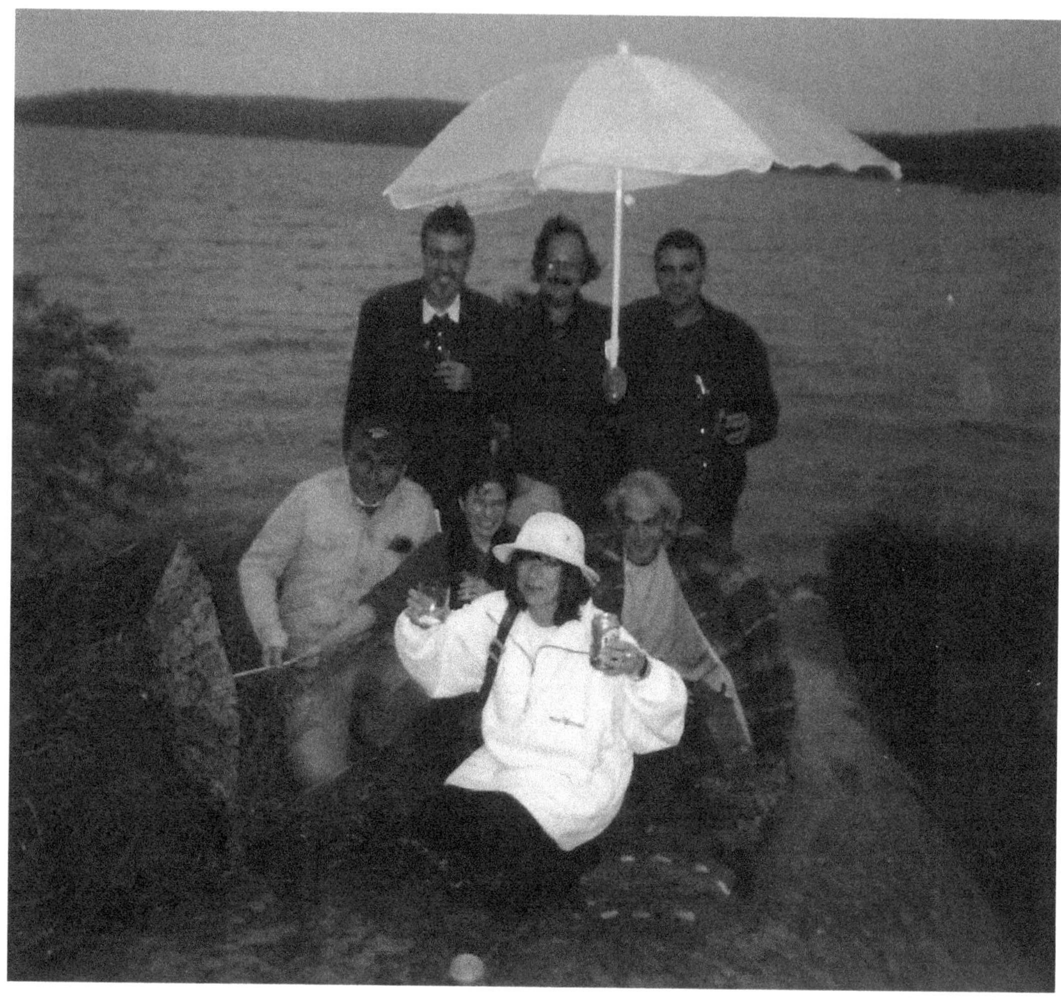

(River people visit the River Thames in Uncasville: Lucien Dimitrov, Richard, Boiko Dimitrov, Marta Levcheva, Lydia Assenova, Niki Marinov)

In 2000, I was very pleased to invite them, as well as Bulgaria's Vice President Todor Kalvadjiev and his entourage to come to the US for an exhibition at the Lyman Allyn Museum and another at the Alexy Von Schlippe Gallery at the University of Connecticut. Et la fete continue, as the expression goes.

Dora Boneva, the wife of Lyubomir Levchev is a dignified and beautiful artist of a different sort. Dora paints portraits with astute psychological insight as well as impressionist landscapes of the highest quality. Classically trained as with artist friends such as Christo, she is an artist of great sophistication and world experience who speaks both French and English and has traveled widely. She seemed ideal to be selected as one of the first Bulgarian fellows at the Griffis Arts Center. She came to us on her own, and that summer William and I invited her to Block Island for a week of plain air painting. The following year, Lyubomir was able to visit and became friends with Niles and Pamela Bond who translated a series of poems he wrote on New London. The community was quite taken with Lyubo, the ultimate diplomat and during this period he and Hughes Griffis began planning the exchange program for American artists to visit Bulgaria.

This international residency program is unique for the loving care Sharon Griffis affords the visitors. As director, she provides cultural activities, exhibitions, intimate, stylish receptions to introduce the guests to the community as well as housing in the beautiful Victorian complex which serves as the center for her program. Board member Hughes Griffis commented once that he, "just writes the checks," but despite his modesty, he clearly takes an interest in the selection of the visiting artists and travels frequently to Bulgaria to meet with his Doppelgänger, Luybomir Levchev. There in the mountain village of Pokolvnik Serafimavo in the Rhodope Mountains near the Greek border, the Orpheus Foundation welcomes American artists at Sharon House, a residence for exchange fellows from the American side of the "bridge of light."

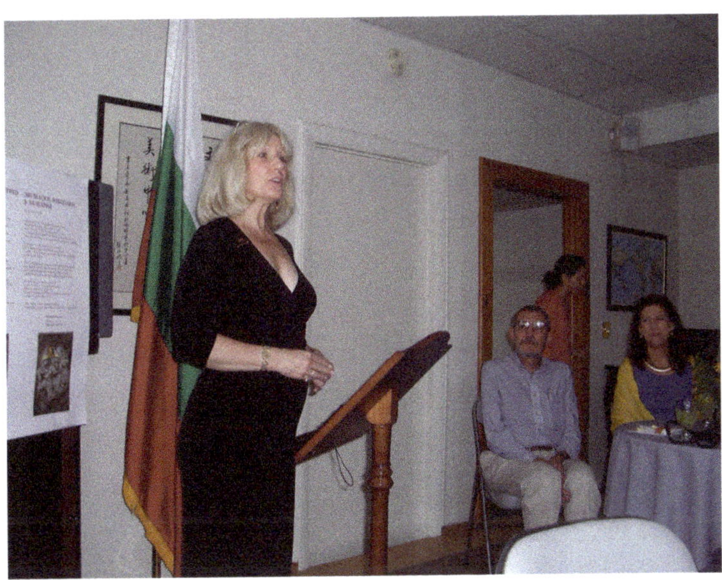

Sharon Griffis greets Ivo Hadhimishev at the Griffis Center

One of the invited artists, Mark Patnode has painted the famous "Dyavolski most" (Devil's Bridge) as a figurative souvenir which serves as the cover of this catalog. Here is another example of his work from his visit to Bulgaria. The back cover has an image of setting up his easel in the mountains to begin his work.

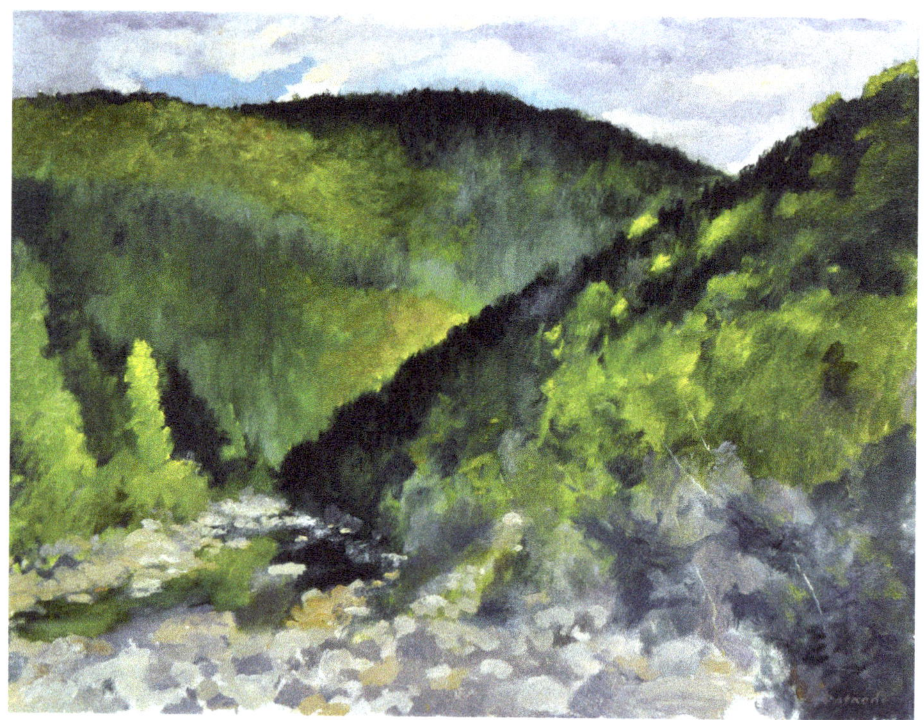

Some of the artists included in the exhibition I know well. Others, I have not yet met. For me, the exhibition has become something like a Whitman Sampler of the many different styles and artistic personalities represented (In the immortal words of Forrest Gump, "life is like a box of chocolates.") - When we were kids, my sister used to turn over the chocolates and stick her finger into the bottom of the candy to see if it was one she wanted. If not, she put it back in the box. But I'm pretty sure you won't find anything here that needs to be put back in the box.

I would like this exhibition to express my great gratitude that I have been able to share in the spirit-sustaining enterprise of art and the chance to get to know so many wonderful artists in my life, especially as a fellow Bulgarian. Moi skuppi saotechestvenitsi, (My dear countrymen) is how I address groups sometimes when I go to Bulgaria. What a gift the universe has given me to be involved this way. And in particular, what a gift the Slater Memorial Museum has given me to have had a hand in sharing these beautiful works.

Perhaps the last word is best given by William Meredith himself in his reflection on time and the artistic process found in his poem, "Two Masks Unearthed in Bulgaria" Here is a photo of the poet Kolyo Sevov in 1984 to whom the poem is dedicated.

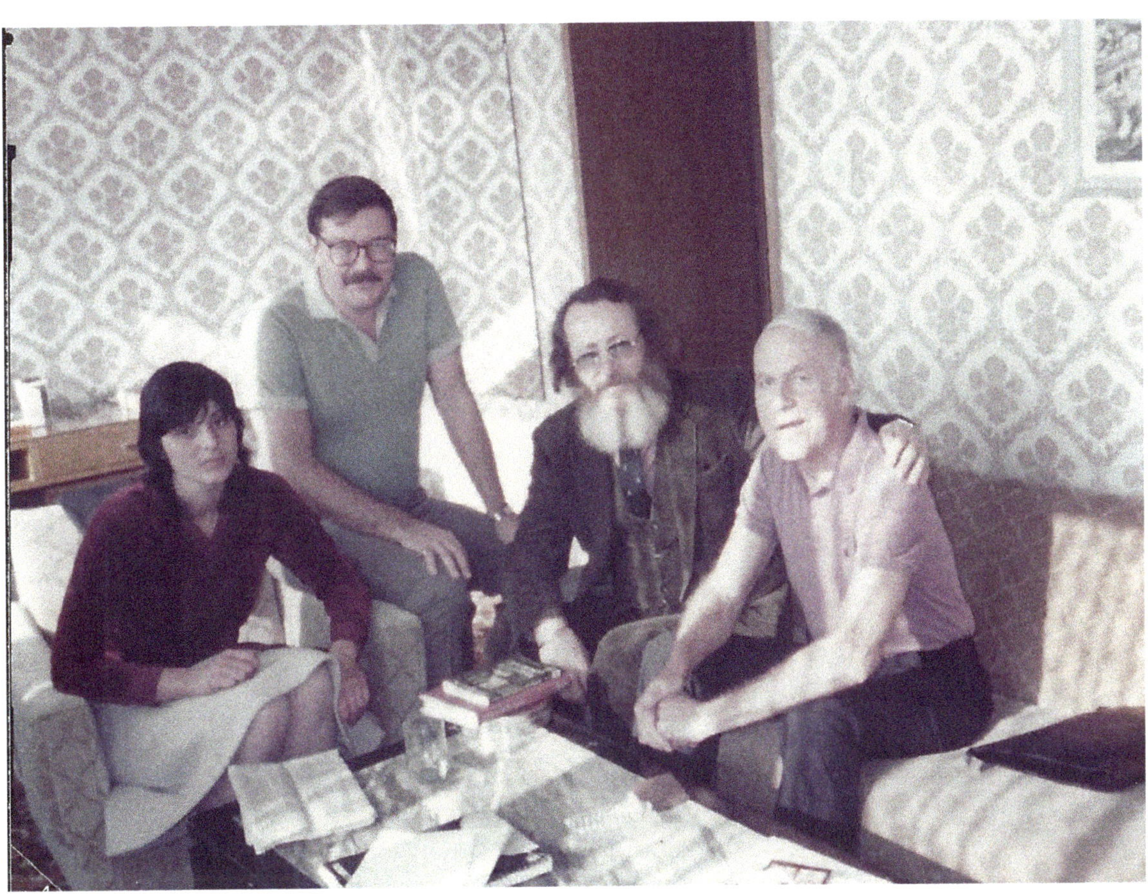

Two Masks Unearthed in Bulgaria":

by William Meredith
For Kolyo Sevov

When God was learning to draw the human face
I think he may have made a few like these
that now look up at us through museum glass
a few miles north of where they slept
for six thousand years, a necropolis near Varna.
With golden staves and ornaments around them
they lay among human bodies but had none.
Gods themselves, or soldiers lost abroad—
we don't know who they are.
The gold buttons which are their curious eyes,
the old clay which is their wrinkled skin,
seem to have been worked by the same free hand
that drew Adam for the Jews about that time.
It is moving, that the eyes are still questioning
and no sadder than they are, time being what it is—
as though they saw nothing tragic in the faces
looking down through glass into theirs.
Only clay and gold, they seem to say, passing
through one condition on its way to the next.

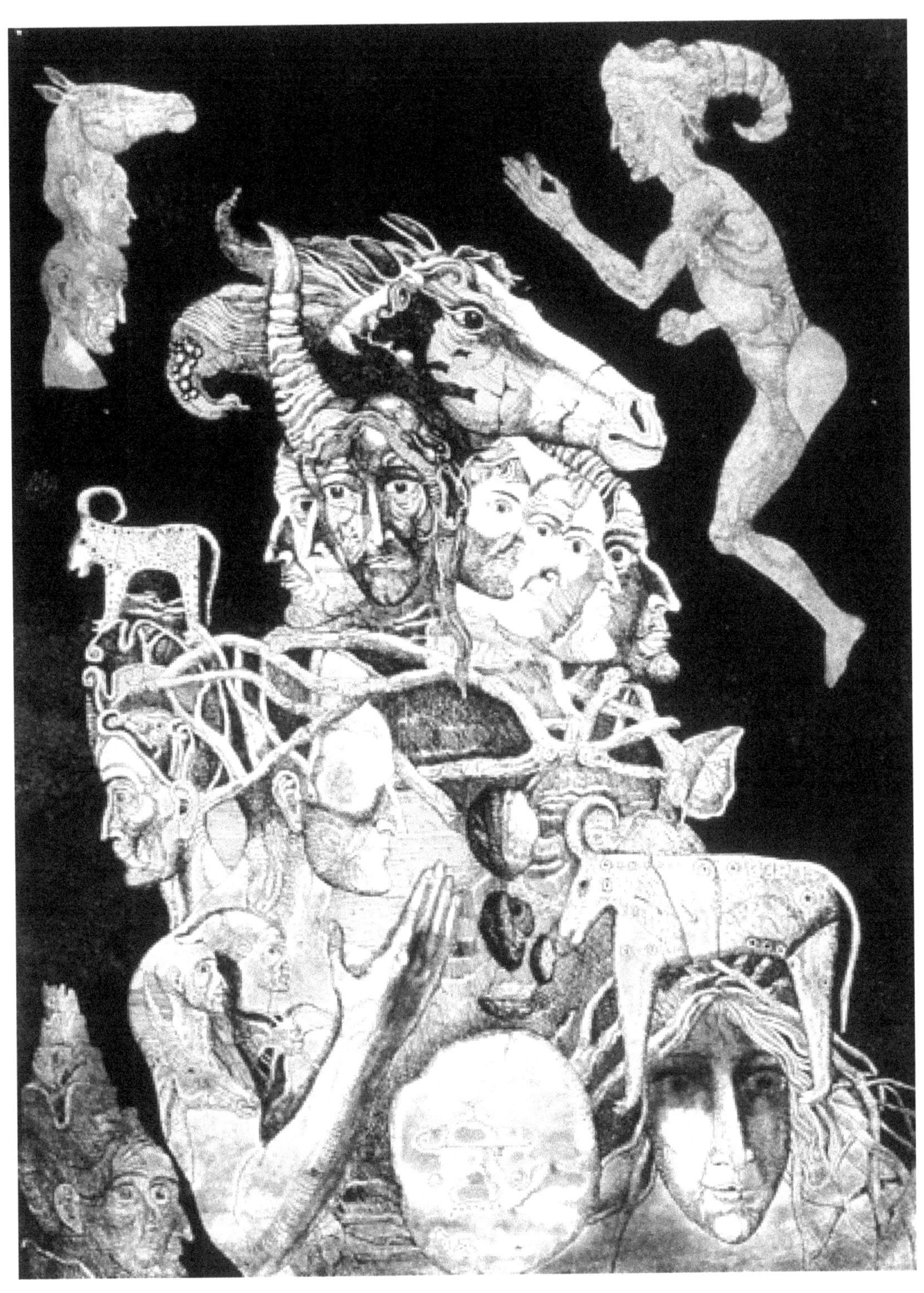

Etching by Stoimen Stoilov for
"Two Masks Unearthed in Bulgaria"

ДВЕ МАСКИ, ИЗКОПАНИ В БЪЛГАРИЯ

На Кольо Севов

Когато се е учил да рисува човешкото лице,
Бог може би създал е няколко от тези,
които сега ни гледат през музейното стъкло,
на две-три мили северно от мястото, където са спали
шест хиляди години – в един некропол недалеч от
Варна.
С обкови златни, покрити с орнаменти,
те са лежали сред тела човешки, самите – без тела.
Самите – божества или пък воини, загубени в чужбина,
кои са те, не знаем.

Тези златни копчета, които са любознателните им очи,
тази древна глина, която е сбръчканата тяхна кожа,
са сътворени може би от същата свободна длан,
нарисувала Адам за евреите приблизително тогава.
Вълнуващо е, че очите още питат
и не са по-тъжни, отколкото изглеждат, предвид стихията
на времето –
сякаш не са видели нищо трагично във лицата,
гледащи ги през стъклото.
Само глина и злато, сякаш казват те,
минаващи през едно състояние на път към следващото.

MEET THE ARTISTS: EAST

Stoimen Stoilov

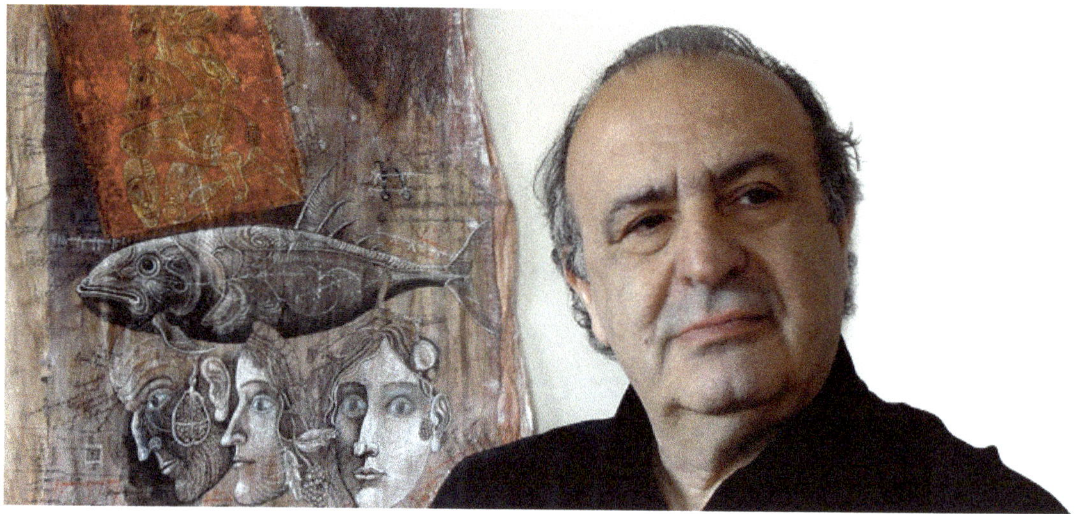

Stoimen Stoilov is recognized as a master painter in Bulgaria and a world-class artist. I wish to give him special attention in this catalog not only for his rank in the world of art, but because he and his family have been such loyal and generous friends over the decades.

William Meredith and I met Stoimen initially in Varna, on the Black Sea. He and his wife and daughter entertained us in the Atelier Vulcan, the studio he established which later grew to such fame for the biennial exhibition this took place at the museum. The reception we were given was very warm and the gifts of his art were generous. Both have continued now for decades.

Stoimen took his wife to Vienna for medical treatment and after she died, he stayed on in Austria where the government has recently awarded him the honorary title of Professor. At one point, he created a phantasmorgic map of the metro system which was found at all the stops along the line in Vienna. At the end of red line, a man with wings carrying books on his back flew down to me and William. Stoimen put us there among Freud, Marx, Klimt, Frans Joseph and other denizens of the capital because it was the line to the airport where he went so often to meet our plane when we arrived to visit him.

Throughout his career, he was always ready to provide art for the publication projects we took on including etchings for the SS Thresher memorial mentioned in the introduction. In 2000, the Lyman Allyn Museum mounted a show of his work, and the heroic canvases were stretched in the museum itself. One of the works, Orpheus, taking its inspiration from Thracian legend can be seen in the Bridge of Light exhibition.

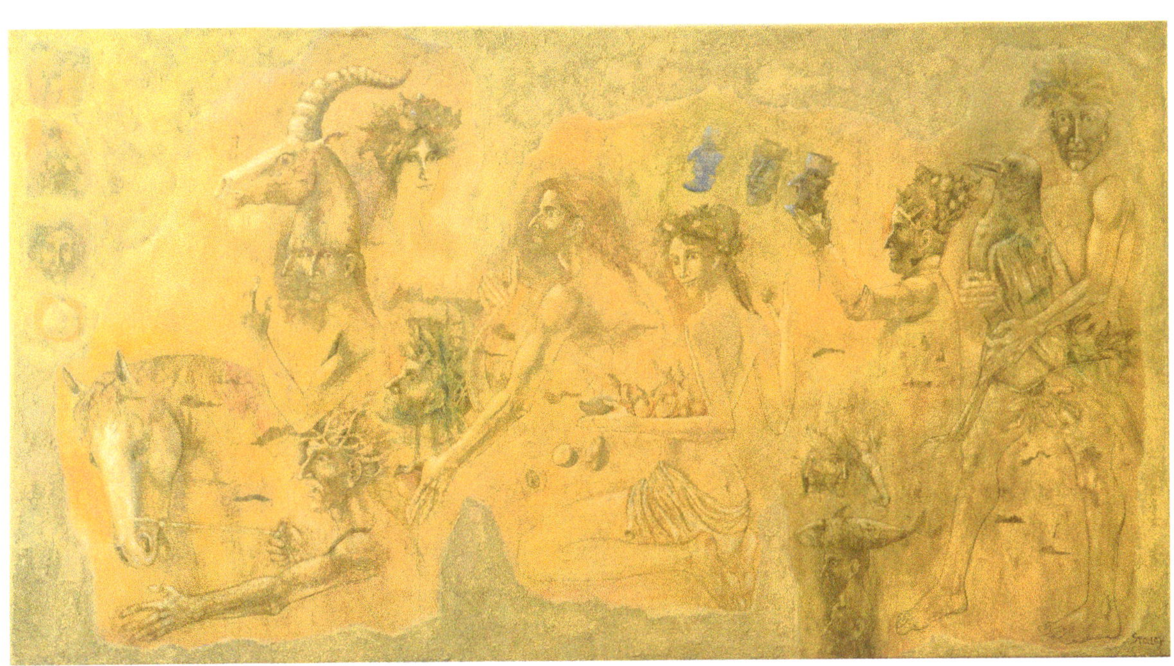

photo: Vincent Scarano

Orpheus, oil on canvas 2.5 x4 meters

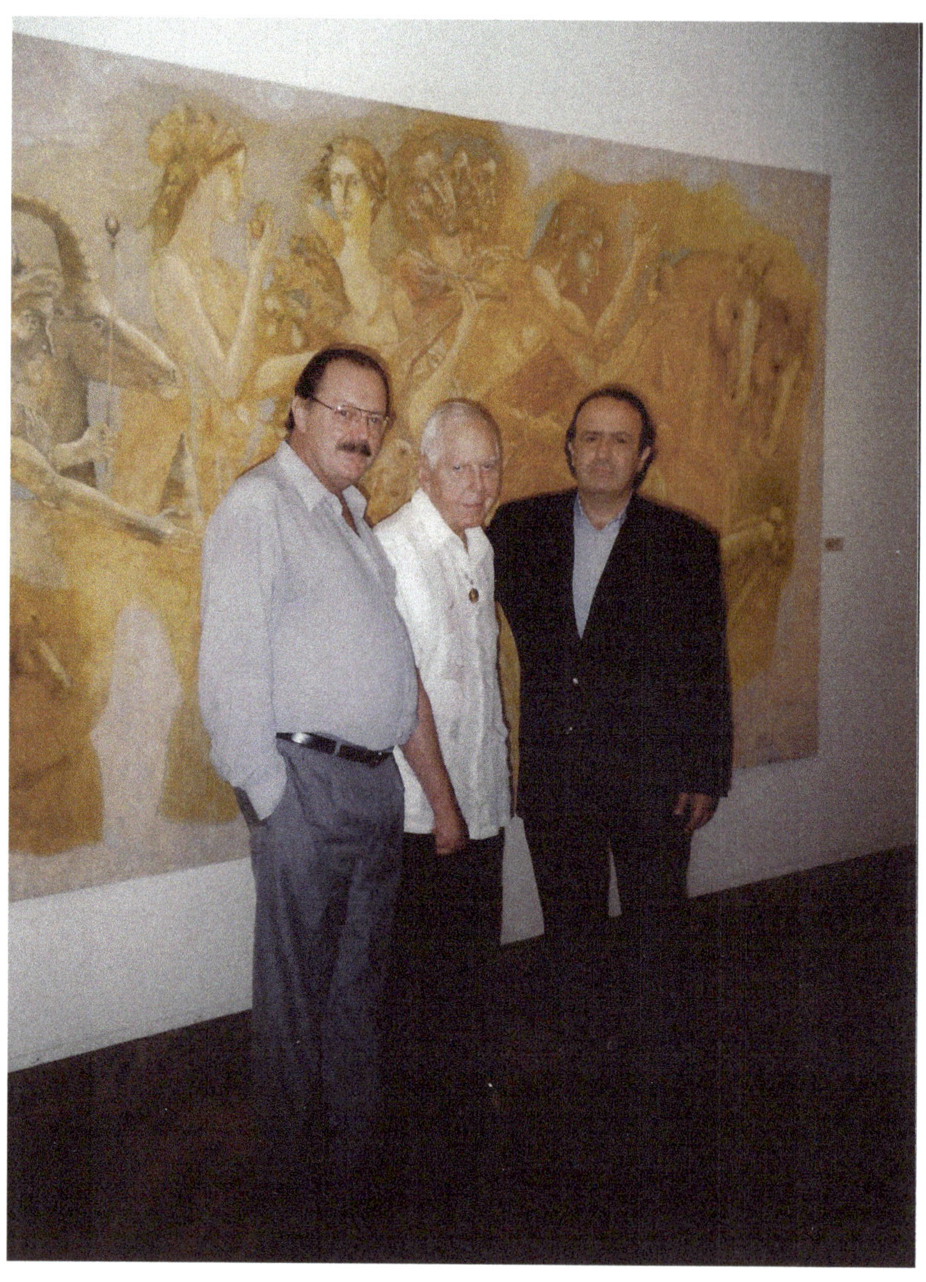

(Richard Harteis, William Meredith and Stoimen Stoilov at the Lyman Allyn Museum. This canvas later found a home with a collector in Switzerland.

Rick Koster of the New London Day wrote a review of Stoimen's exhibition at the Lyman Allyn which is included here as well as an appreciation of Stoimen's work I wrote when I taught at the American University in Blagoevgrad. Here are several more images of Stomen's work which are not included in the exhibition.

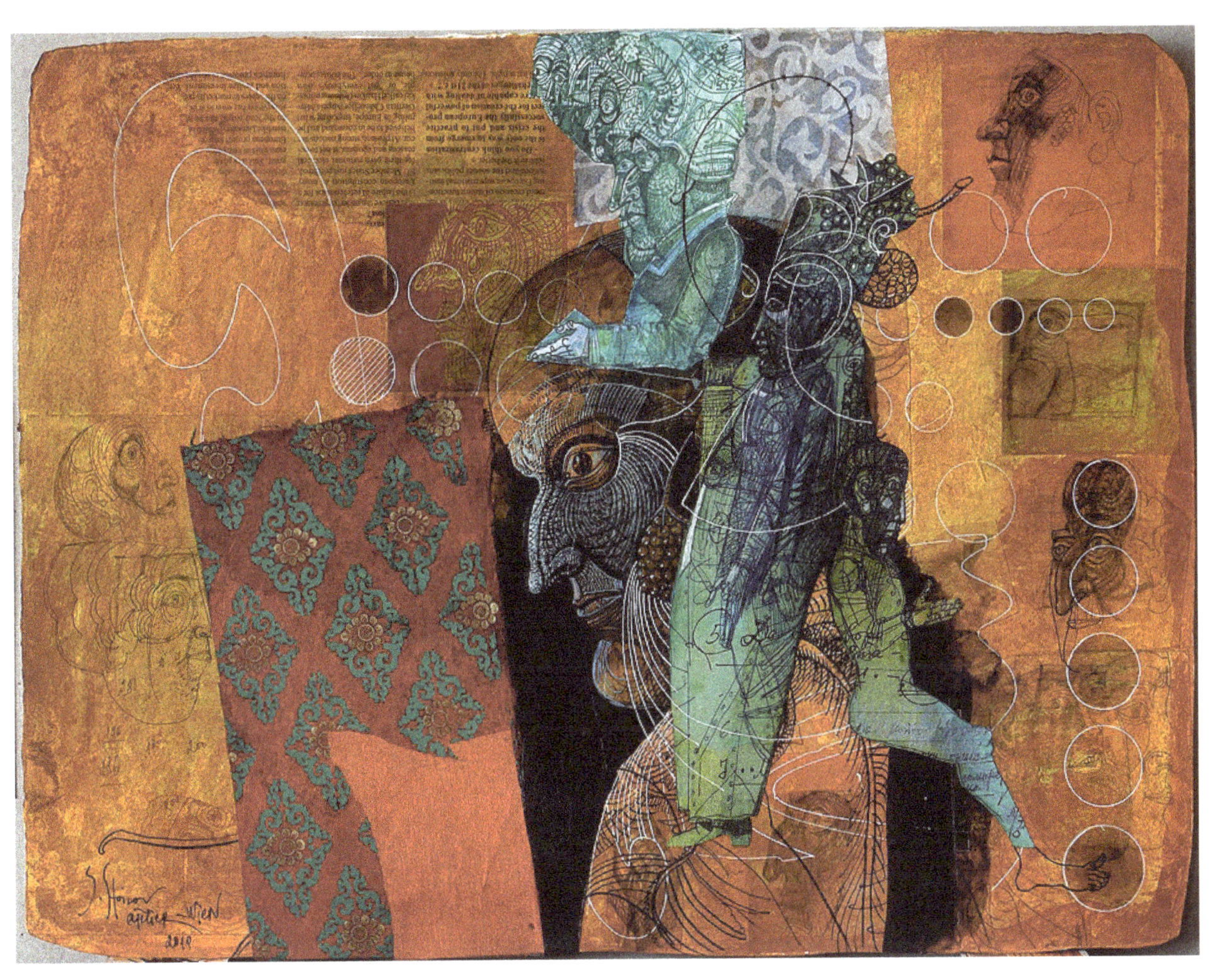

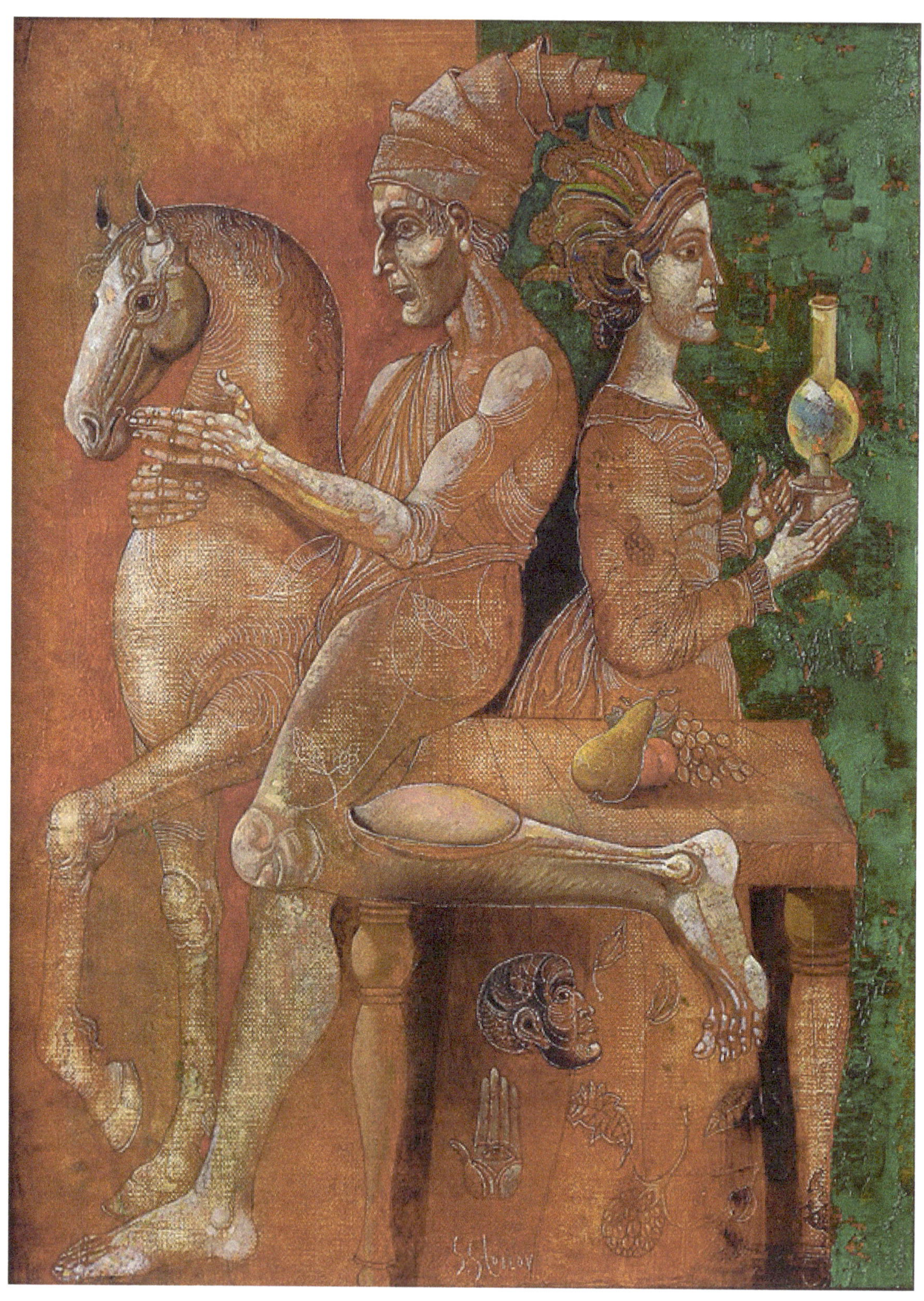

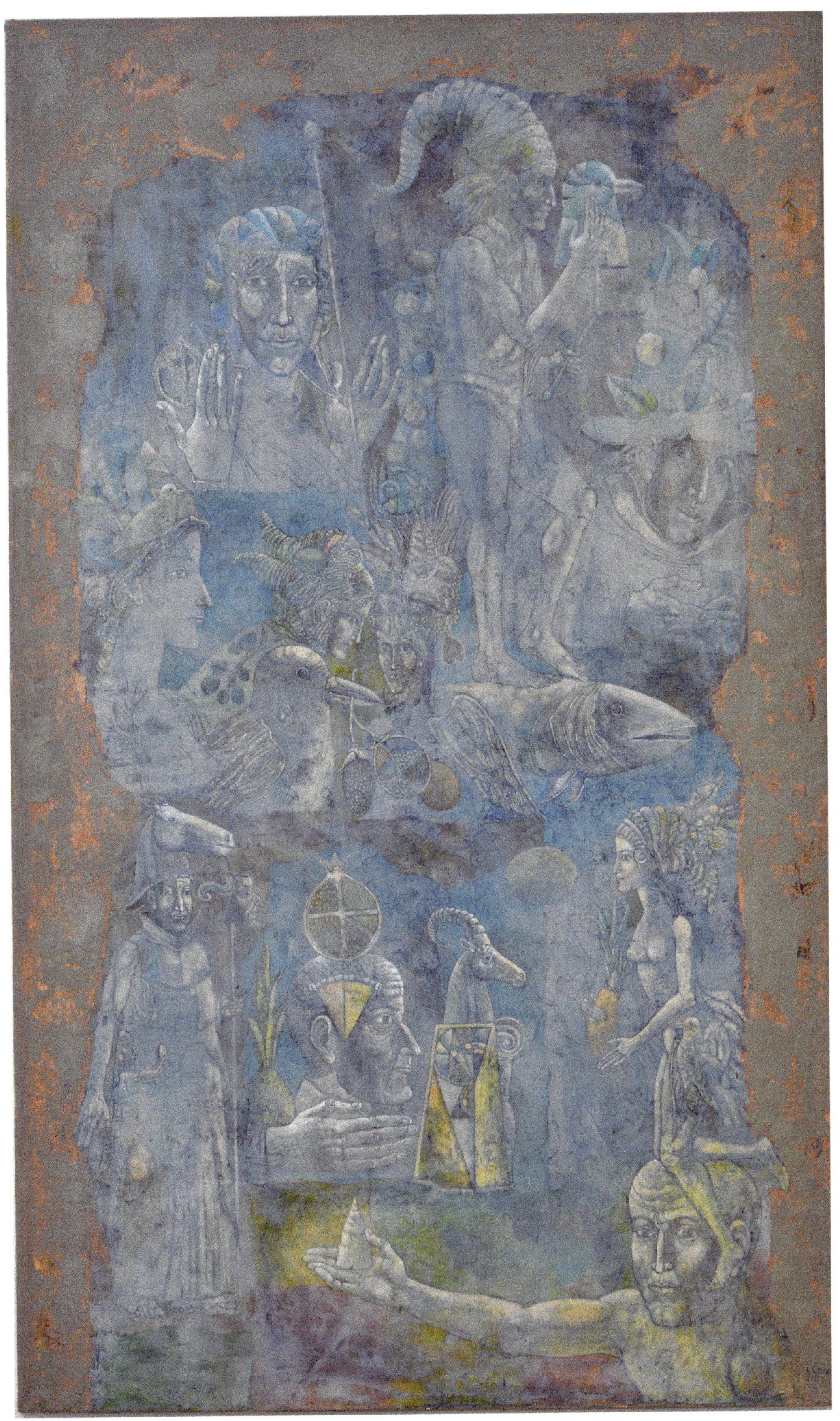

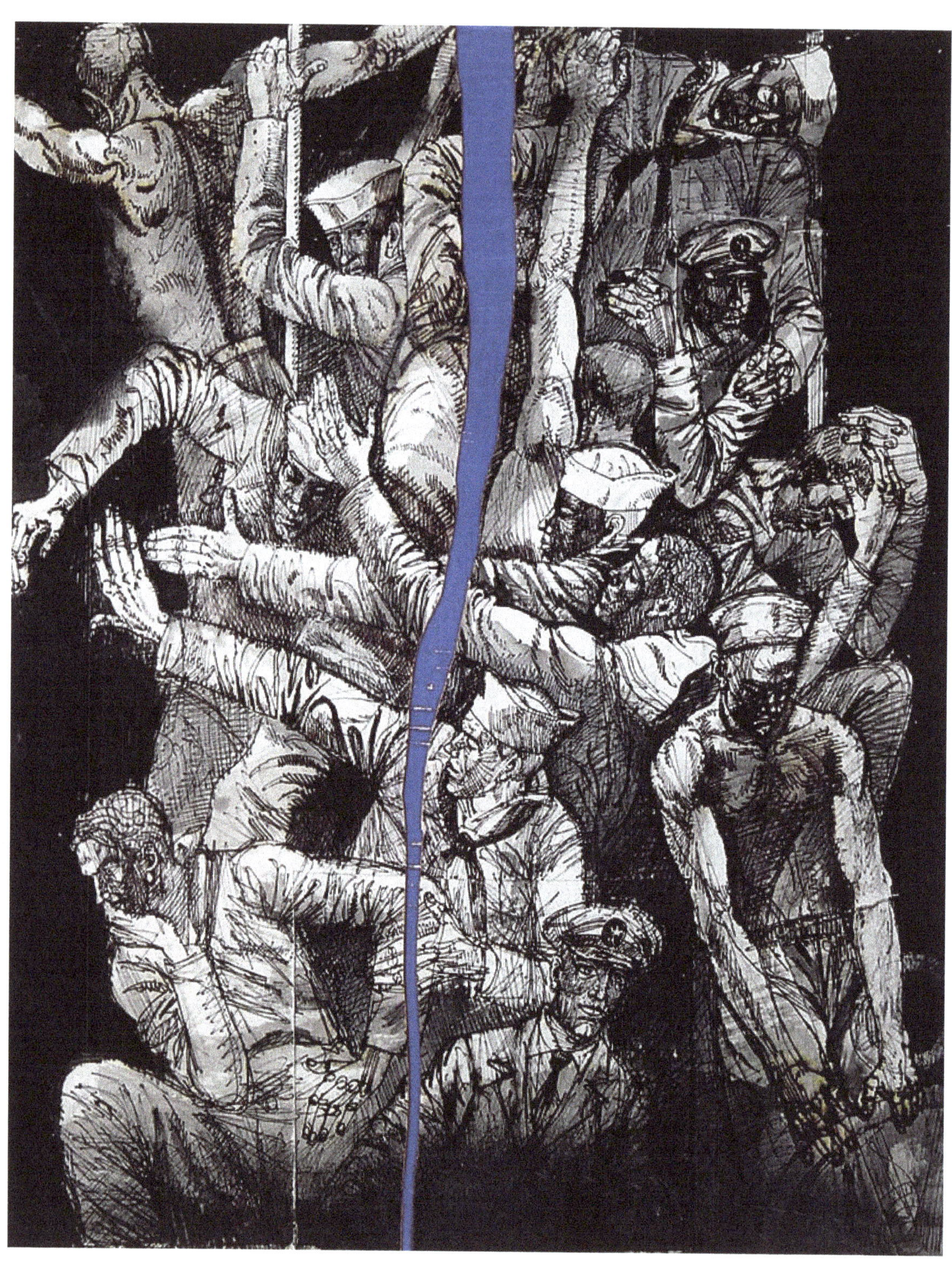

Stoilov etching to illustrate the William Meredith Poem,
"The Wreck of the Thresher"

Stoimen StoilovBiography

1944 Birth in Varna (Bulgaria)
1972 Graduates from the Academy of Fine Arts in Sofia (Bulgaria).
1991 Settles in Vienna (Austria). Lives and works in Vienna (Austria)

PRIZES

2009 The title Professor
1991 Gottfried von Herder Prize for his complete works, University of Vienna (Austria)
1991 Price at the 2nd Print Triennale, Chamallières (France)
1985 Grand Prix for Bulgarian Participants at the 3rd Print Biennale, Varna (Bulgaria)
1984 Price at Art Expo, New York (USA), granted by the foundation Bilan de l'art contemporain.
1983 The 'Iliya Petrov' Grand Prix for Mural Painting awarded by the Union of Bulgarian Artists, Sofia (Bulgaria)
1982 Silver Medal at the International Exhibition in Leipzig (Germany)
1976 Grand Prix of the Biennale, Brno (Czech Republic)

Has been awarded many other national prizes for print and drawing.

PRIVATE COLLECTIONS AND MUSEUMS

Austria
Museum of Graphic Art Albertina, Vienna
Vienna Ministry of Foreign Affairs, Vienna
Artothek, Vienna
NÖ Landesmuseum, St. Pölten

Bulgaria
The National Art Gallery, Sofia
Municipal Museum of Art, Varna

France

Bibliothèque nationale de France, Paris
Fonds national d'art contemporain, Paris
Art Dialogue Foundation, Paris

Germany
Museum of Art Villa Merkel, Esslingen
Museum of Graphic Art of the Schreiner Foundation, Bad Steben
Ludwig Forum, Aachen

Russia
Pushkin Museum of Art, Moscow

USA
The Library of Congress, Washington DC
New York Public Library
Princeton University
Yale University
Florida State University (Strozier Library)
Florida Atlantic University (Jaffe Collection)
Middlebury College (Starr Library)

Website: www.stoimen-stoilov.com□□□

New Works from Europe Combine a Master's Touch with an Arresting Vision

By Rick Coster
The Day, New London, Ct.

The title of the mightily compelling Stoimen Stoilov exhibit at the Lyman Allyn Museum of Art in New London, "Window on the Black Sea – New Works," is perhaps confining. The collection of murals, etchings and lithographs might better be described as, "The Carnival Ride We Call Stoilov's Brain" since, unlike many artists who paint only what they see or who deal in sheer abstractions, Stoilov filters both such sensory perceptions through the exotic baggage of his mind.

A contemporary Bulgarian painter and lithographer, Stoilov was born in Varna, Bulgaria, in 1944 and grew up on the coast of the Black Sea. He graduated from that country's Academy of Fine Arts and is now a resident of Vienna, Austria. His works are exhibited in many public and private collections throughout the world, and they display a paradoxically futuristic interpretation of the mysticism and mythology appropriate to both eastern and western Europe.

Fasten your seatbelt, then, and join the ghosts of other travelers who've apparently been inside his brain a while: Hieronymous Bosch, Albrecht Dürer, Pan and his eclectic and recurring entourage of Greco-Roman deities and myth-makers, Leonardo DaVinci and maybe the painter/patricide Richard Dadd.

Book-ended at either end of the Lyman Allyn's McKee and Chapel Galleries are two of Stoilov's massive murals. Along with a third, displayed at the top of the stairs leading to the exhibit proper, these murals serve as stylistic sentinels for the show. Actual rollable canvases, the murals appear, through the artist's skill and technique, as though they're actually frescos painted on some decaying wall certainly not found in the likes of Mystic or Darien. "Aged" through faux graffiti, cracks and coffee-like stains, the canvases are also fully realized and compellingly colored studies of various recurring motifs and allegories that pepper the smaller works comprising the rest of the collection.

The show is rife with images of various gods and a jester-hatted Everyman, horses and unicorn-like creatures, large Boschean birds, fish, fruit, flying machines, conical shapes, seashells and enough masks to supply the whole county for Halloween.

Said likenesses range in technique from the cartoony (as in "Horseman," pastel and gouache on paper-mounted canvas) to what seems like anatomy-textbook realism overlaid on graph paper ("Icaria" and "Mechanical Fish," both etchings with aquatint). Many of the lithographs are frequently depicted in triptych fashion – again a heavily and no doubt conscious reworking of the Bosch influence.

In companion pieces like the three lithographs in the "Mythology" series, there is a phantasmagoric discipline, as gleeful as it is ordered. The larger painting "Pandora" adds to the nervous freneticism with the suggestion of motion in stuttered images. On the other hand, Clearly, some of the early, smaller works are at least in part studies for the murals that came later. It's interesting to see how the fragmented ideas actually blossom years later. It should also be mentioned that, in addition to his skill at rendering characters and objects, Stoilov's mastery of lithography – where, for example, with a simple, pale yellow wash and a few inspired slashes of red and gray, he suggests whole worlds of color that aren't really there – is extraordinary.

What does it all mean? Can you look at any of the pieces like a Rockwell painting and say, "Oh, gosh, is it already Groundhog Day again!?"

Hardly. It's easy enough to discern the tension and joy perpetually busy in Stoilov's muse. Sometimes they work together and sometimes not, but he's not afraid of the possibilities in either case. What the viewer takes from these rich and speculative histories is of course interpretive, but "Window on the Black Sea" is a nourishing exhibit.

WINDOW INTO TIME:
The art of Stoimen Stoilov

By Richard Harteis

Fulbright Poet-in Residence 1995-96
American University in Bulgaria

Aside from his paintings, the best way to get to know Stoimen Stoilov may be to have lunch with him some aquamarine afternoon along the Black Sea Coast in Varna, the town of his birth. There, over fish and white wine, he will tell you stories of this ancient sea coast like some modern day Carl Jung or cultural historian. But Stoimen's vision is that of the poet, not the scientist. The freighter drifting by on the horizon with the barely discernable and oddly-shaped boxes on deck is carrying sheep to Perth, he will explain. Sheep, of all things. It could as easily be a Phoenician cargo ship or Argonauts sailing on their way to war. He knows all the many civilizations that have made their home in this region. Orpheus was born in the Rhodope mountains, he explains, and even now archeologists are searching for the lost city of Atlantis in the depths of the Black Sea. As in India, these lands have been inhabited for so many centuries the air is thick as a winter fog with human spirits.

In the Balkan tradition of mystics such as Vanga, or the earlier oracle found at Delphi, Stoimen Stoilov seems able to tap this collective unconscious, moving in and out of time, backward and forward like the great white fish that swims through his paintings these days, carrying all of civilization on her back. One recalls the great turtle of Pacific Ocean legend which shoulders the whole universe, or even Melville's great white whale - similar archetypes for the mystery of our tenuous human condition. The passengers astride Stoimen's great fish, a rowdy band of Mardi Gras revelers, toss off a cornucopia of human artifacts, soiling her wake as she makes her way through the oceans of the cosmos. And if these oceans seems vast and empty, there is the consolation that we are all traveling together, have each other at least, for better or worse, as company on the journey -- it was his making as an artist, Stoimen will tell you, when his professors dismissed him from engineering school for drawing caricatures in class, letting him spend a year's sabbatical on the beach listening to the song of that beguiling creature.

Watching Stoimen's eyes scan the waves that afternoon, I thought of William's poem recounting the two masks unearthed in Varna, the poet's awe for those ancient masks whose curious eyes are fashioned from the oldest known gold ever to be worked by prehistoric artisans.

When God was learning to draw the human face I think he may have made a few like these that now look up at us through museum glass a few miles north of where they sleptfor six thousand years, a necropolis near Varna. What was Stoimen watching, what did the artist intuit as his gaze drifted out to sea?It is moving, that the eyes are still questioning and no sadder than they are, time being what it is—as though they saw nothing tragic in the faces looking down through glass into theirs.

This same humanity, the same outward longing is transparent in Stoilov's work through the clear window of his imagination. But his is not a facile optimism despite the sympathy one finds there for his fellow human beings. Like William Meredith, Stoimen does not shy away from the dark underbelly of life. For two years Meredith lay unable to move or speak after his stroke. At the heightof his career Stoilov's studio was mysteriously burned to the ground along with his life's work. Each man has had his share of trouble you might say. How does one transcend such history, achieve the sort of grace with which each man now lives his life?

The early work, in particular seems to tell a more ominous tale. Were those rigid characters with fractured faces and stately miters in etchings he did before 1989 actually symbols of tyranny, I asked him, thinking how poets were forced to speak in metaphor during the Stalinist period of Bulgaria's history?" Art responds to politics, of course, he agreed, but his concerns seem to run deeper than the vagaries of political life.

Only clay and gold, the ancient masks seem to say passing *through one condition on its way to the next.*

And what of the strange animals that seem to pervade so much of his earlier etchings? Like Picasso and other contemporary masters, Stoilov's work sometimes takes its inspiration from more primitive cultures - he has, in fact, lived among aborigines in Australia - where the experience of the tribe seems at once most simple and most profound, where the human river seems to run its deepest. The paintings come magically alive like the beasts on the walls of the caves of Lascaux in the firelight. We may have no idea of what language our primitive ancestors may have spoken, though the images they created to "name" the beasts, or bring them down, tame or even worship them haunt us still. In Stoimen's work we are entranced by the creature's bright eyes, so tender and strange, that seem to look on with such wonder and pity for the evil man does to man in the name of authority.

Far from naive, these works reflect a richness and a mystery that flows out like the rings on the surface of a lake when a heavy stone is dropped into the center, or if you wish, Pandora's box, spilled out onto our laps, helter skelter, come what may. Though bruised by what they see, the eyes are filled with compassion finally, that remarkable charity that informs all truly great art.
After lunch the day we visited Stoimen - fact always stranger than fiction, as though it were ordained - I chanced to meet a woman swimming in the ocean named Stoimenova. As we swam, she explained that the name Stoimen in Bulgarian meant something like "stay name" in a household where too many children had died young, an injunction that the child live on and his reputation not die. I thought how aptly named our painter friend is, for certainly Stoimen Stoilov will not be forgotten any more than other native sons of Bulgaria who have become citizens of the world and masters of their art.

“The Academic management of the University of Economics - Varna has the great honor to invite you to the grand ceremony for the opening of the monumental paintings by the artist Stoimen Stoilov created in honor of the 95th anniversary of the University .

The event is on 29 April 2015, 16.00 at the central hall of the University of Economics – Varna. The paintings measure 4 X 4 Meters

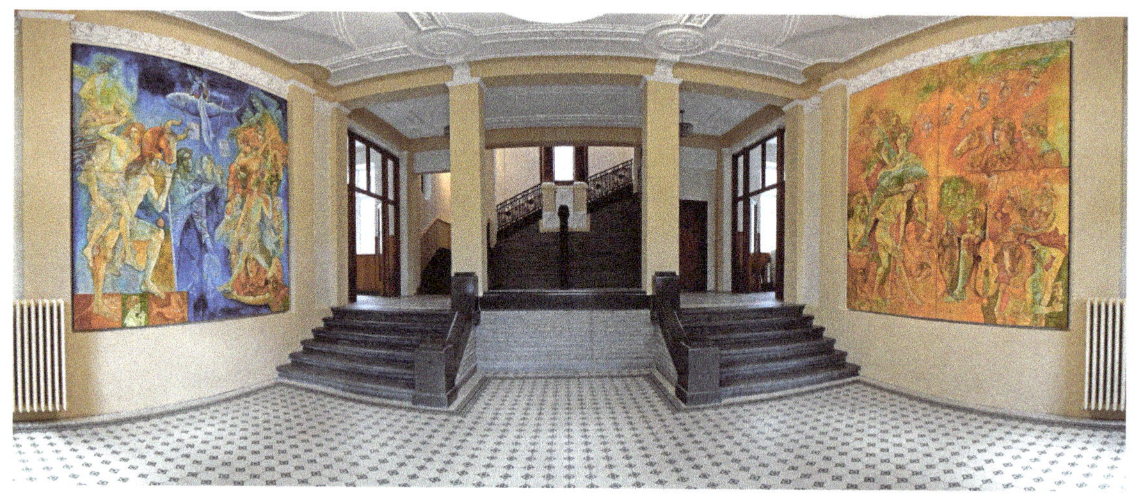

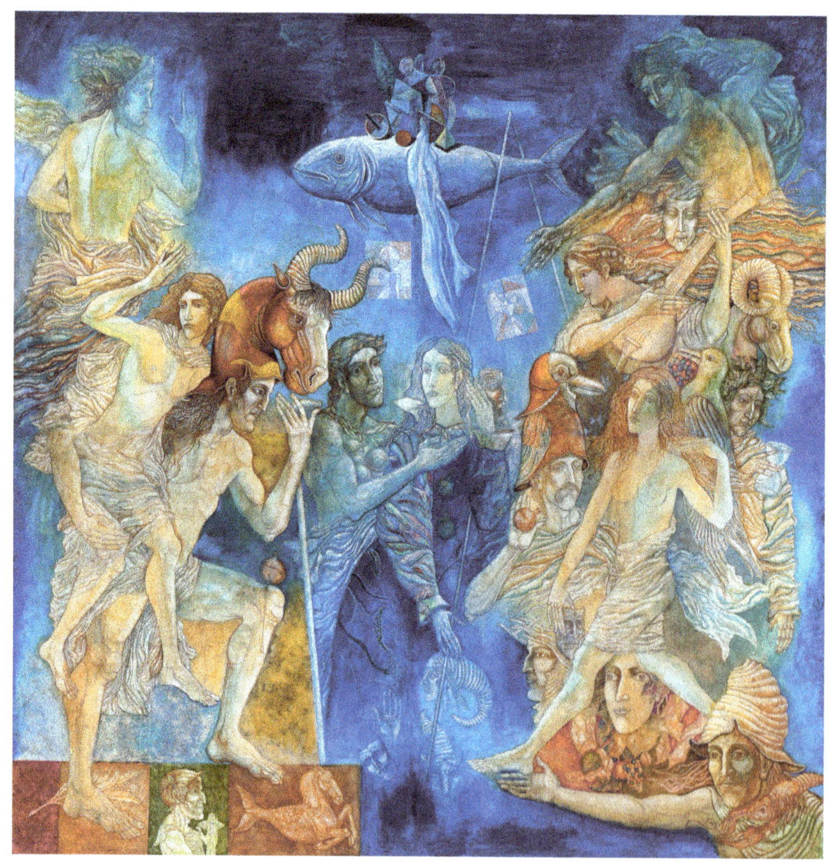

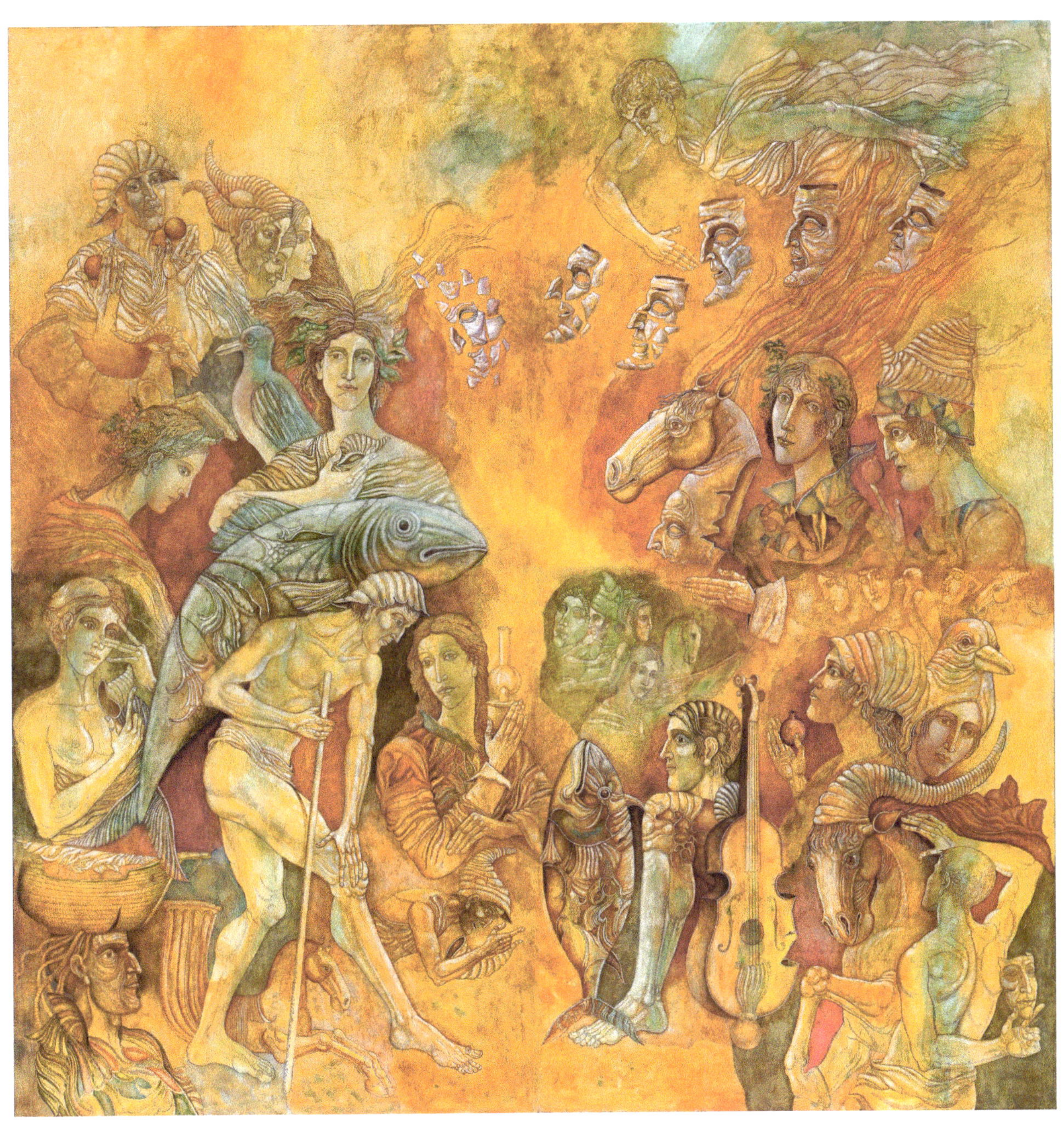

LYDIA ASSENOVA

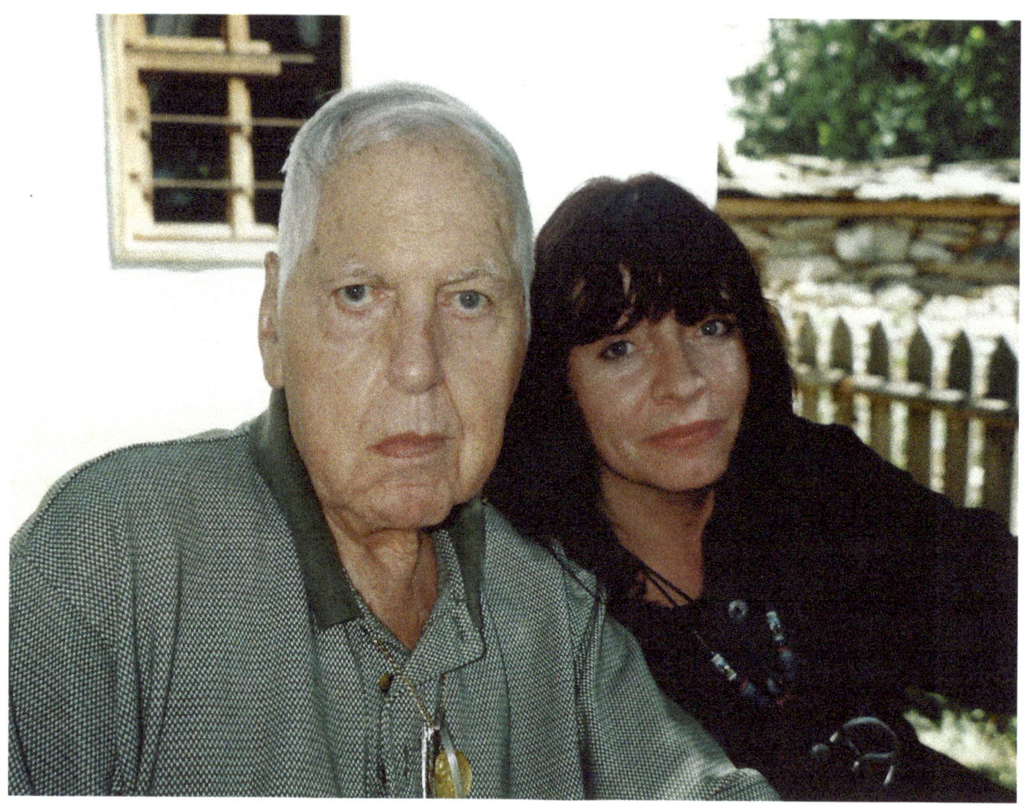

Lydia Assenova and William Meredith, 1996

When I accepted a Fulbright Fellowships to teach at the American University in Blagoevgrad, in 1995, I had a lot to consider. I wanted William to join me in Bulgaria, but since his stroke in 1982, he still was challenged with aphasia. I needed to find someone who could work with him on speech therapy and keep him engaged while I met students and taught my classes. Lydia Assenova was introduced to us and proved to be a charming person who had great regard for William and his poetry. One project they deisigned was a for Lydia to paint William's portrait. That painting became the logo for a dessert wine we contemplated producing when the foundation was in the wine business.

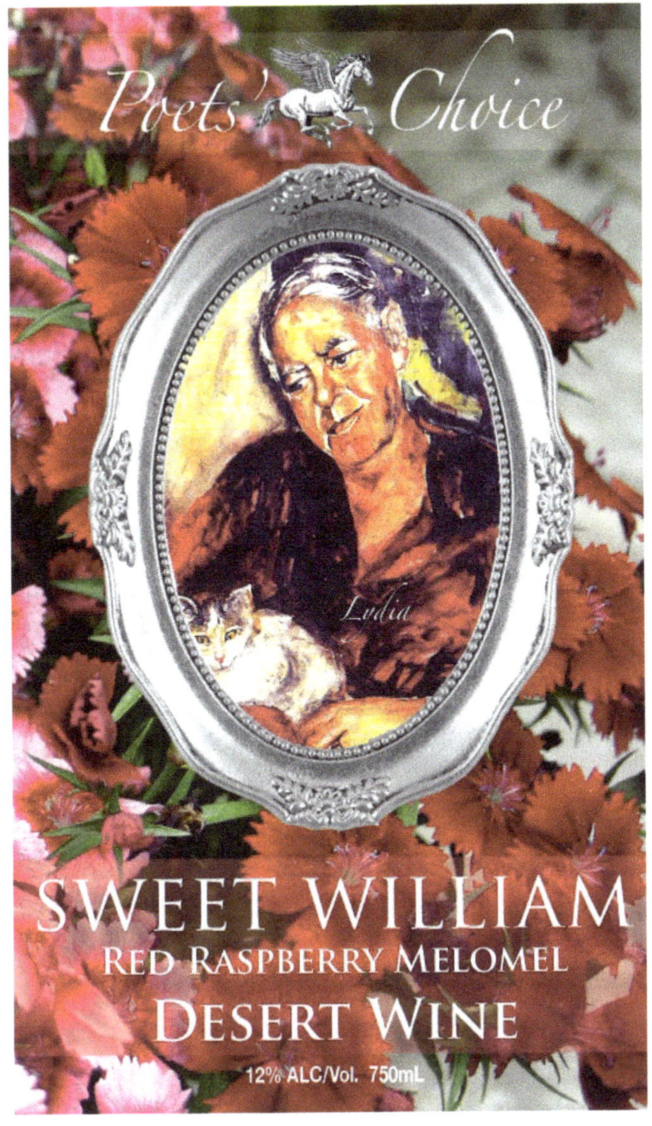

Lydia was such a charming companion and they spent afternoons together while I taught my classes. Occasionally, William would join me to meet students and we worked on translations of his poetry into Bulgarian. For a while, Lydia was like many Bulgarians who hoped the return of King Simeon would unify the country and solve the solve the economic and political morass the country had fallen into. We often hung out at the "king's Club" restaurant in the section of the town where Lydia taught art to young students.

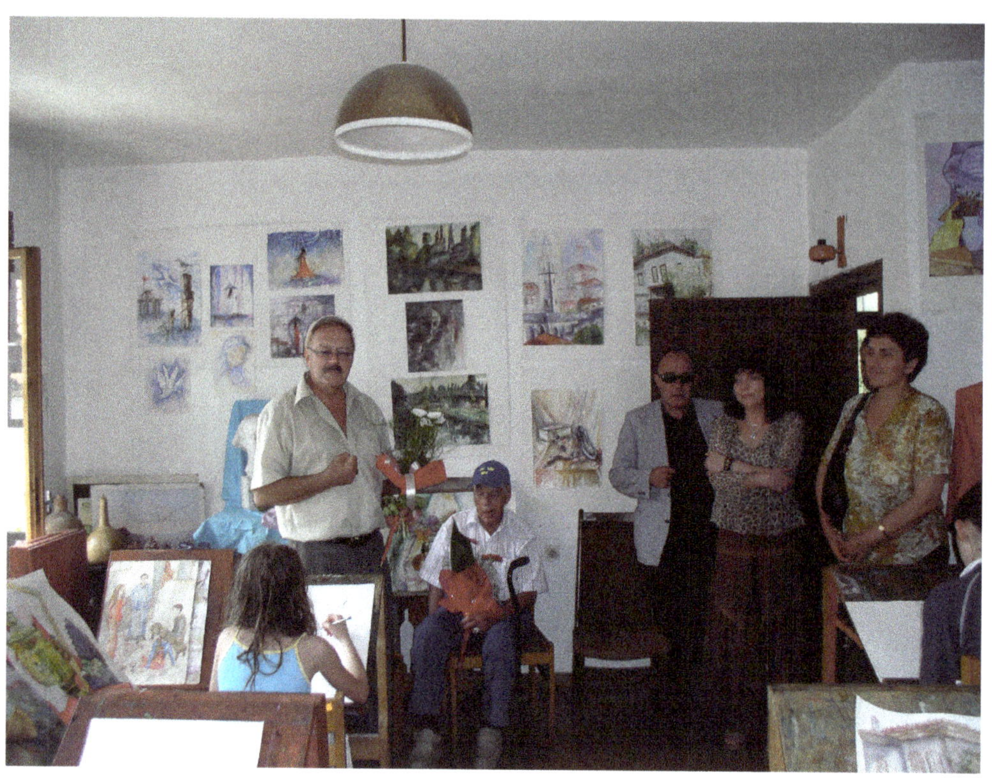

When the King visited Blagoevgrad the town turned out as though it were the second coming. But he could not wave a magic wand and solve the country problems. Lydia gave up politics like so many people of her generation and focused on her art. The top shot here is of me and William in my office during a visit by the sculptor, Nancy Frankel. The lower photo shows the people swelling the plaza in front of the American University during the King's visit.

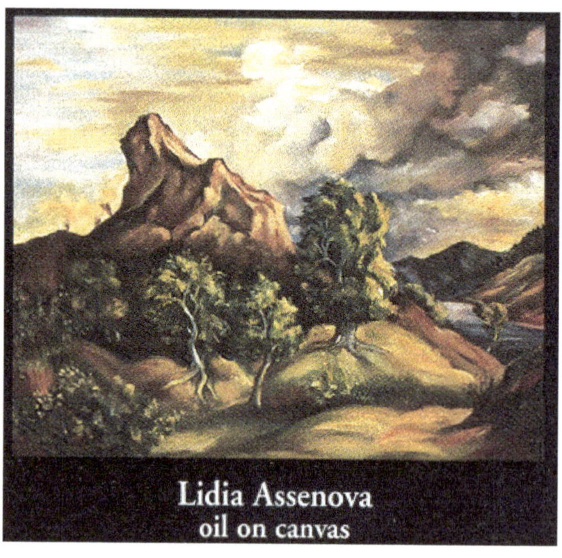

Lidia Assenova
oil on canvas

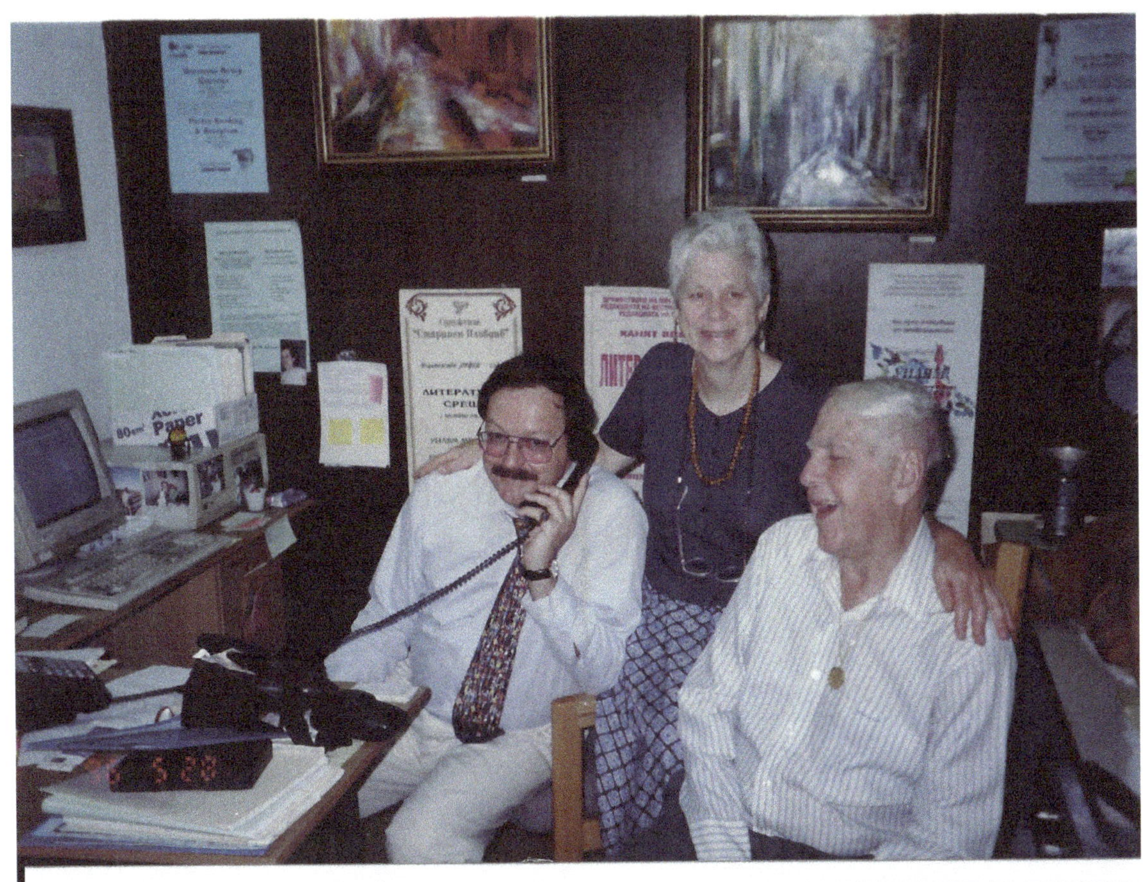

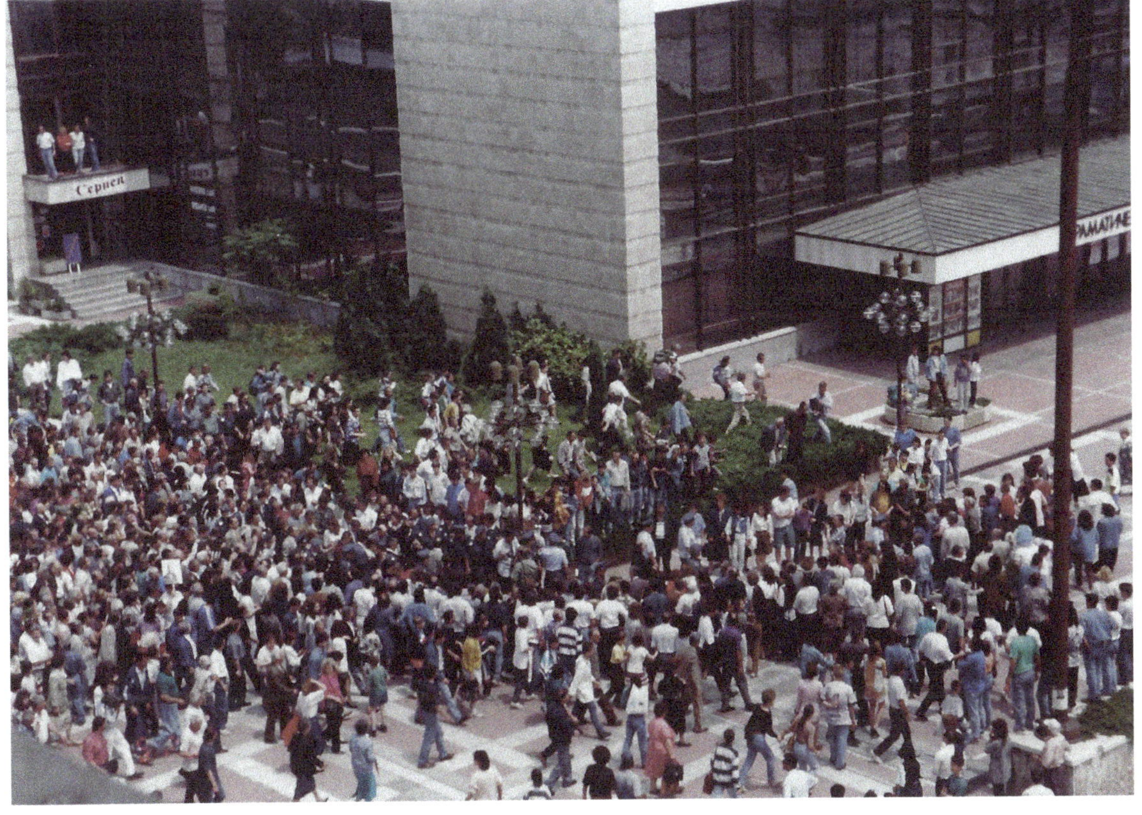

Years later we were able to invite Lydia for a one man show at the Norwich Arts Council which was a success and a great opportunity for her to return to the US "on her own" and not as part of the River People exhibition at the Von Schlippe Gallery. Besides the romantic landscapes she is well known for, Lydia is also a fine portraitist as seen in her painting of Niki Marinov and another local friend.

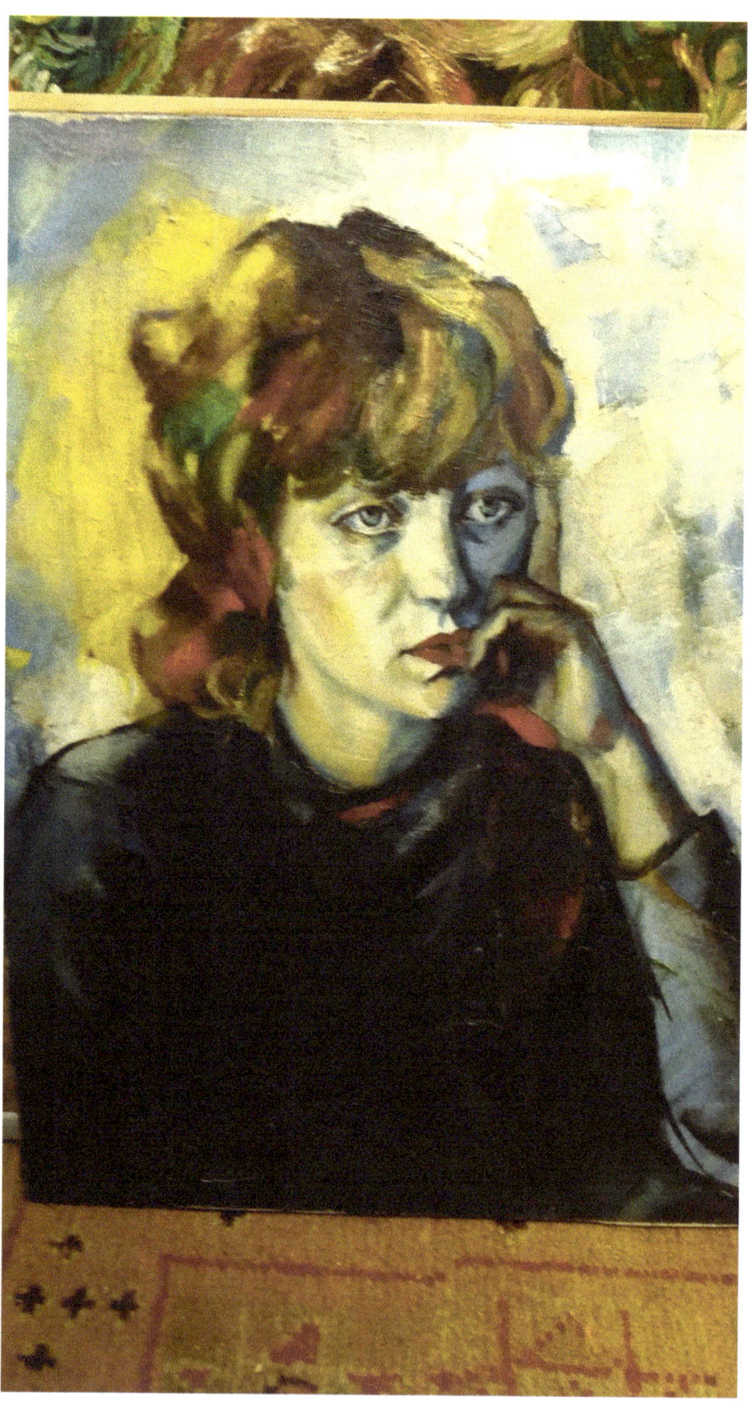

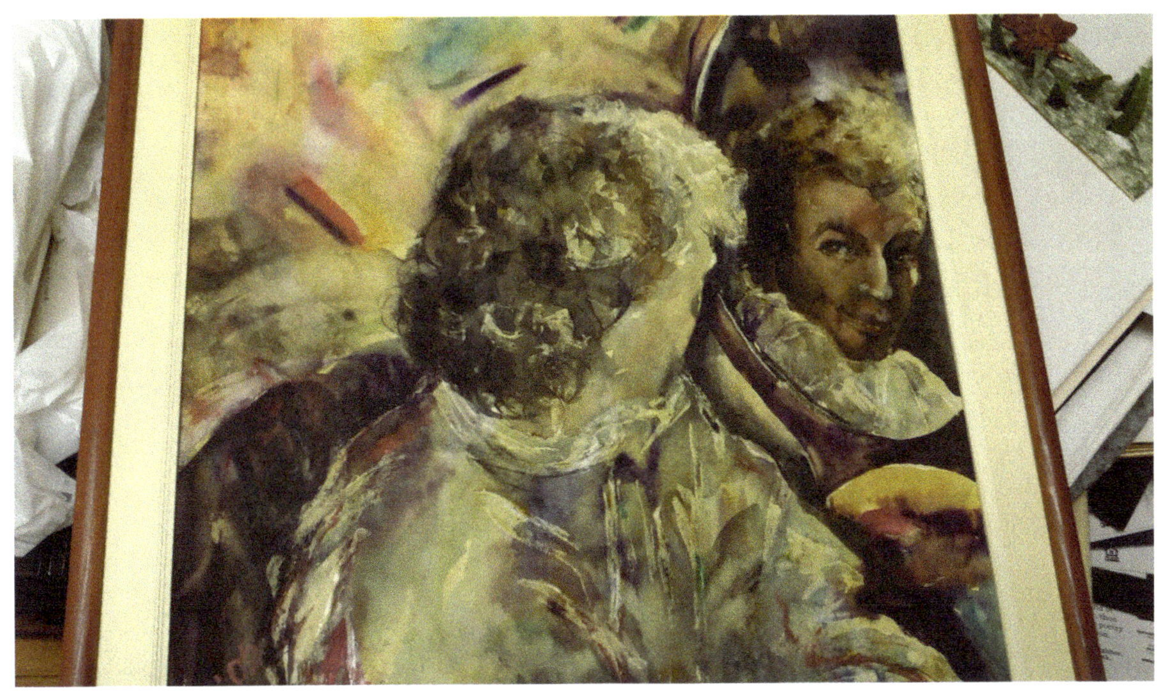

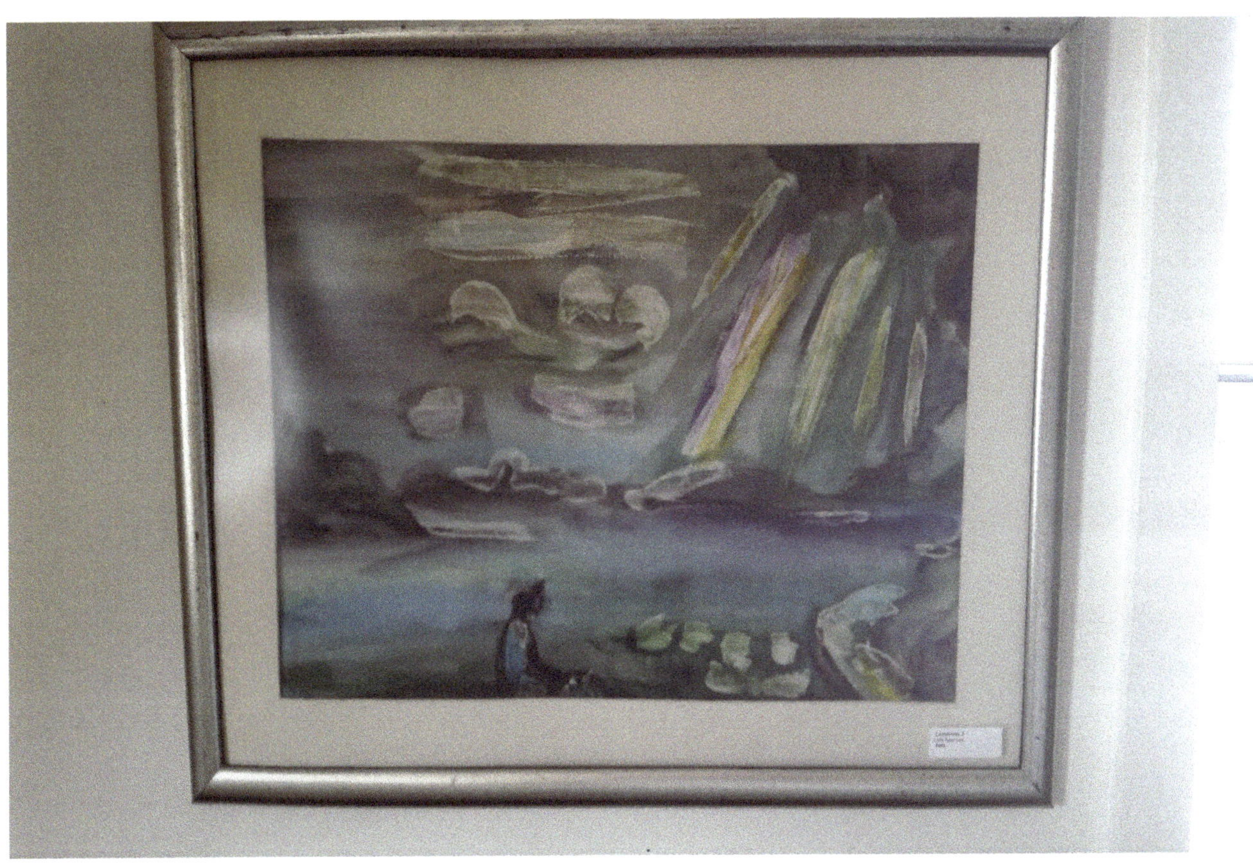

At this writing, I have not received her bio data (very river people) but all I can say is that she is a beauty, does beautiful work, and if you want to buy a painting, we know how to find her!

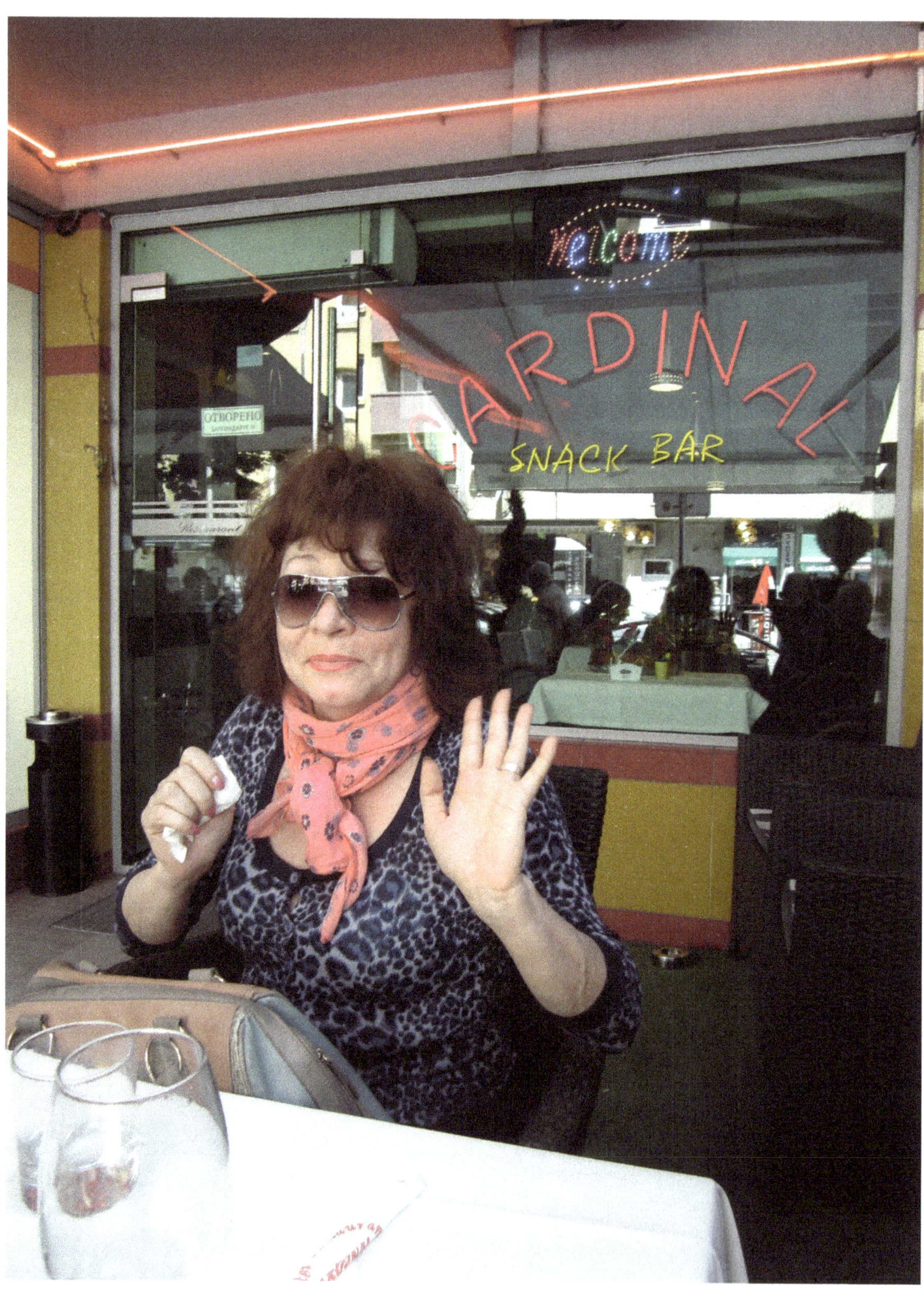

BOIKO DIMITROV

This spring Boiko drove up from Miami to buy me dinner and catch up. I hadn't seen him since wedding in Chicago that Nancy Frankel and I were able to attend. He lives in Canada now since the marriage to his Canadian wife. But he had come to Florida to work on a mural for which he had been commissioned.

Boiko likes a good joke and I reminded him that Nancy and I made a few faux pas during our visit. At one point, we saw him dancing with his new bride and thought we would join him to get the party rolling. Suddenly, the master of ceremonies announced that the father of the bride would now have the next dance. We had stumbled into the wedding ritual when the family was introduced one by one, and we hurried back to our table, tail between legs. We got a lot of strange looks too when we walked down the aisle of the church to take a seat and discovered we were treading on a trail of rose petals meant for the bride's entrance. Well, none of this bothered Boiko. Here is a shot of him carrying his bride out of the church.

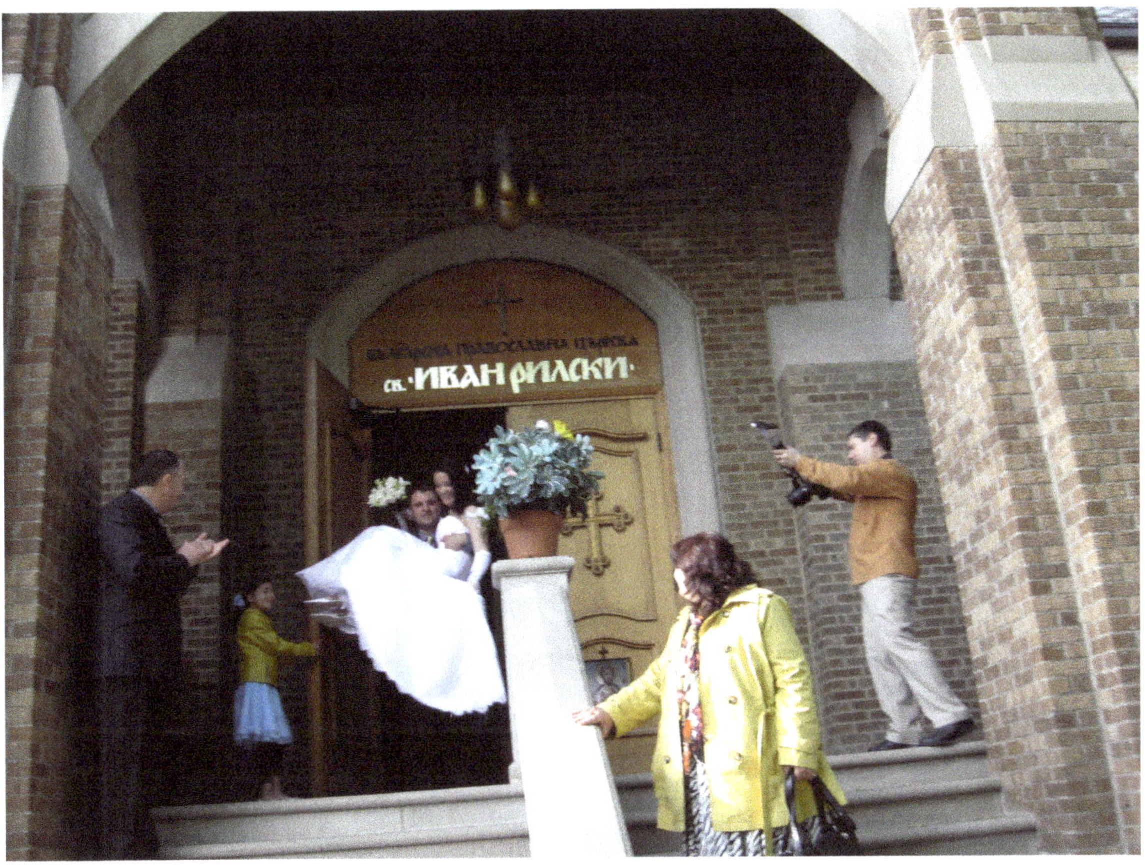

Everyone agrees that Boiko is a kind of a little devil. He cracks himself up when he makes a joke, and he likes to play tricks. For a number of years apparently he was in the monastery and because of this the icons he paints are authentic and receive the blessing of the church. He was accepted as the official iconographer and muralist when the church in Blagoevgrad was being refurbished. But I can't imagine how he had it as a monk. In one painting that was shown at the Von Schlippe God seems to be of two minds when he considers the church.

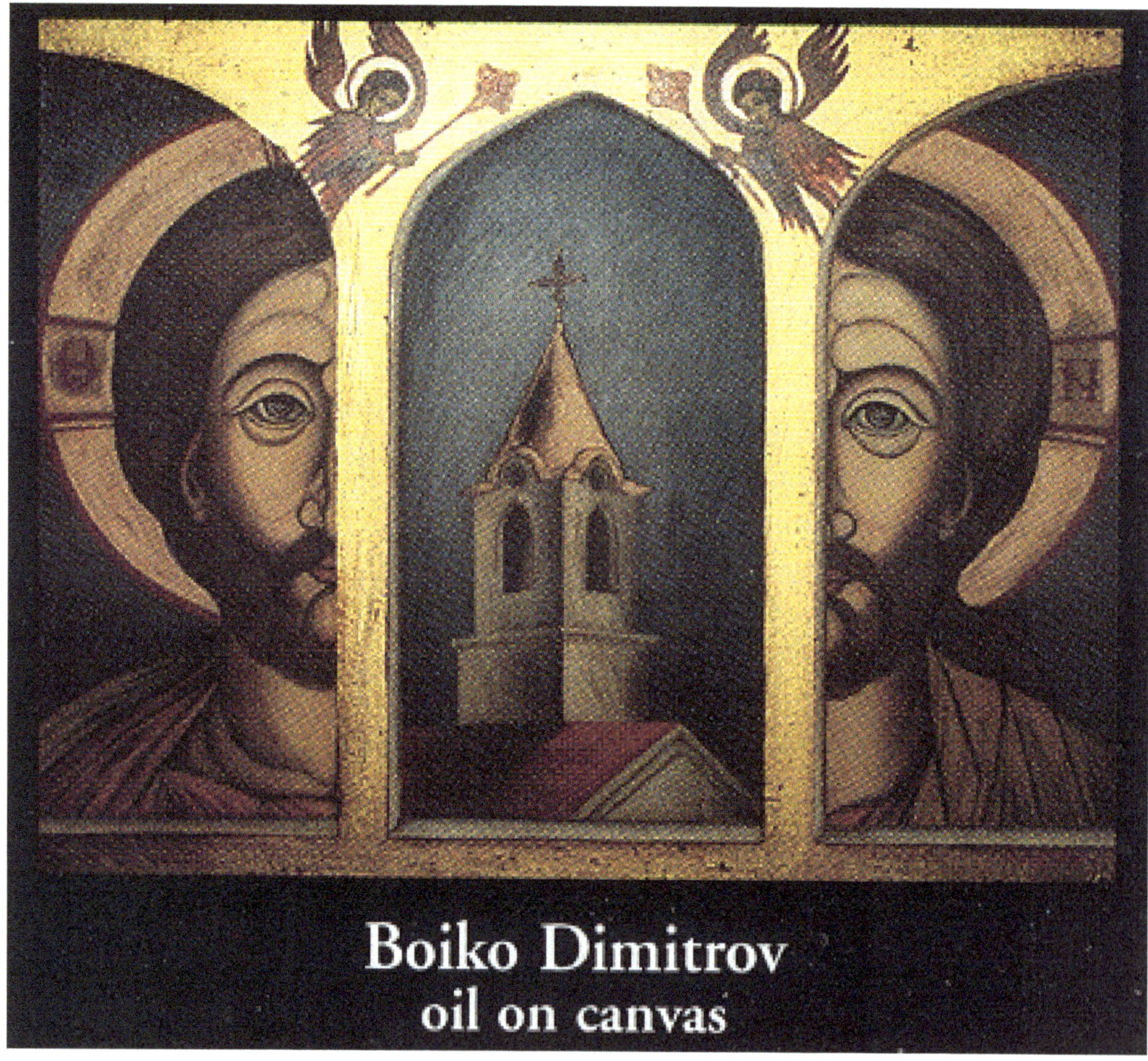

Boiko Dimitrov
oil on canvas

One painting he gave me as a gift I have called Mr. and Mrs. Fish and her lover after Boiko told me their story. Seems Mr. Fish found out his wife was having an affair so he went to the fishermen and told them where to find him. You can see him in this photo caught in a net at the bottom of the ocean. The guy sleeping with the fish at the bottom of the photo is Patrick Carmichael, dreaming of God only knows what.

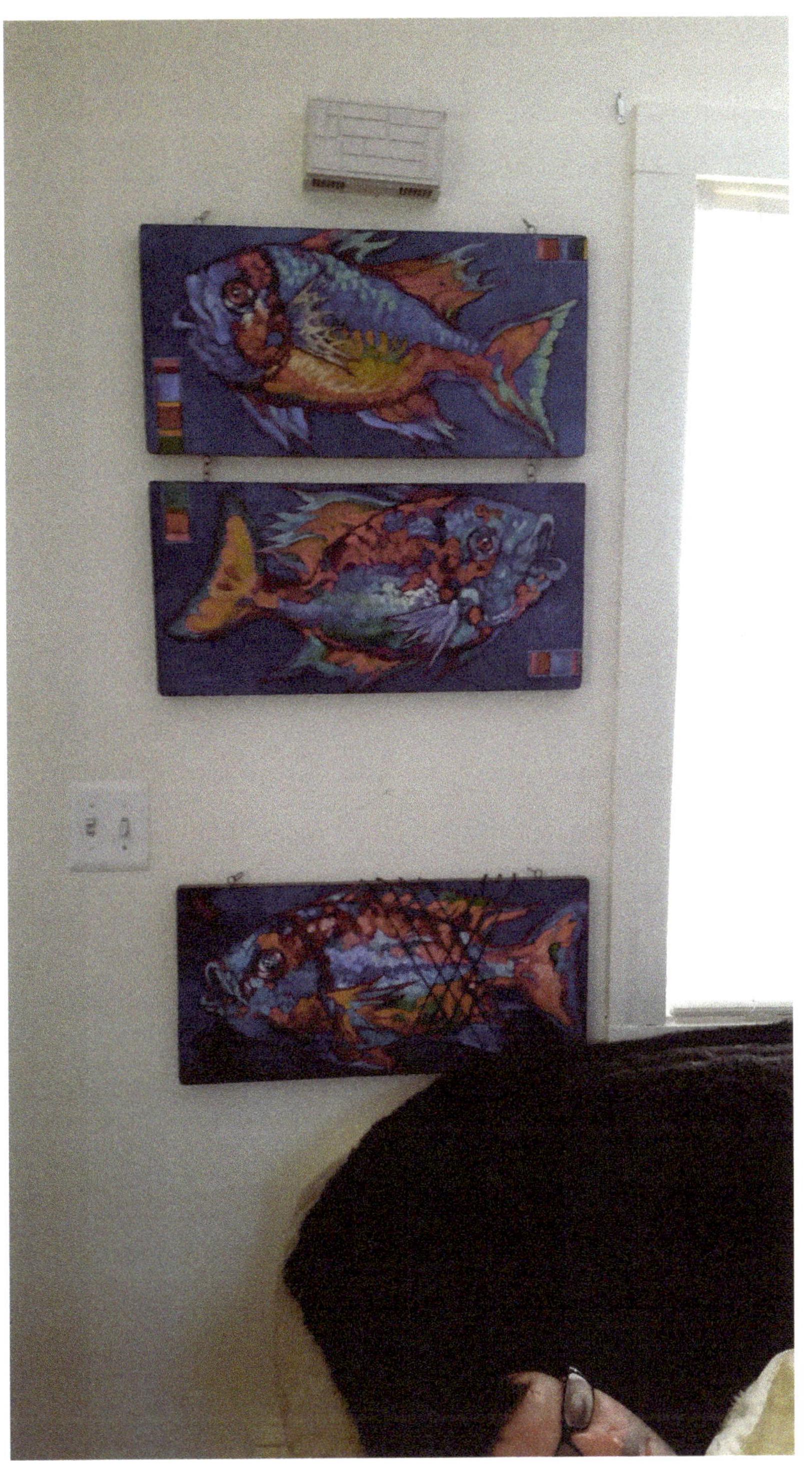

Here is an example of the kind of guy Boiko is. At William's funeral at St. James in New London, I looked at the back of the church and there was Boiko looking very disheveled like one of the homeless guys the church looks after. He had driven all night to be at the morning funeral and when it was over, he got into the old bomb of his car and drove back to Chicago. We have been very lucky in our Bulgarian friendships.

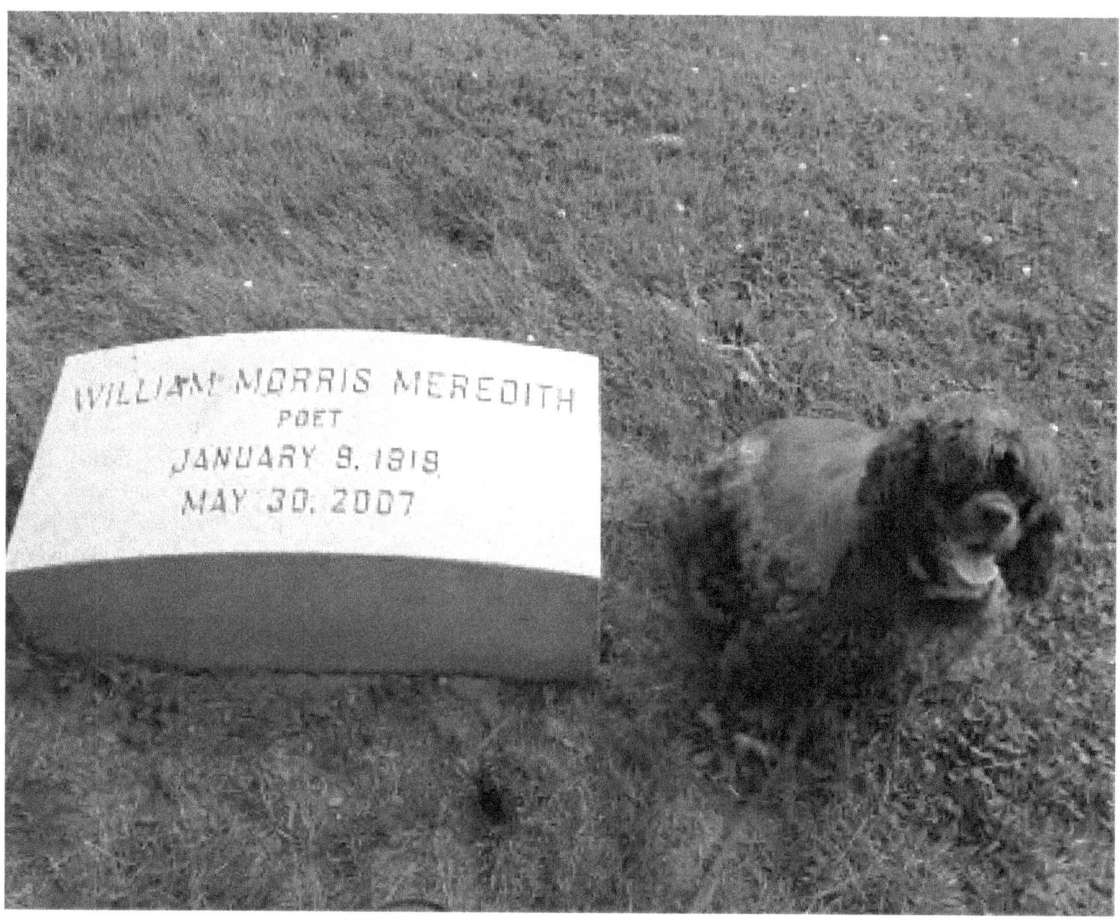

My little dog Daisy at William's grave in Valhalla in Philadelphia

LUCIEN DIMITROV

No relation to Boiko, it is a very common name in Buglaria like Smith or Jones or Washington which is perhaps why Lucien goes by the name Liko when he wears his artist hat. Lucien is a much milder mannerd fellow, almost shy, proud of his beautiful two daughters and wife Ellie. He's a very sweet guy.

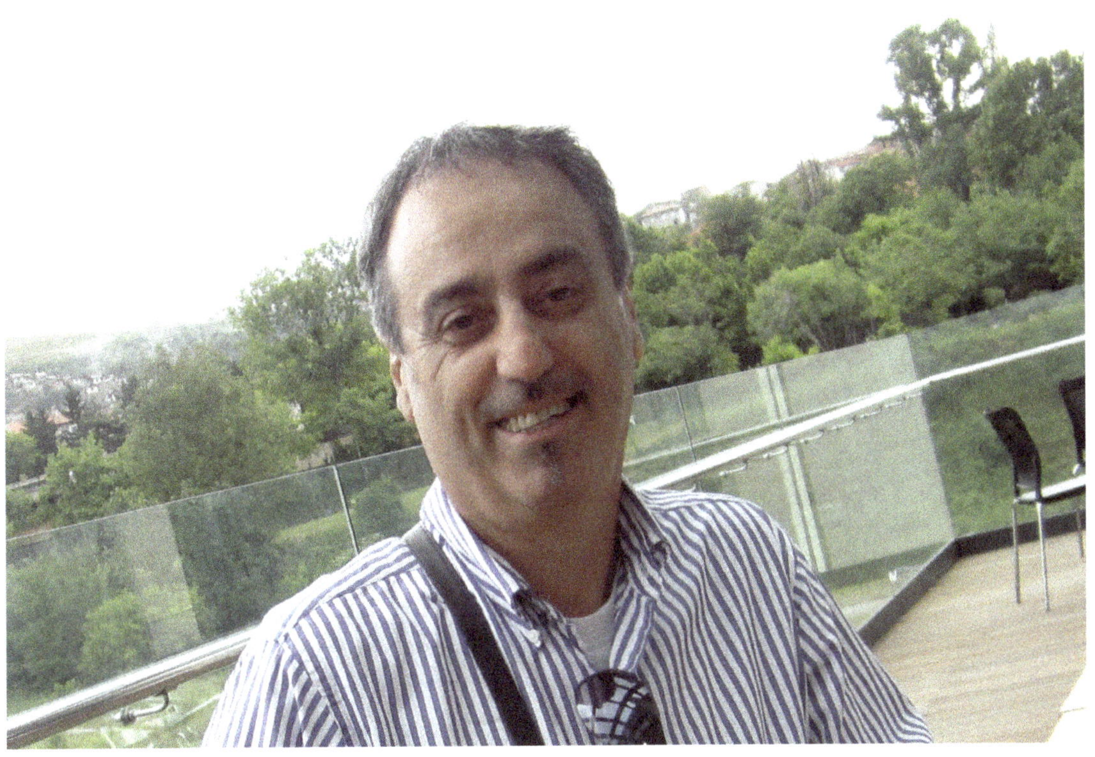

Lucien draws heavily on legend and folklore in his art and some years ago I tried to give an interpretation when he had an exhibit in Italy.

The Art of Lucien Liko
By Richard Harteis

Often in world culture, great art takes its rise from folk traditions and mythology, for such hard-won legends incorporate the tribe's wisdom garnered throughout the centuries. They are a way of teaching our children and ourselves at a level which is both simple and profound. The courage to kiss a frog may reveal a handsome prince, taking care of others may save you from the oven yourself when the witch temps you with a gingerbread house, best not lie, or your nose may grow and grow. A simple tune may swell to a Dvorák symphony, or inspire Motzart's magic flute. The tempo of the lullaby is the human heart.

So it is in the art of Lucien Liko. Like Geppetto at his work bench, this master sculptor brings Bulgarian and Thracian traditions to life through great technical acumen informed by love and compassion. What are these delicate creatures that come to us from the forest of his imagination, so gentle and at peace as they feed at the water's edge, standing on impossibly long legs, and banded by stripes of rainbow. Is it priest or shaman that looks impassively at us from behind the mask? As with all great artists, there is a mystery about his work that can not be solved, but nevertheless delights. You want to stroke the gentle creatures, touch poor Icarus who lies broken on the shore, yet struggles with one wing to rise. The famous actress named X wears a hat as big as Sicily, as big as her ego. She is funny, she is laughable, and she is, and she knows it, beautiful.

The legend of Icarus is a popular story in Bulgarian arts and one wonders if the appeal does not come from the half a century of isolation the artists felt under Communist rule. Exiled from the larger world, unable to travel freely, they drew on their own legends and inner resources, created wings to fly and escape the grey world in which they were forced to live. That they could achieve such remarkable art, both stoic and exuberant, is nothing less than a testament to the human spirit and its capacity to create beauty out of the world's rubble, like a flower pushing through the concrete of their lives. In one Liko sculpture, a handsome youth wearing a pharaoh's hat, rides a magic bird with grace and perfect balance. It is an apt metaphor for the dignity and skill in Lucien's work. He reads the wood and translates it into poetry, he adds color, but with great sophistication and subtlety, the marks of his scalpel give a texture to the surface like impressionist brush strokes. Many artists are technically skilled but only the great ones create works that come from a life which has overcome great challenge and can still take joy from the world. The engine which drives such talent is love, a gift given to the artist and one he returns to us, completing the circle of communication that is art.

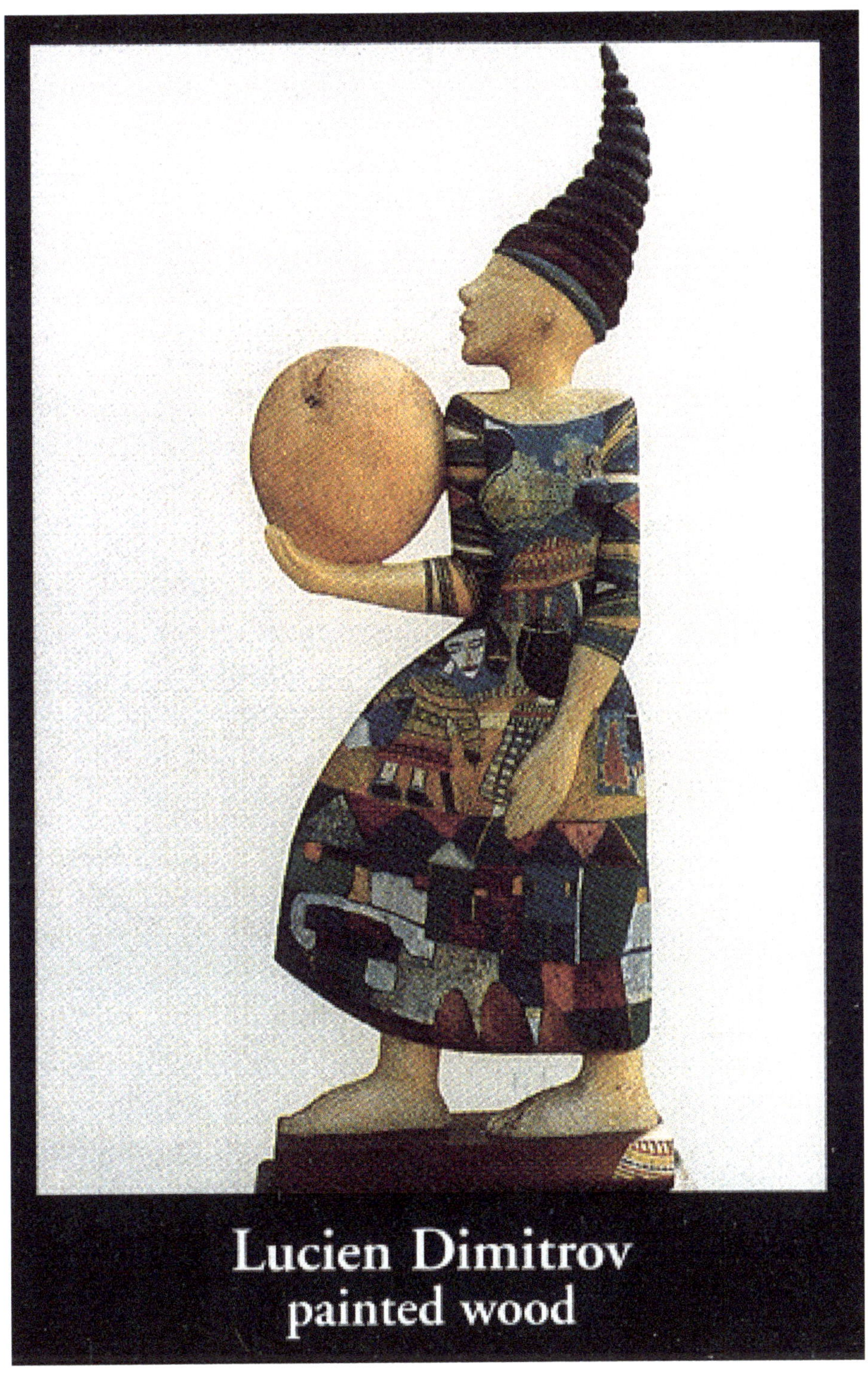

Lucien Dimitrov
painted wood

A gift he made to William is that of a seabird, very strange, unlike any bird you will find on the Black Sea.

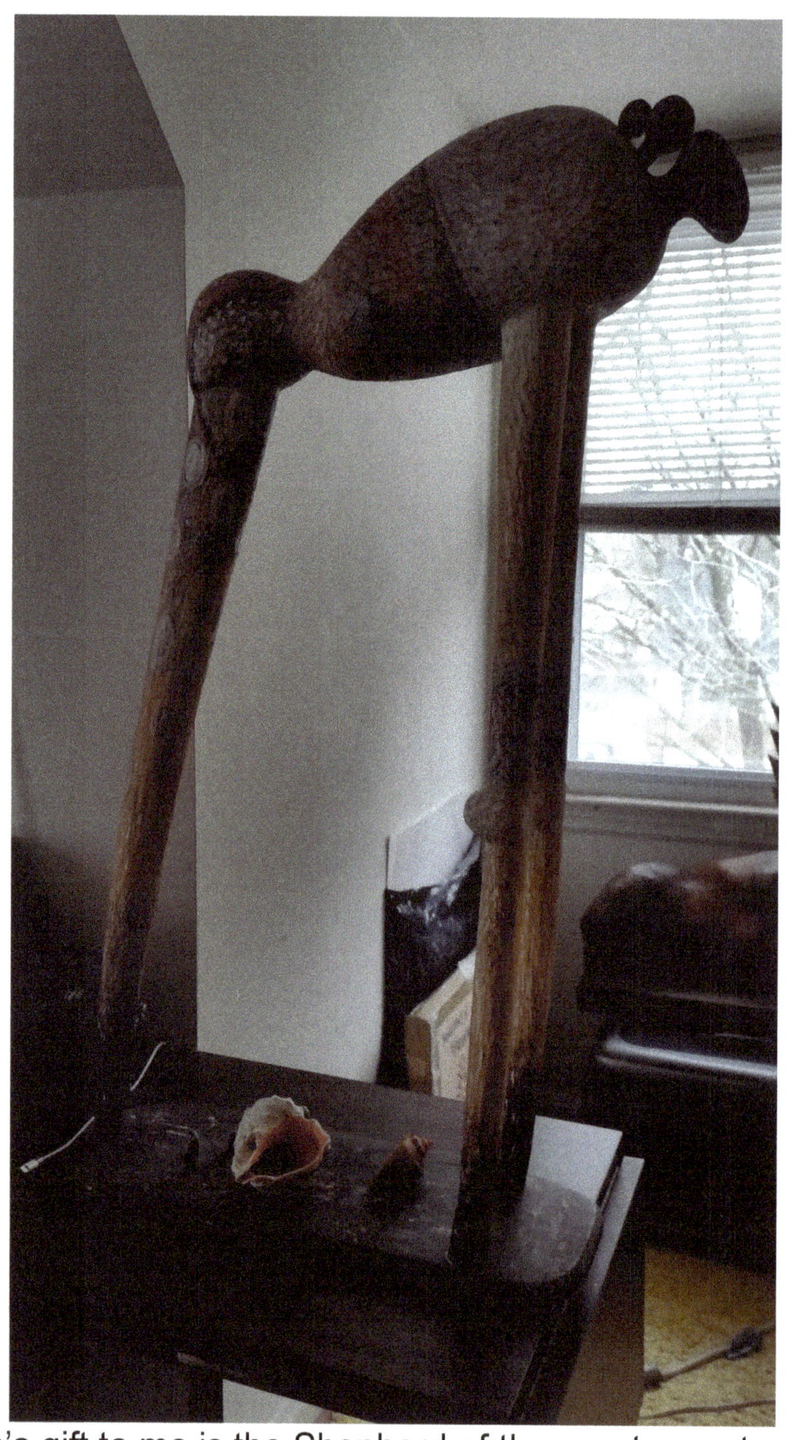

Lucien's gift to me is the Shepherd of the great moustache.

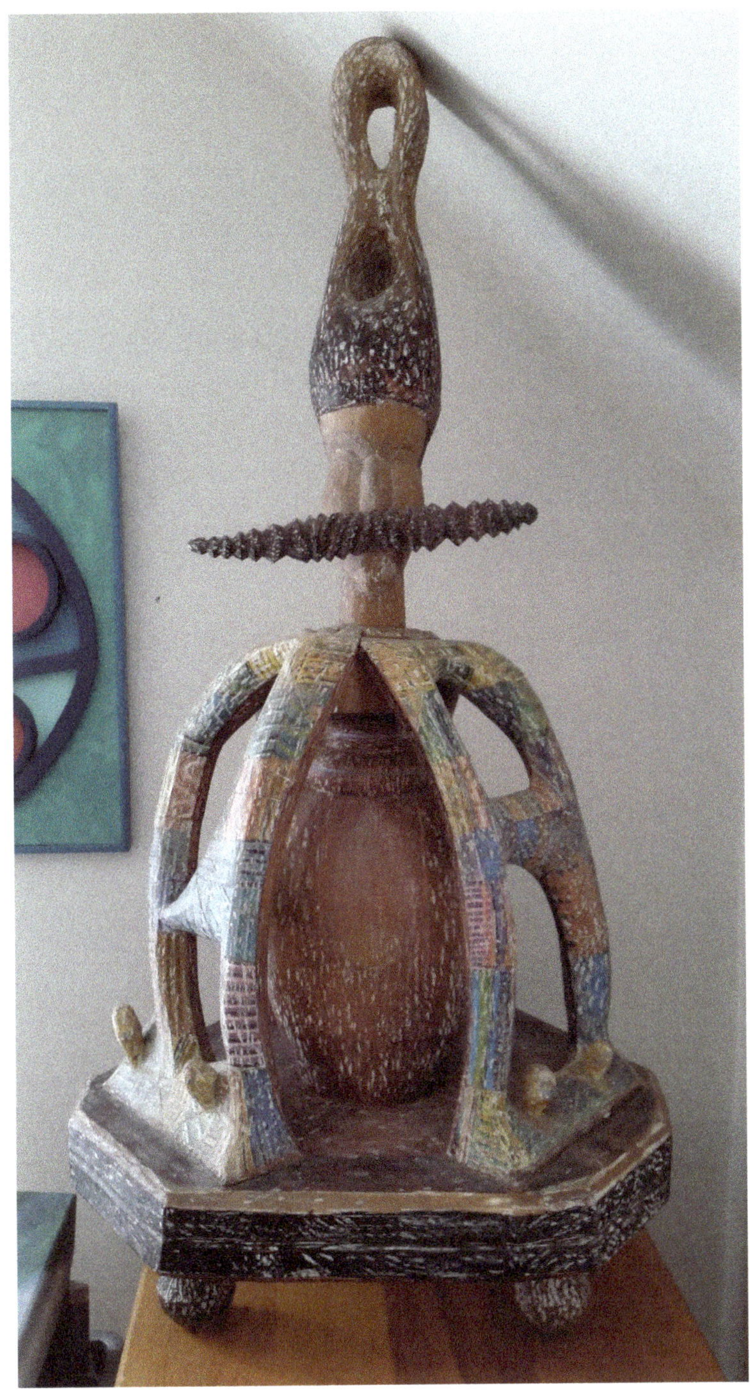

The life these friends share in Blagoevgrad is modest, but when you see them at the café or in their studios, you get the feeling that these people really know how to live, know what it is all about. Here we are during a recent visit to present Lyubomir Levchev with the 2013 William Meredith Award at the American University.

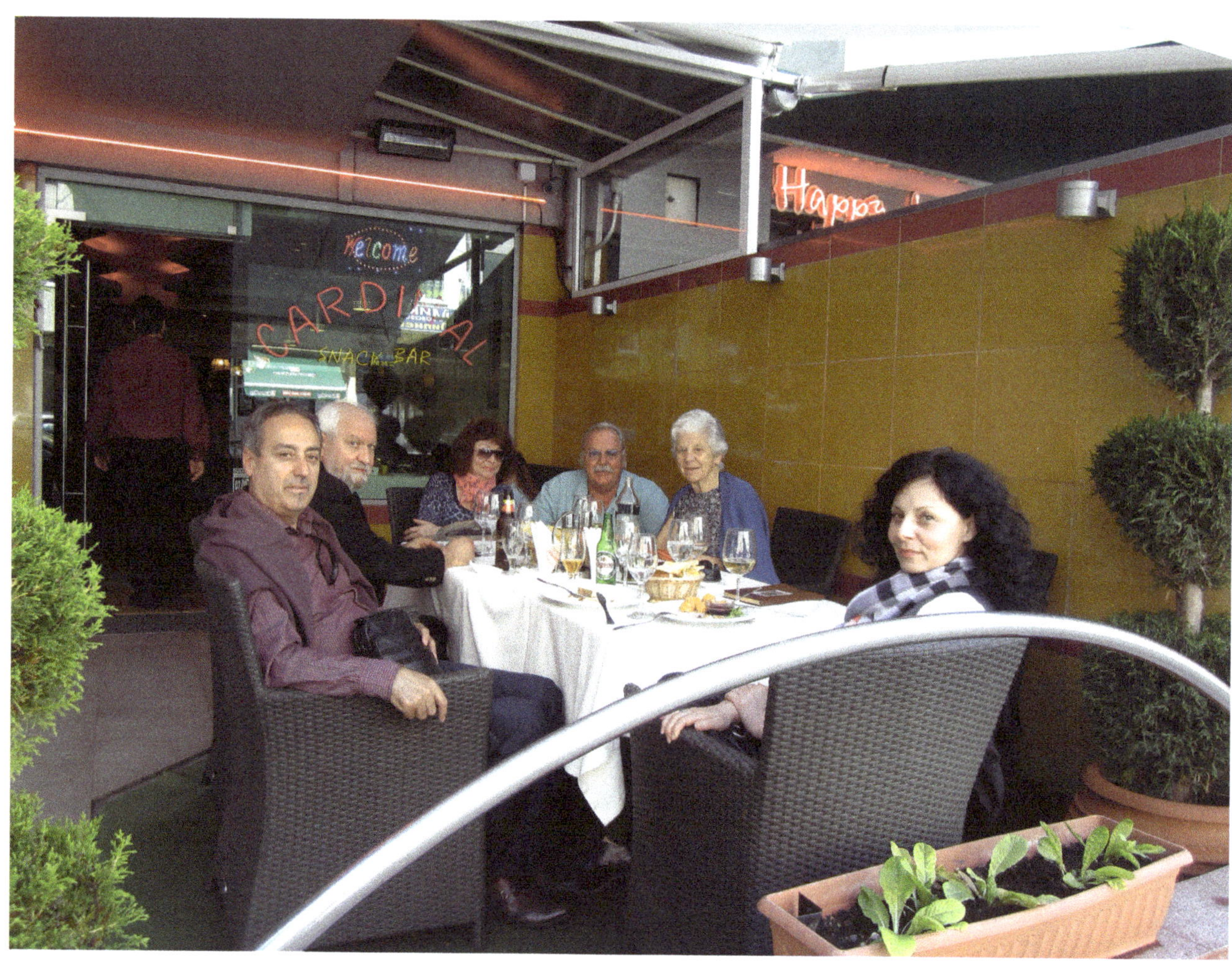
Welcome
SNACK BAR

NIKOLAY MARINOV

Though Nicky Marinov lives in Gotze Delchev down near the Greek border, he is often in Blagoevgrad where he finished his studies at the Pedogogical Institute. He walks the plaza in flowing robes designed especially for him in Poland. One thinks of Salvator Dali when one considers both the art and the man. At first the works look to be a kind of one liner, or visual punning, but they have staying power like Wharhol's Cambells' soup can or Robert Indiana's sculpture of LOVE. He is considered an aesthete in the best sense of the word for his sensitivity to beauty and the seriousness with which he takes his work. His series on umbrellas is remarkable for its inventiveness and wit. Individual paintings such as a butterfly landing on a sunflower tell the story of a soul at rest, a flock of flamingos morp into the sunset over Key West. His metaphorical vision is arresting and thought provoking. He has shown his work in Germany, Ukraine, Poland, New England, Seattle, and even in West Palm Beach Florida.

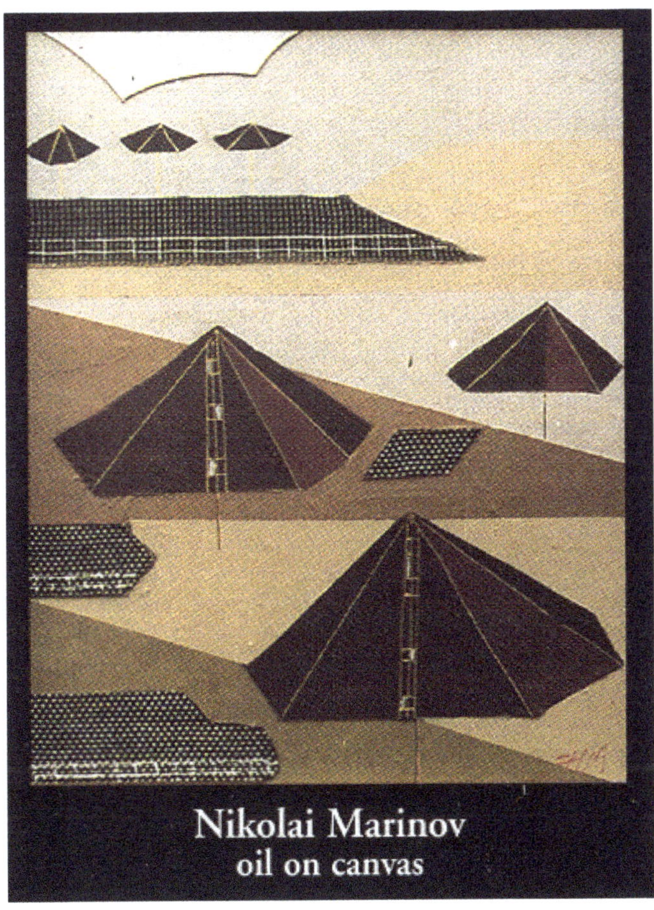

Nikolai Marinov
oil on canvas

Visitors to Gotze Delchev find him to be a remarkable host. I recall visiting there once and jogging through the village. I stopped at one point and gave an impromptu bouquet of wild flowers to a very old lady who was spying me from her balcony. "Grandmother, how old are you," I asked. She had no idea. Time in this part of the world is not seen as linear. The blind soothsayer Vanga lived in a village named Rupite also down toward the Greek border in the center of a semi active volcano. It is said when the Russian's tried to tape the conversations of the generals who came to her to have their fortunes told, the tapes were filled with nothing but white noise. Lyubomir took me and William to see her once, but I did not ask her a question, at least not in words.

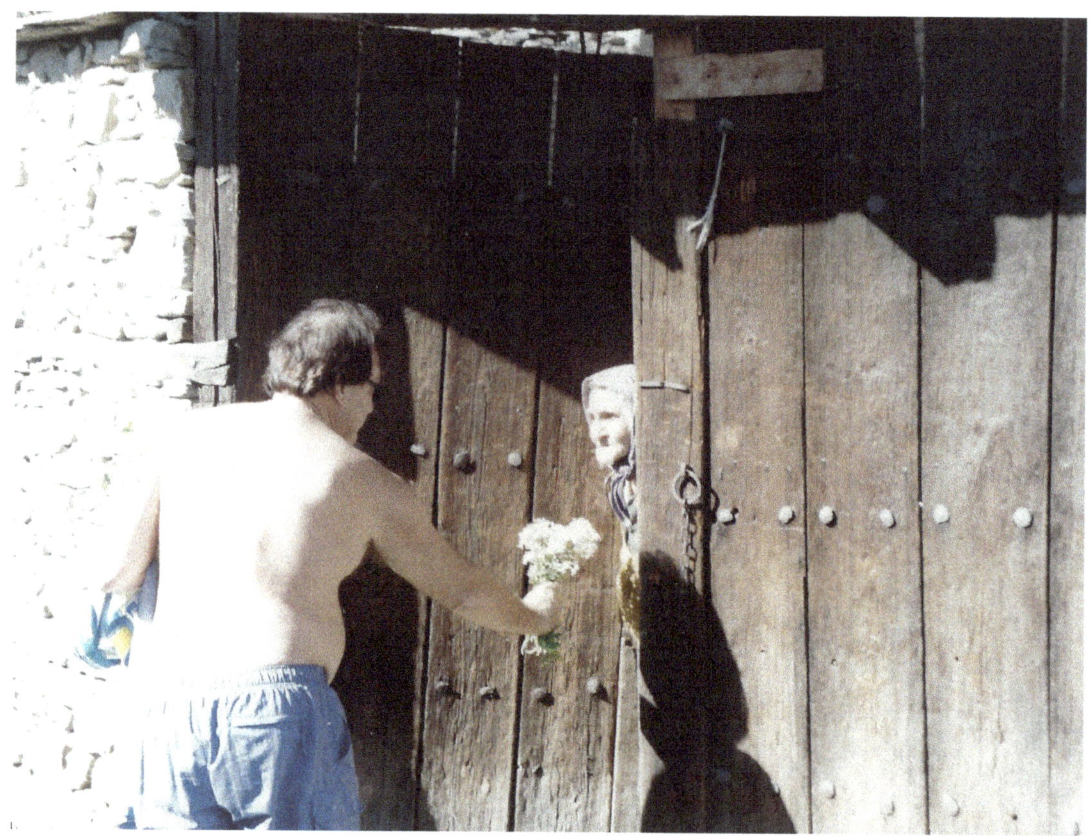

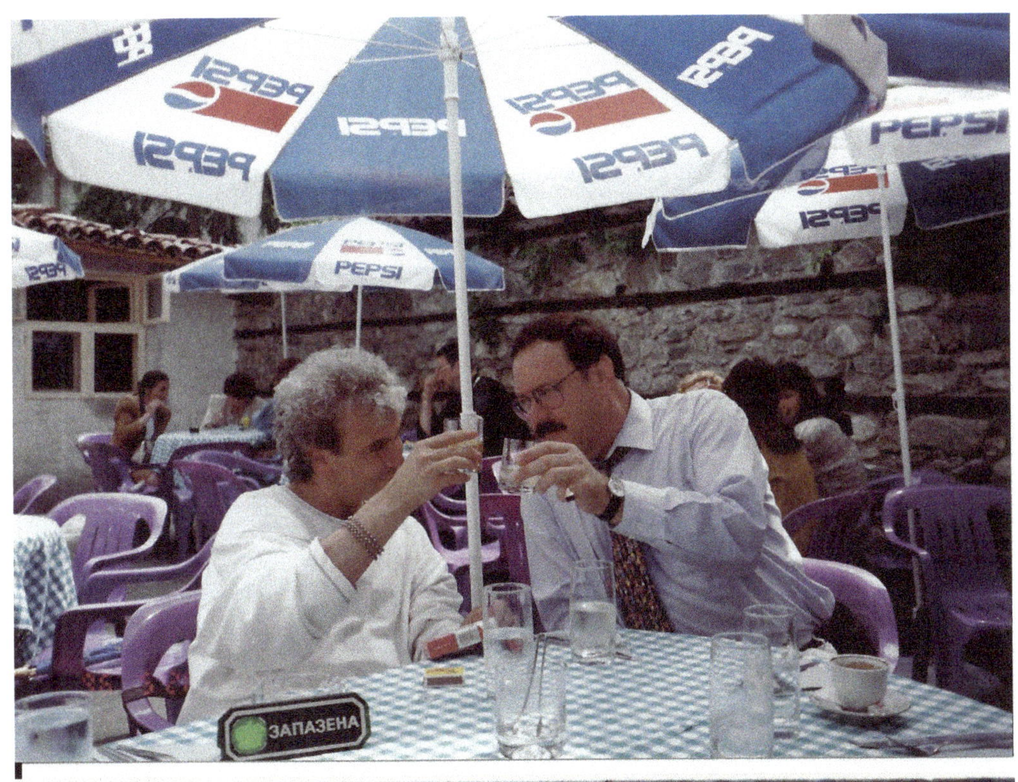

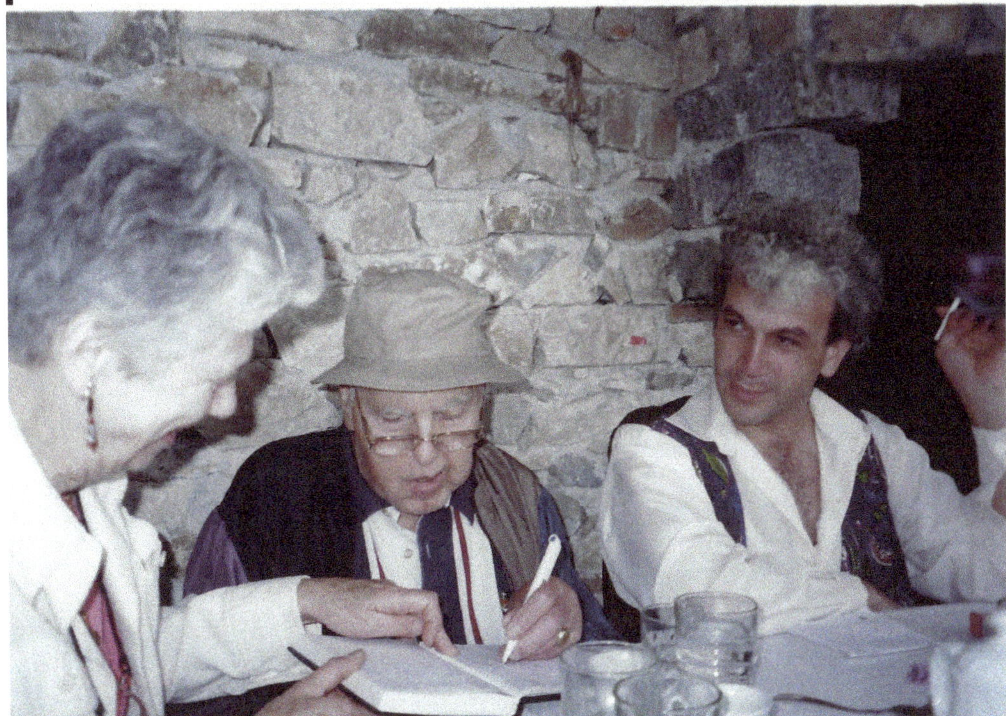

Visiting Nicky with Nancy Frankel and William

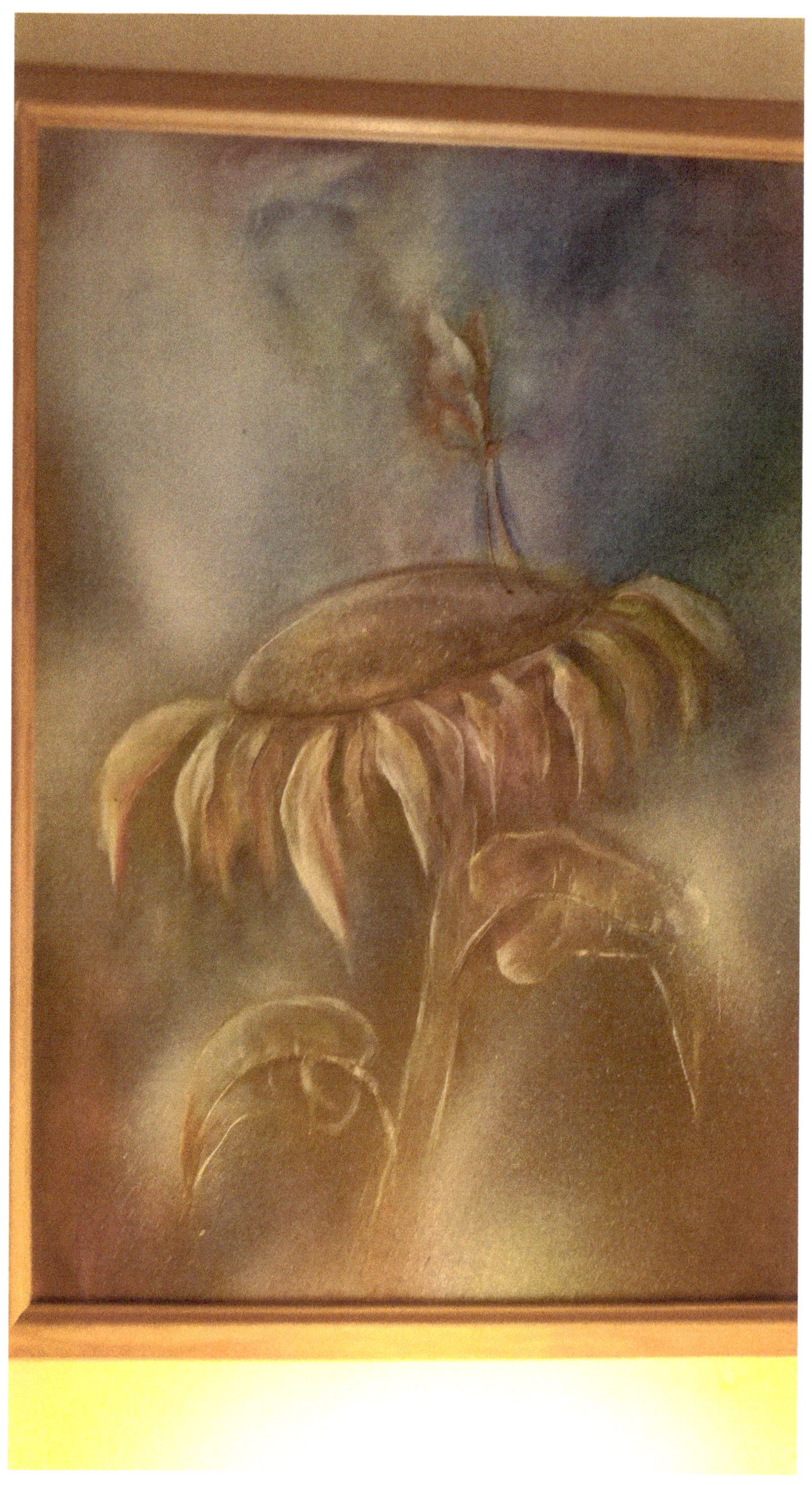

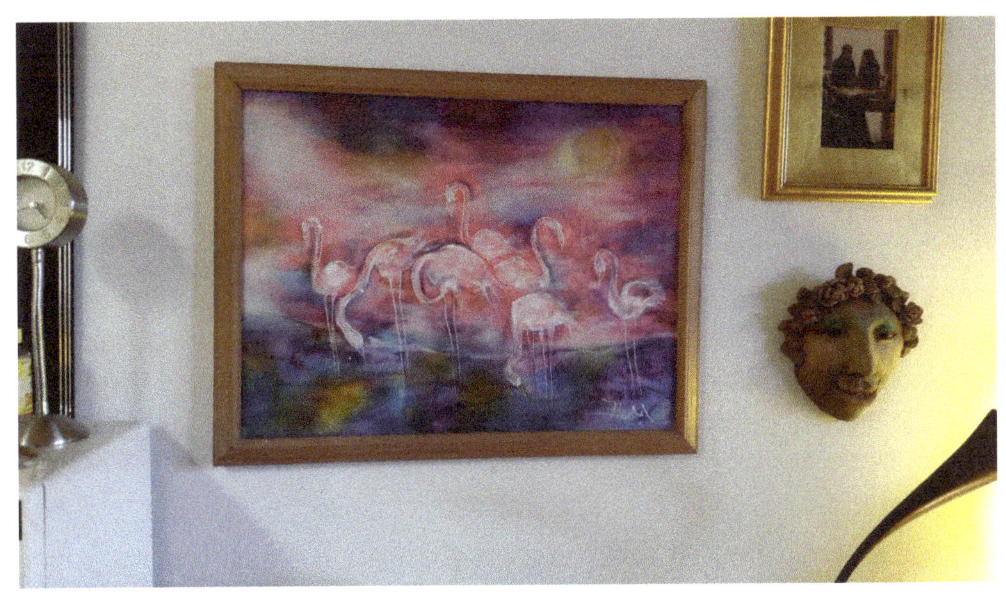

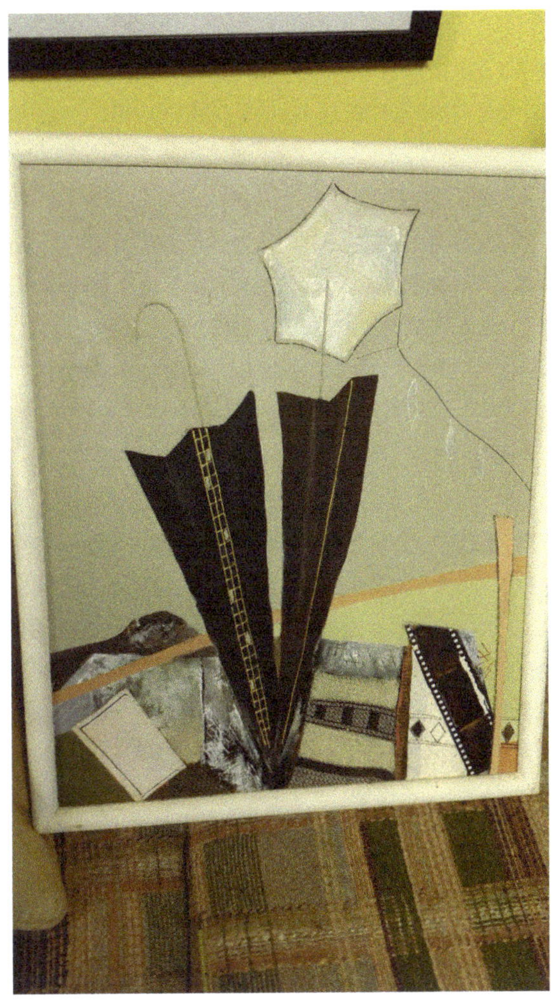

DIANA STOILOVA

In Bulgaria, a wife or a daughter adds an "a" to the end of the family name to make the gender distinction. I imagine some women artists might choose to take a professional name other than the family name, but in Diana's case, pride in the family name of her famous father may have kept her from such a decision. It is certainly a remarkable family, when one considers that her aunt Margarita is also an exquisite painter living and working in Varna. The art gene seems to have expressed itself formidably in this family's DNA. One thinks of another family – the Bach musicians in Germany where such talent runs deep in the blood.

In 1994, Diana studied at the Academy of the Beaux Arts in Sofia, Bulgaria, where she attended a Master Class for Pressure Graphics. When Stoimen took the family to Vienna, father and daughter stayed on after the death of his wife. In 1997, she studied at the Applied Arts in Vienna. She now shares her talent as a professor at the university.

Like her father, Diana's work is highly influenced by mythology. For Bulgarians, the legend of Icarus, exiled on an island prison, appealed to many Bulgarian artists dreaming of freedom as they lived their lives behind the iron curtain. But Diana's work often uses Eurydice as a subject for her work, a story that undoubtedly speaks to her. The bride of Orpheus lives in two worlds caught between light and darkness. When she leaves Hades, her mother rejoices and spring flourishes on the earth. Diana's vision captures both worlds in exquisite almost unimaginable detail in the etchings. Her paintings are filled with light and joy. Though inspired by her father's craftsmanship and vision, she has discovered a voice of her own as artist which has found a highly appreciative audience. Her works can be found in the collections of the Graphics Museum Carpenter, Bath Steben, Germany, the Dialogue Foundation, Paris, France, the Griffis Art Center, New London, CT, and in other private collections around the world. When one considers her talent and the delicacy of her spirit, nineteenth century beauties such as Fanny Mendelssohn or the Bronte sisters come to mind. It is charming to see how carefully she and her aunt look after Stoimen as he ages and faces the challenges that aging brings. Beyond what she brings as an artist, anyone would wish to have such a daughter in their lives.

Diana Stoilova

1994 Graduated from the National Academy of Art in Sofia, speciality Graphics.
1997 Graduated from the University of Applied Arts, speciality Painting and Graphics.

Works in the fields of graphics, painting and collage.

Solo exhibitions (selection)

2010 "Graphics, Painting and Objects", Gallery 10, Varna

2007 "Watercolours and Objects", Gallery Kavalet, Varna

2006 "Symbols of Wisdom", New Haven Art Gallery, USA
"Bulgarian Spring", Amtshaus Wieden, Haus Wittgenstein,Vienna

2004 The Hoxie Gallery, Rhode Island, USA

2003 Art Gallery UNO City, International Centre Vienna
Galerie Haslinger in Schülke und Mayr Company, Vienna

2000 Galerie Lehalle, Paris, France
Alexey von Schlippe Gallery, Connecticut, USA

Group exhibitions (selection)

2012 “So Close, So Far”, Contemporary Bulgarian artists abroad, National Palace of Culture, Sofia
Salon du Dessin et de la Peinture à l´eau, Grand Palais, Paris

2010 "Touches", Gallery Bulgari, Sofia
Salon du Dessin et de la Peinture à l´eau, Grand Palais, Paris

2009 "Painting, Graphics, Ceramics ", Haus Wittgenstein, Vienna
Salon du Dessin et de la Peinture à l´eau, Grand Palais, Paris

2007 "Graphics Exhibition", Offizin für Druckgraphik, Vienna
7. Biennale Internationale d`Art Contemporain, Senlis, France

2006 "Days of Culture", Bank Austria, Vienna
"Woman and migration", Gallery Lendava Castle, Slovenia

2005 VI. Women's International Conference, Künstlerhaus Graz, Graz, Austria
Cultural Centre "Ursulinenhof Linz", Linz, Austria

2003 5. Biennale Internationale d`Art Contemporain, Senlis, France
"Kunst ist gleich Seele", Stadtgalerie Vienna, Vienna

2002 "Window on the Black Sea", Delight Hamilton Gallery, Seattle, USA
"Joint exhibition", Der Kunstraum, Vienna
Frankfurter Buchmesse, Frankfurt, Germany

Works of the artist are included in the collections of the Graphics Museum – Schreiner Foundation, Bad Steben, Germany; Art Dialogue Foundation, Paris, France; The Griffis Art Center, USA; and private collections in Bulgaria and abroad.

Lives and works in Vienna, Austria

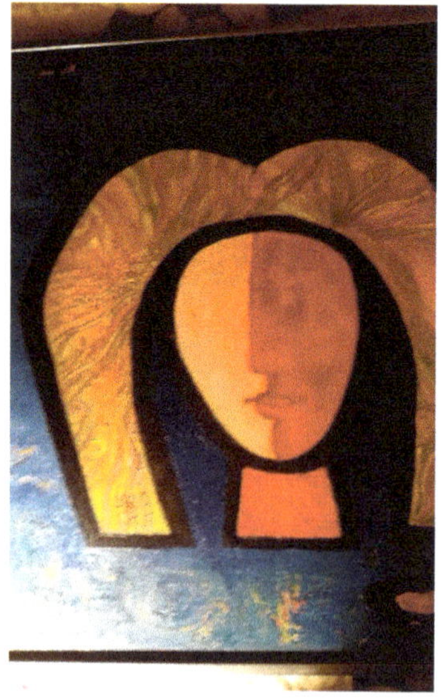

The work of Diana Stoilova

Diana Stoilova works in the areas of graphic art and painting and lives in Vienna, Austria.

Her work is rich in archaic and semantic signs in which abstract and figurative meanings are interrelated. The foundation is the historical and cultural rendition of mythological and psychological themes. In this way symbols of human culture are weaved with abstract signs.

Diana Stoilova has developed a unique painting technique where pasty and semi-translucent strokes are homogenously connected to clear or muted tones.

The simplicity of shapes bound in a collage is the other expressive means in the artist's work.

Diana Stoilova draws from her huge artistic potential and in-depth research of the classical modern art, the Surrealism and the French school of Ecole de Paris.

Alongside with her paintings, the artist is engaged with the graphic art. Her etchings reveal perfect implementation in both black-and-white and colour techniques worked on a couple of plates and demonstrate the potential of the mysterious printmaking process.

Another special interest of Diana is her involvement with the theory and history of art, which inspires her creativity.

Diana Stoilova studied Graphic Art in the National Academy of Art in Sofia and Painting and Graphic Art in the University of Applied Arts in Vienna.

Her works have been exhibited on multiple exhibitions in Austria and worldwide.

Prof. Ulrich Gansert
June 2010, Vienna

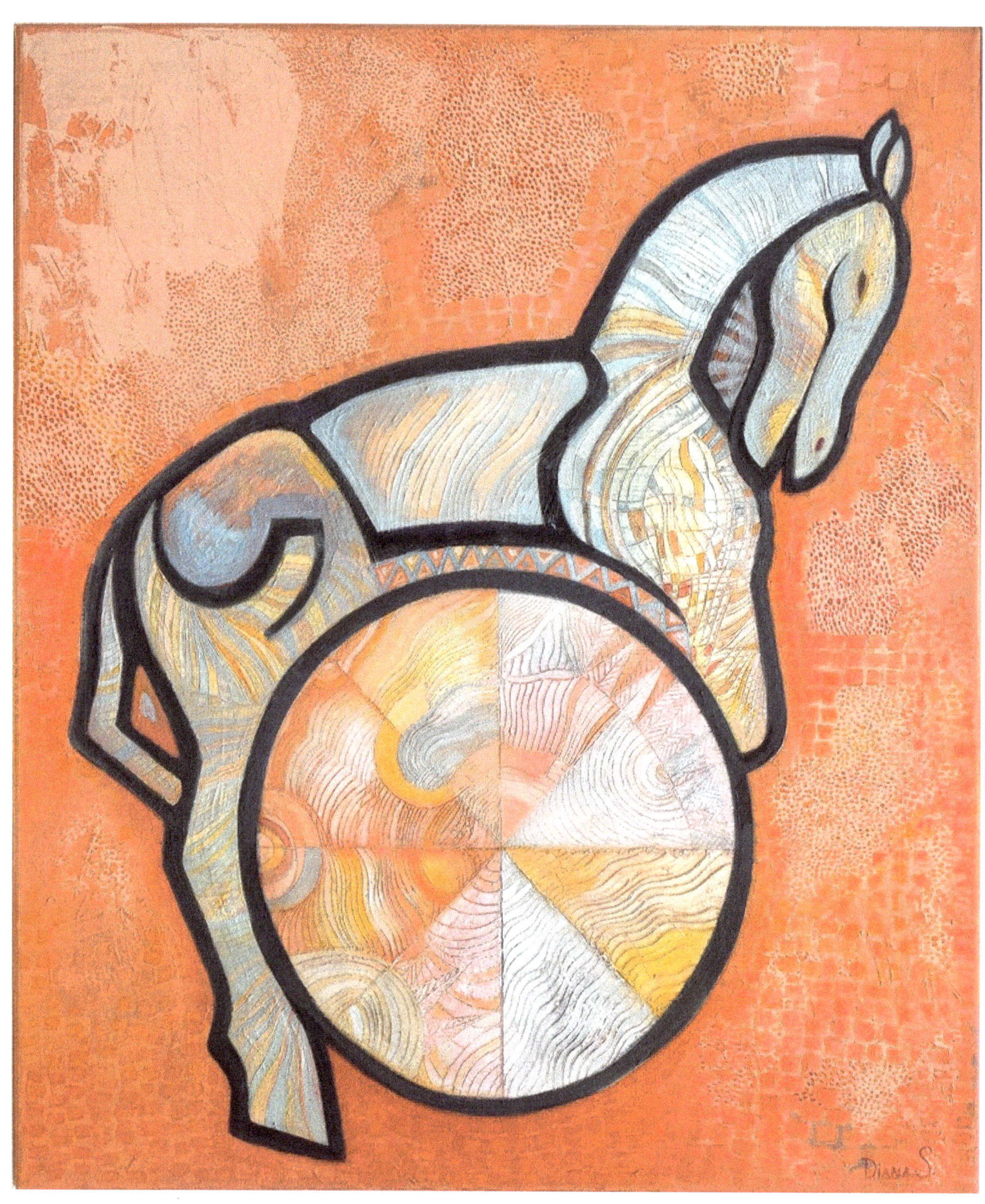
DIANA S.

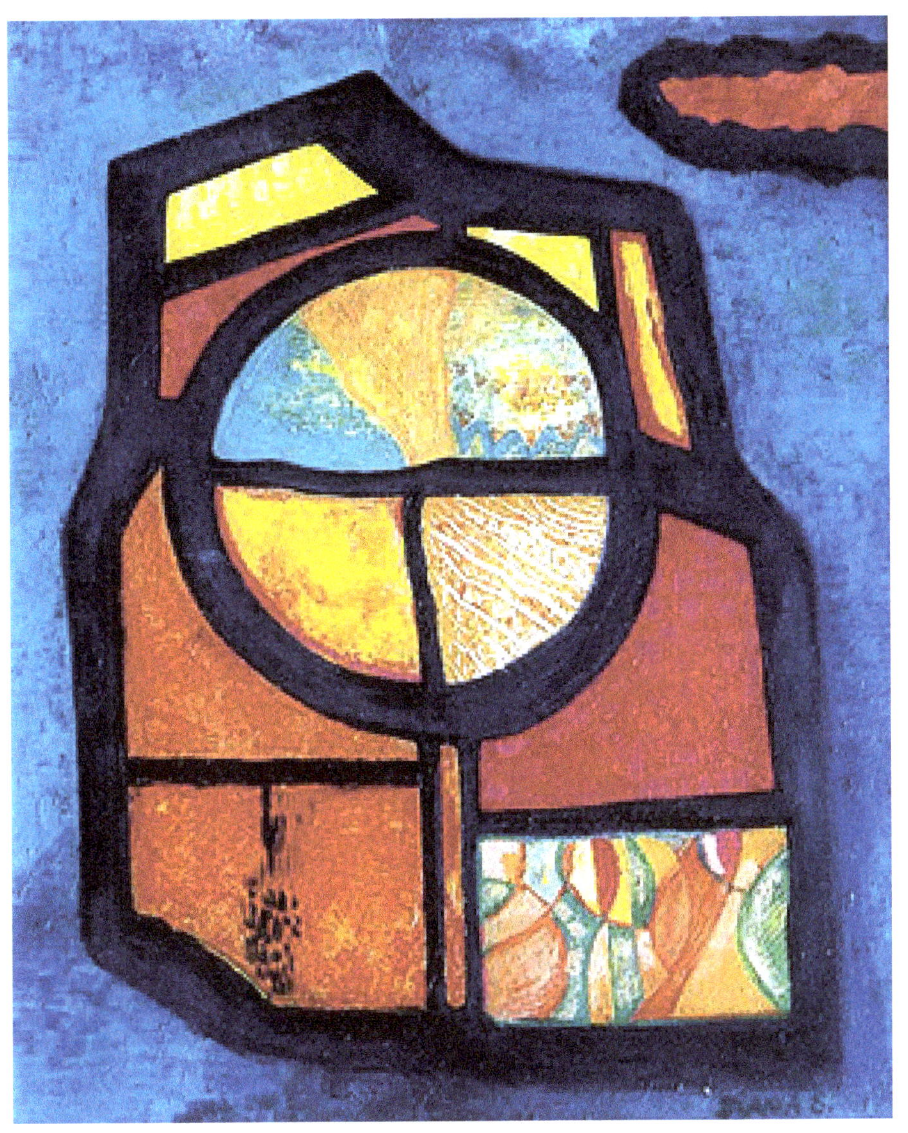

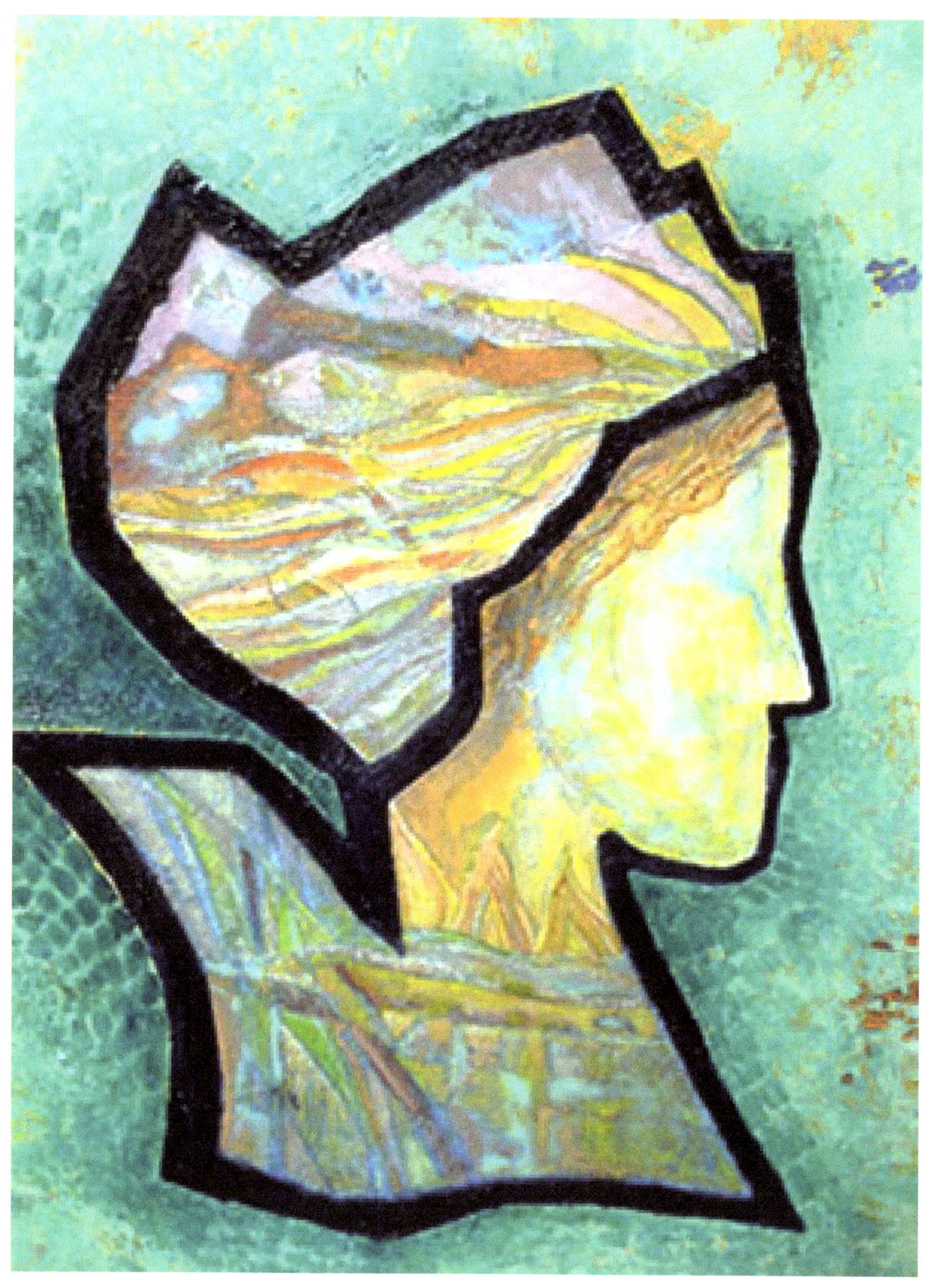

MARGARITA VOYNOVA

Margarita, like me, is a Leo, which is perhaps why we get on so well together. During many visits to my favorite city in Bulgaria, her home town of Varna, we have spent many happy days visiting her and her family. She is a remarkable, can do person and loves to take charge. She is Stoimen Stoilov's younger sister, and shares the loving attention the family pays to the "patriarch." She has remained a bon vivant throughout all the years we have known her and her optimism and vitality shine forth in her work. She is the perfect foil to her psychiatrist husband who has looked after the many broken souls that came as a result of Bulgaria's political and economic challenges throughout the years. These folks are examples of families that make me proud to be a Bulgarian. Here is her biographical information and artist statement. Unlike the river people, she is so capable and responded immediately to my request for information in English for this catalog.

BIOGRAPHY

Margarita Voynova
Born on 11 August 1952 in Varna, Bulgaria.

Specialized painting and aquarelle in Varna and Vienna under Prof. Stoimen Stoilov – bearer of Herder Prize.

Since 1980 Margarita Voynova is member of the Union of Bulgarian Artists.

Solo exhibitions:

2014 – Varna, "Old Varna" Gallery

2013 – Sofia, "Maestro" Gallery

2012 – Shumen, "Iva Gallery" Art Centre, painting, drawing and aquarelle

2012 – Varna, "WinArt" Art Centre, painting, collage and aquarelle

2012 – Varna, "Old Varna" Gallery, painting, aquarelle

2011 – Sofia, "Arthur" Gallery, painting, aquarelle

2010 – Varna, "Largo" Gallery, painting, aquarelle

2009 – Sofia,"Azza" Gallery, painting, collage

2009 – Sofia, "Arte" Gallery, painting, aquarelle

2008 – Varna, "Kavalet" Gallery, painting, aquarelle and collage

2008 – Varna, "Old Varna" Gallery, painting, aquarelle

2007 – Varna, "Yuka" Gallery, painting, aquarelle

2005 – Frankfurt, Germany, "Ude" Gallery, painting, aquarelle

2004 – Vienna, Austria, Art Exhibition of the UN, painting, aquarelle

2003 – Connecticut, USA, "Alva Gallery," painting

2003- Connecticut, USA, "Alexey von Schlippe" Gallery of Art, painting

2002- Lyon, France, "John Dort" Gallery, painting, aquarelle

2001 – Lyon, France, "Georges" Gallery, painting, aquarelle

1999 – Burgas, Ruse, Varna and Albena, painting, aquarelle, woven textile and stained glass

1998 – Istanbul, Turkey, Journalist Centre, painting, aquarelle

1997 – Amman, Jordan, The Royal Art Centre, painting

1996 – Sofia, “Interart” Gallery, painting, aquarelle

1995 – Varna and “Dobrudzha” Hotel, Albena, aquarelle

1994- Vienna, Austria, “Kavalier” Gallery, painting

1994- Perth, Australia, “A Shed” Gallery, painting, woven textile

1993 – Varna, City Art Gallery, painting

1991 – Berlin, Germany, Schlesische Gallery, woven textile

1989 – Albena, woven textile

1987 – Varna, City Art Gallery, woven textile

Margarita Voynova works in the areas of painting, aquarelle, drawing, ceramic, stained glass, mural painting and woven textile. She has implemented dozens of large-scale stained-glass and mural-painting projects, theatrical sceneries and woven textile designs for hotels and public buildings by the Bulgarian Black Sea coast. Her works can be seen at: www.Saatchi-gallery- Margarita Voynova, http://www.art.ida.bg/facebook-Margarita Voynova artist painter.

In 2006, Margarita Voynova published her first novel “Alsario” and in 2008 wrote a screenplay based on the novel. She is author of essays and short catalog.

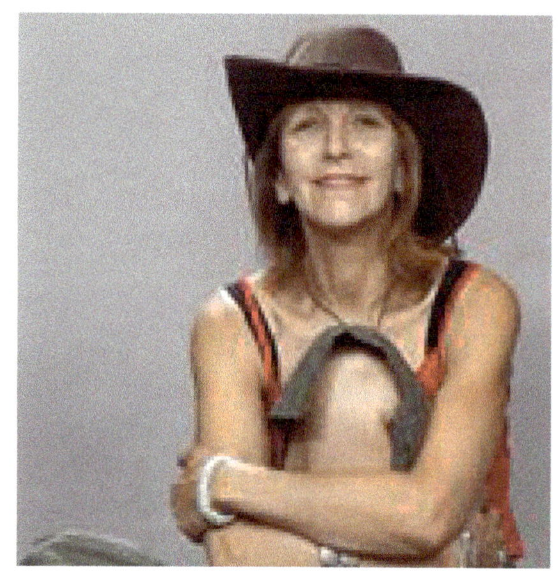

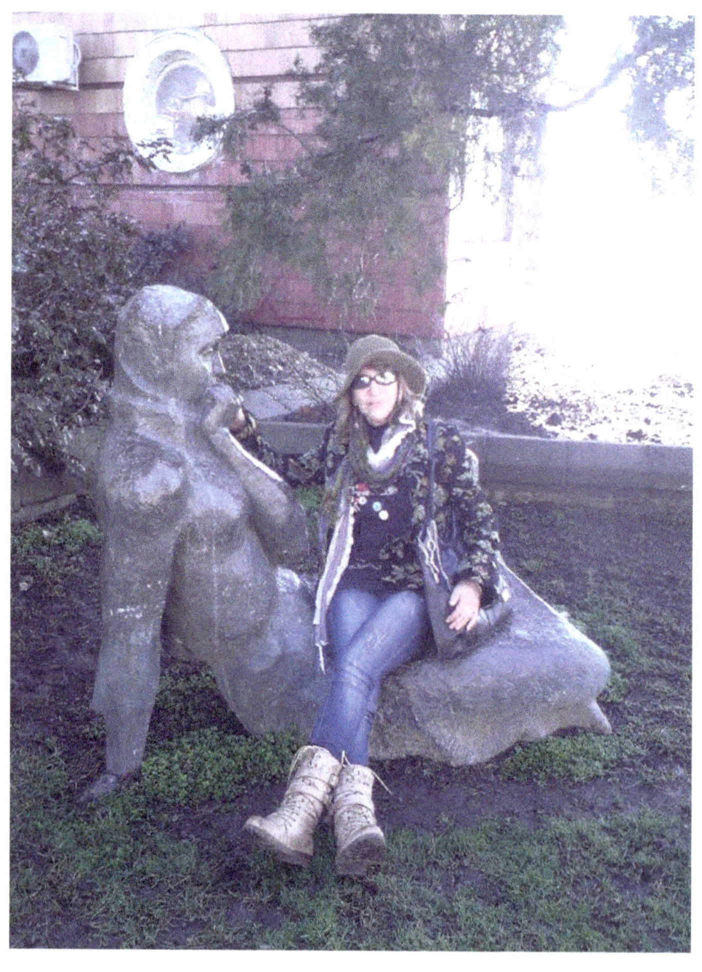

About the work of Margarita Voynova

It is not by chance that Margarita's works contain so much warmth, optimism and fairy-tale feel. This is her way to "retell" Nature. Voynova presents the cross-sections and the meeting points of different cultures in a unique amazing way. The wonderful harmony of colours, fantasy and improvisation mesmerize the viewer. Voynova depicts emotional states through a modern plastic language, which brings her art closer to her public. She has an original artistic expressivity, which acts like a poetic message full of optimism and vitality and communicates the rich Slavonic spirituality.

Andre Mur, writer and art critic
Lyon, France, 2000

Margarita Voynova depicts primary signs stylized in a fantastic way– exotic animals, birds, fishes and flowers that originate from a world bound with the myths about the Earth, Nature and Air. These signs are the archetypal concept of the universe and a symbiosis of the nature that surrounds us. These are calm, focused and accessible symbols understandable by everyone. The artist finds these signs in her engagements with the traditions of the world cultures and in the exploration of her own self. Her works are a vivid exemplification of the Jungian philosophy.

The harmony of colors and shapes is breathtaking, surprising and convincing. The artist speaks through her works, which communicate with ancient civilizations and draw from a shared archetypal culture, which has universal cultural, historical, ethnographic and emotional roots.

The seemingly naïve style of her symbolism, of the signs and expressive language, direct the viewer to a forgotten primeval essence of matters and thus evoke the joy of memories, which spring from the universal history of humankind.

Prof. Dr. Philipp Maurer, art critic and culture expert, Vienna

Sofia, 26 May 2009

I do not observe rules and do not follow formulas in my creative process. I would like my audience to feel pleasure when seeing my works, the way I do when painting them. I love art in all its forms and I know that many people love it, too. In fact, Art is a huge illusion and those who believe in it are true connoisseurs.

Margarita Voynova

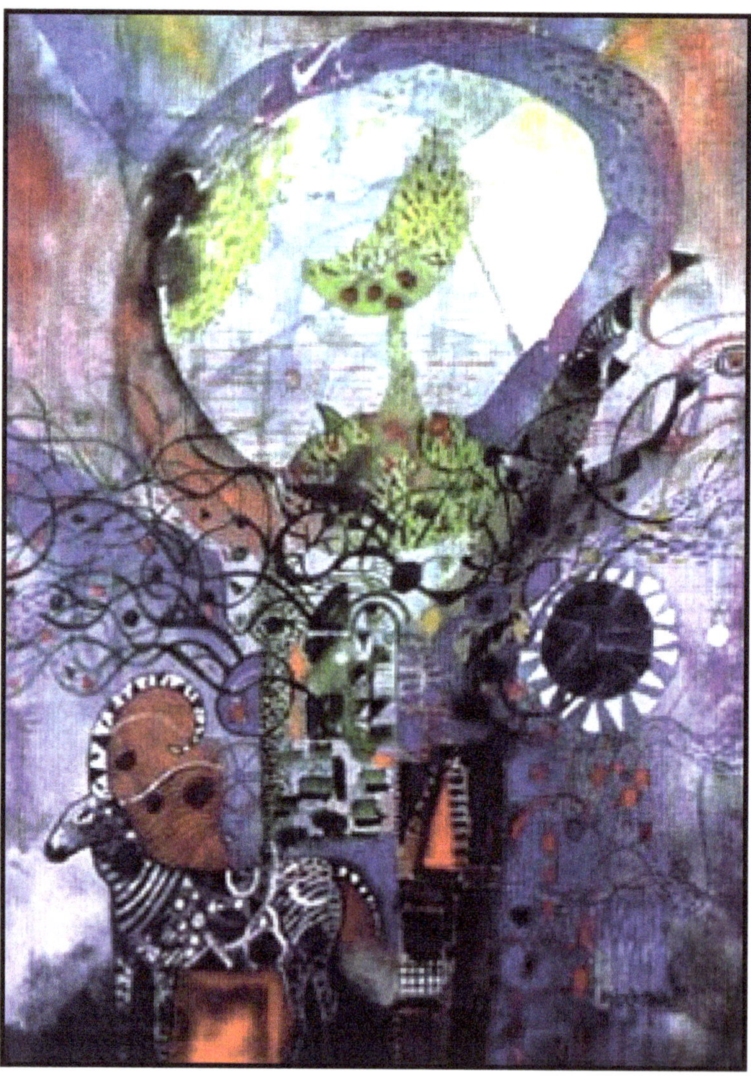

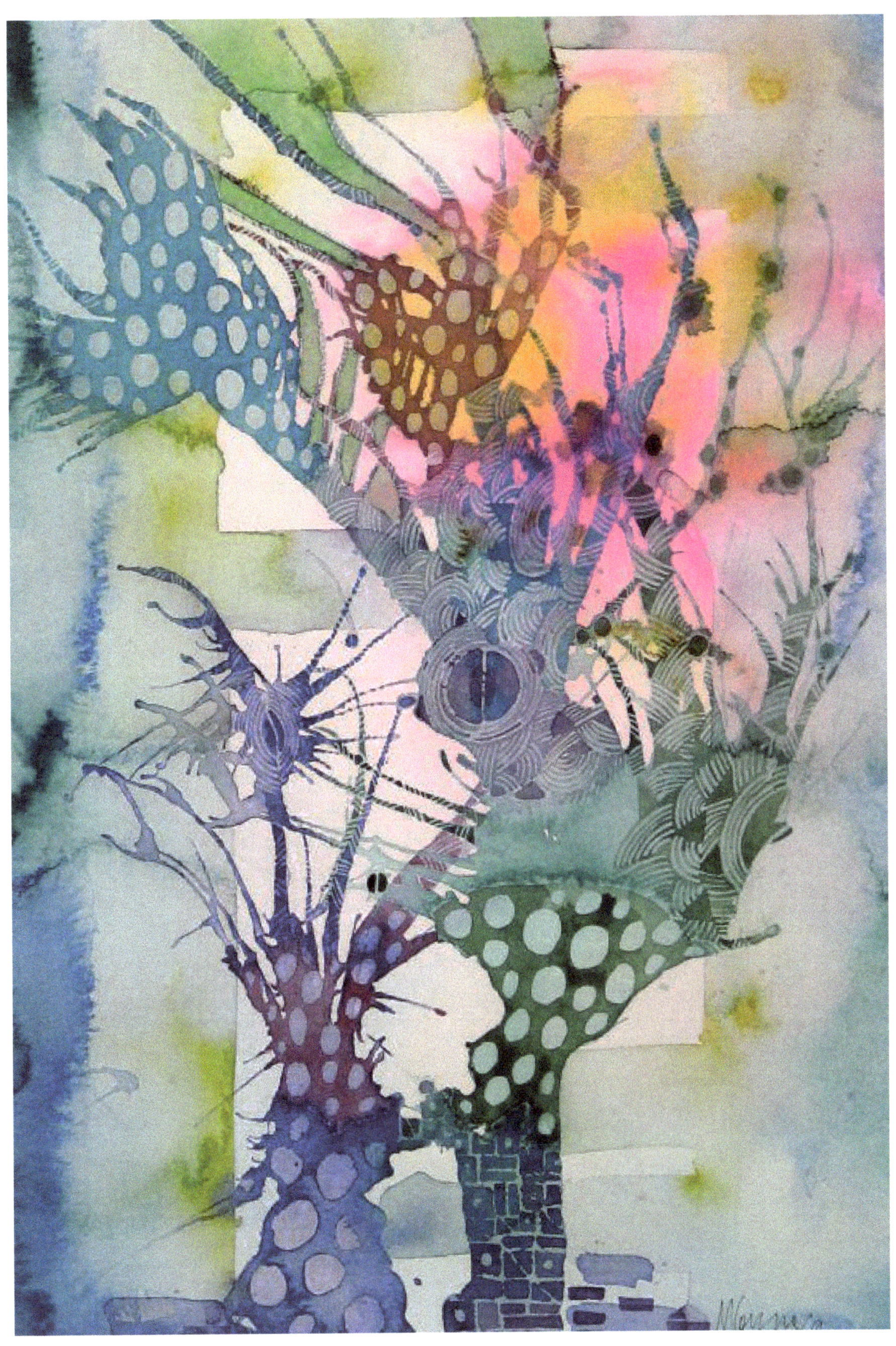

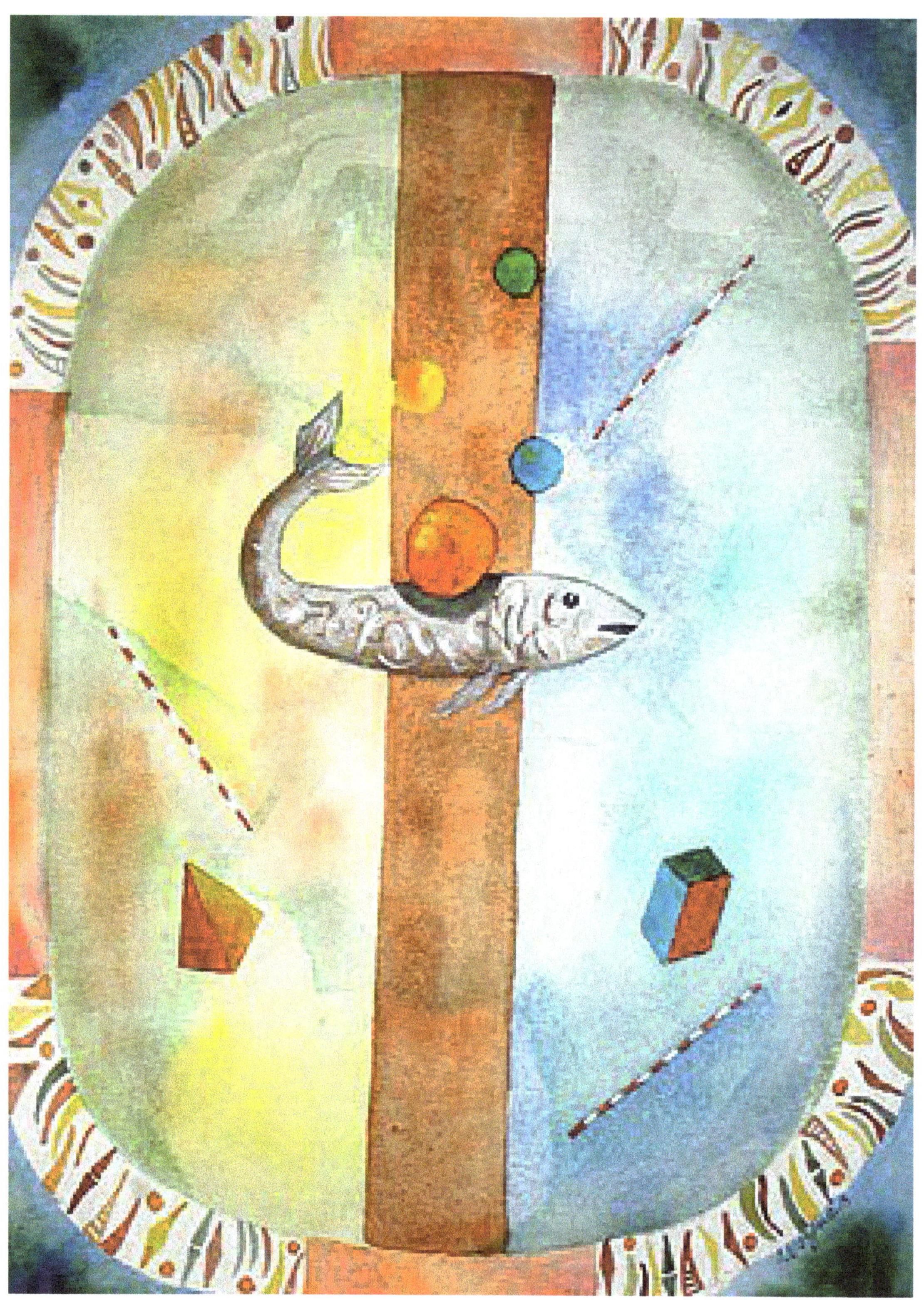

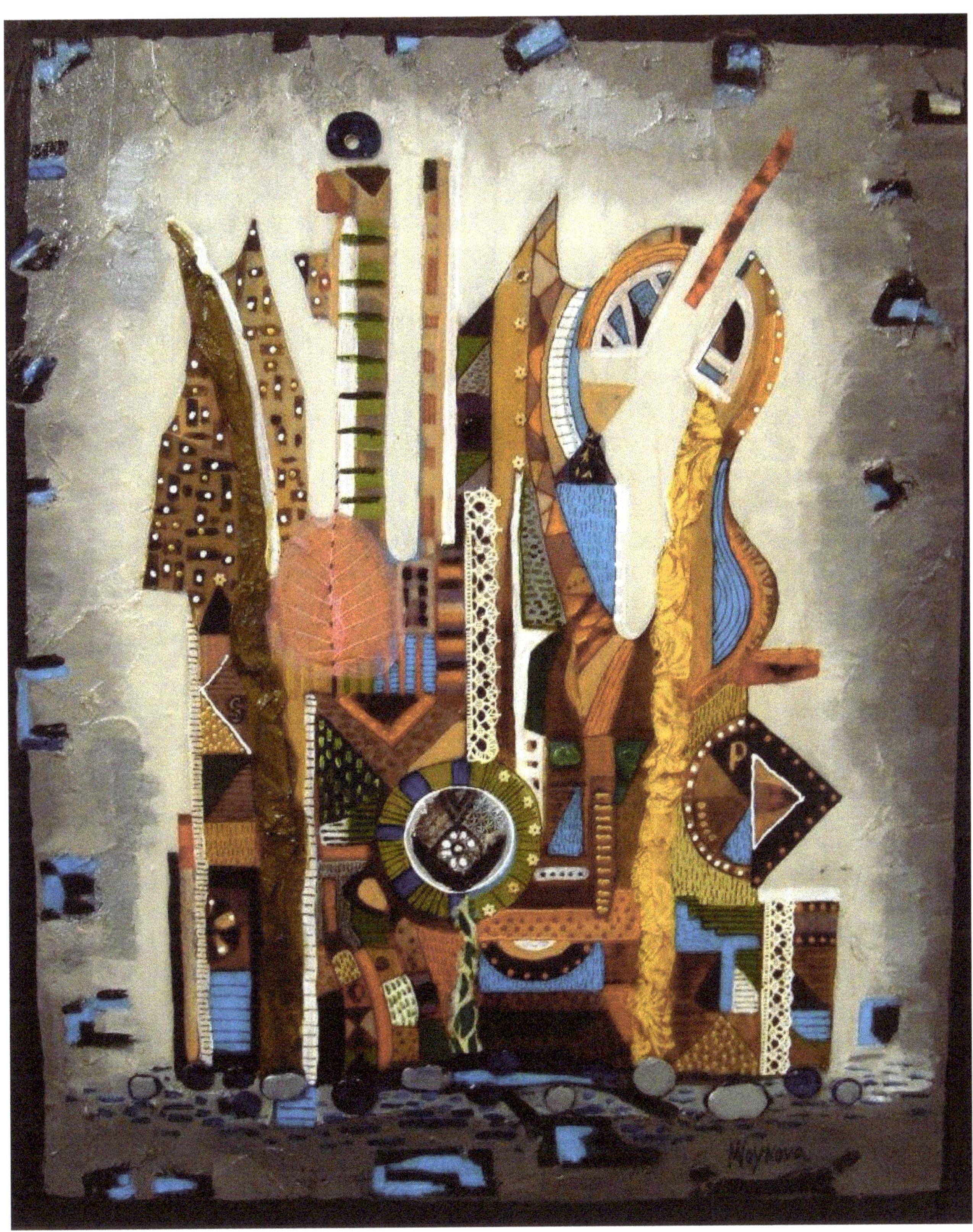

PANCHO MALENZANOV

Pancho is an honorary "River" person though he lives in Sofia, and lately in London. He is sort of the Lone Ranger in the group, just as zany, but with a lot of attitude. He takes great pleasure in his daughter and the various women in his life. One thinks of cool black private eye John Shaft in the film series, or possibly Doc Martin in the BBC sitcom. Pancho is hip, in the know, and doesn't suffer fools gladly. He's not mean, just worldly wise. You would know none of this from the brilliant, cubist paintings he produces which are filled with such animation and joy in life. He has a fauve's love of color and you probably would never know he was Bulgarian if you only saw his canvases. Pancho is an original.

CURRICULUM VITAE

Pancho Malezanov

Born in Sofia in 1964.
Graduated from Secondary Art School in Sofia in 1984.
Participated in general exhibitions in major galleries in Sofia in 1988-1989.

SOLO EXHIBITIONS
2014 – Artamoncev Gallery Sofia Bulgaria
2011-Anima Art Gallery Hilton Sofia Bulgaria
2011- Bulgarian Embassy – London, England
2008- Gallery Ikar Sofia Bulgaria
2007- Bulgarian Cultural Institute-Berlin Germany
2004 - Avant-garde Gallery, Plovdiv
2004 - Apollo and Mercury Gallery, Sofia
2003 - Iridium Gallery, Sofia
2003 - Draca Gallery, Sofia
2001 - Monitor Daily Gallery, Sofia
2000 - Municipality Gallery, Varna

2000 - Art 36 Gallery, Sofia
2000 - Draca Gallery, Sofia
2000 - Romfeya Gallery, Plovdiv
1998 - Art Club Gallery, Sofia
1998 - Gallery of the Bulgarian National Assembly
1997 - Ata-Ray Gallery Sheraton Hotel, Sofia
1997 - Macta Gallery, Sofia
1996 - Ata-Ray Gallery, Sofia
1995 - Macta Gallery, Sofia
1994 - Macta Gallery, Sofia
1993 - Ata-Ray Gallery, Sofia
1992 – Mericas Gallery, Athens, Greece

SELECTED GROUP EXHIBITIONS

2014 – Hay Hill Gallery London U.K.
2013 – Hay Hill Gallery London U.K.
2013 Makta Art Gallery Kempinski Hotel Sofia Bulgaria
2005 – Apolonia Arts Festival, Bulgaria
2003 – Delight Hamilton Gallery, Seattle, WA (US)
2002 – Gettysburg, PA (US)
2001 – Washington, D.C.
2001 – Aleksey von Schlippe Gallery, Univ. of Connecticut, New London, CT (US)

The prominent art critic Maximilian Kirov writes about the author:

..."As an artist Pancho Malezanov always prefers to interact with nature directly, but it is difficult to call him a landscape artist in the exact meaning of the term. He is not interested in particular details, but prefers to unite the entire scenery through a randomly situated point of view, which does not take into account the horizon line or the static position from which each natural object is seen. This point of view almost always has a peculiar "bird's plan view", which allows him to contemplate a panoramic scene. This is a "bird's eye vision" where the retina captures separate aspects of reality during the very flight. Consequently, it is difficult to imagine the author's micro cosmos via traditional concepts as up, down, left or right. In Bulgarian painting only the Great Kazakov has ever dared to depict nature in this way. Nevertheless, Malezanov is not his imitator but a true continuer of this graphic principle."

A NOTE FROM PANCHO:
"Painting has been always my 'calling'," he says. "In my teenage years I was strongly influenced by the Bulgarian artists Greddy Assa, Roumen Rachev, and Hundertwasser. My first paintings were mostly abstract landscapes, painted with oil and pastel. For me, nature is large part of my inner peace; therefore painting nature brought out my 'self.' I would dare to call them ‘flying landscapes'. I see most images in my head from a bird's point of view. Also, for me, the presence and inspiration of a loved one plays an important role, and it is then that I do my best work."

Malenzanov also paints "machineries": laptops, airplanes, boats, and submarines, with a special vision on how to incorporate those objects. "Music plays a very important role in my life and work : Jazz gives me a lot, so I feel obligated to 'give back' to jazz through my paintings."

His graphic designs and logos can be seen on major ads and publications in Bulgaria

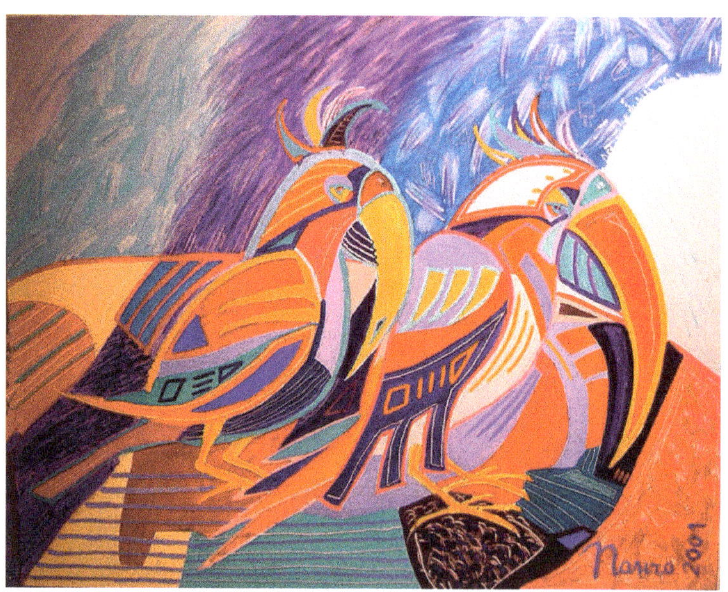

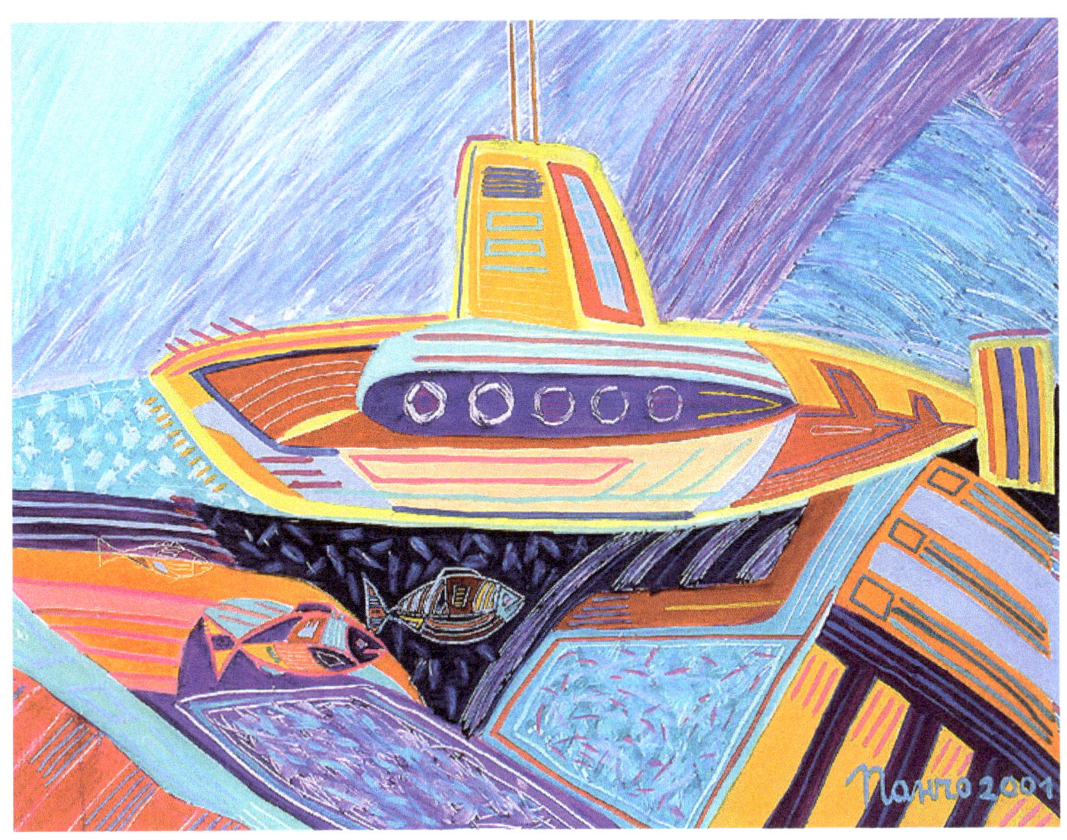

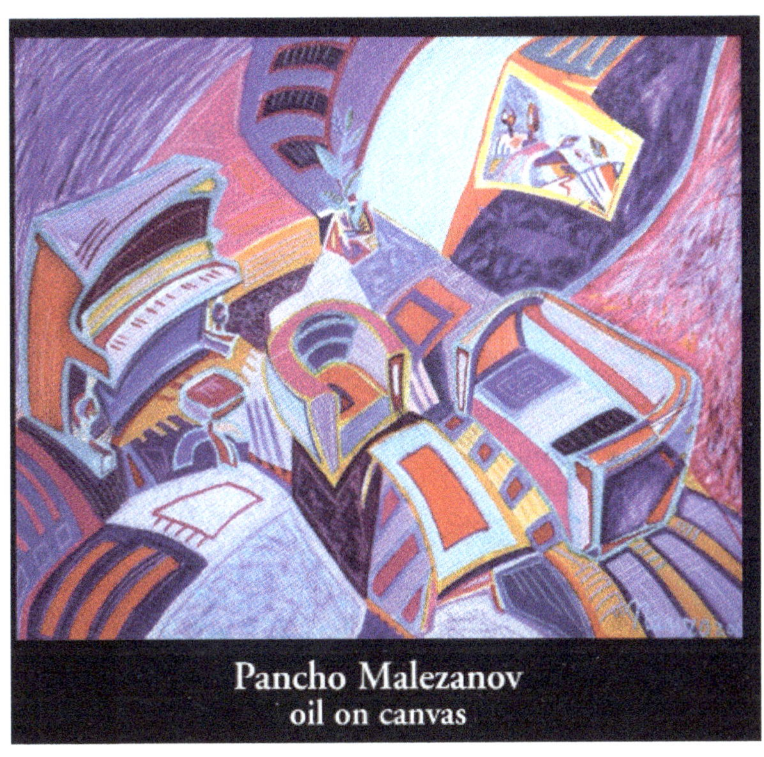

Pancho Malezanov
oil on canvas

Ivo Hadjimishev

An example of the really fun sort of encounters Sharon Griffis arranges between her Center and people in the community is the day she brought Ivo to lunch at Wiliam's home at Riverrun. We were prepared with enough scotch to satisfy Sharon and Ivo and despite the terrific downpour that threatened to wash out the afternoon, Ivo was in paradise. They came dressed for an elegant meal but after enough encouragement from Johnny Walker, we all decided to go down to the point on the river, Ivo the proverbial kid in a candy shop. The contrasts he was able to achieve in black and white because of the storm kept him enthralled, and we almost had to foce him back into the house. We all went traipsing down to the river, flood be damned like Gene Kelley dancing in the rain. Some weeks later he mailed me back the socks I had lent him. Here is a shot he took of me, umbrella tiled in the wrong direction, checking out the heavens. It seems slightly prophetic when I consider the challenges of keeping the foundation center afloat, glass half full, half empty as it were as I look to the clouds for some sign of where the weather is going.

Artistic biography
Personal Data: Born 12.09.1950, Sofia
Education:
1975 Graduated from College of the Arts "Bournemouth and Pool College of Arts", UK, majoring in photography
Professional performances: Professional dealt with photography since 1969
1973 Artist-photographer of the promotion of the Ministry of Culture
1975-1989, the editor of "Homeland" Since 1975: Honorary life member of the Royal Photographic Association, UK 1990-94 Assistant to the Associated Press
Since 1991, the founder of "FOMUS" Ltd. - the official distributor of KODAK for Bulgaria. Consultant "Professional Products" in the company.
1995-99 Co-founder of "Now" - "Build Editor".
1999-2003, editor of "Woman Today" magazine and "Our House".

Since 1996: Co-founder of the Bulgarian Photographic Association (BFU). Since 2000 the Association Pretsedatel
2003 Head of "Artistic Photography" at the National Gallery of Art
Exhibitions: He has over 20 collections of photographs and fotoeseta presented primarily in Europe: UK, Austria, Holland, France, Italy, Lithuania, Poland, Nigeria, Hungary, Mexico, USA. Has donated his original collections of the Universities of Leeds, UK Leiden, Netherlands, Pisa, Italy and the Museum of Photography in Lithuania.
1974 His first exhibition was displayed in the halls of the Royal Photographic Association in England.
1990 established permanent contact with the Department of photojournalism at Columbia University in Missouri.
1991,92,93,94, the initiator of a series of seminars in Bulgaria on professional photojournalism with speakers from the "National Geographic", "Time", "Life", "Washington Post", "Star Tribune", "US News and World Report "and others.
1992, 93, 2003 With his active participation for the first time in Bulgaria, visit the publications of the famous Foundation "World Press Photo", whose exposures are represented in the National Palace of Culture.
1994 Participated in the creation of the First Bulgarian photographic collection at the National Art Gallery (Donation)
1996 Participant in the collection "Portrait photography in the Bulgarian" - National Gallery of Art
Completed in December 2000 the Bulgarian-Dutch project "Bulgaria - Identity and Tolerance" - Euro-
Bulgarian Cultural Centre, Ministry of Culture, Sofia, 2002 Europe, Belgium
Books:
1982 "Bulgaria", album, 100 color and black and white illustrations
1986 "Rila Monastery"
1996 "Rogozen treasure"
1998 "Thracian culture in the Bulgarian lands"-album catalog, 500 p

Sky half full, half empty?

MARTA LEVCHEVA

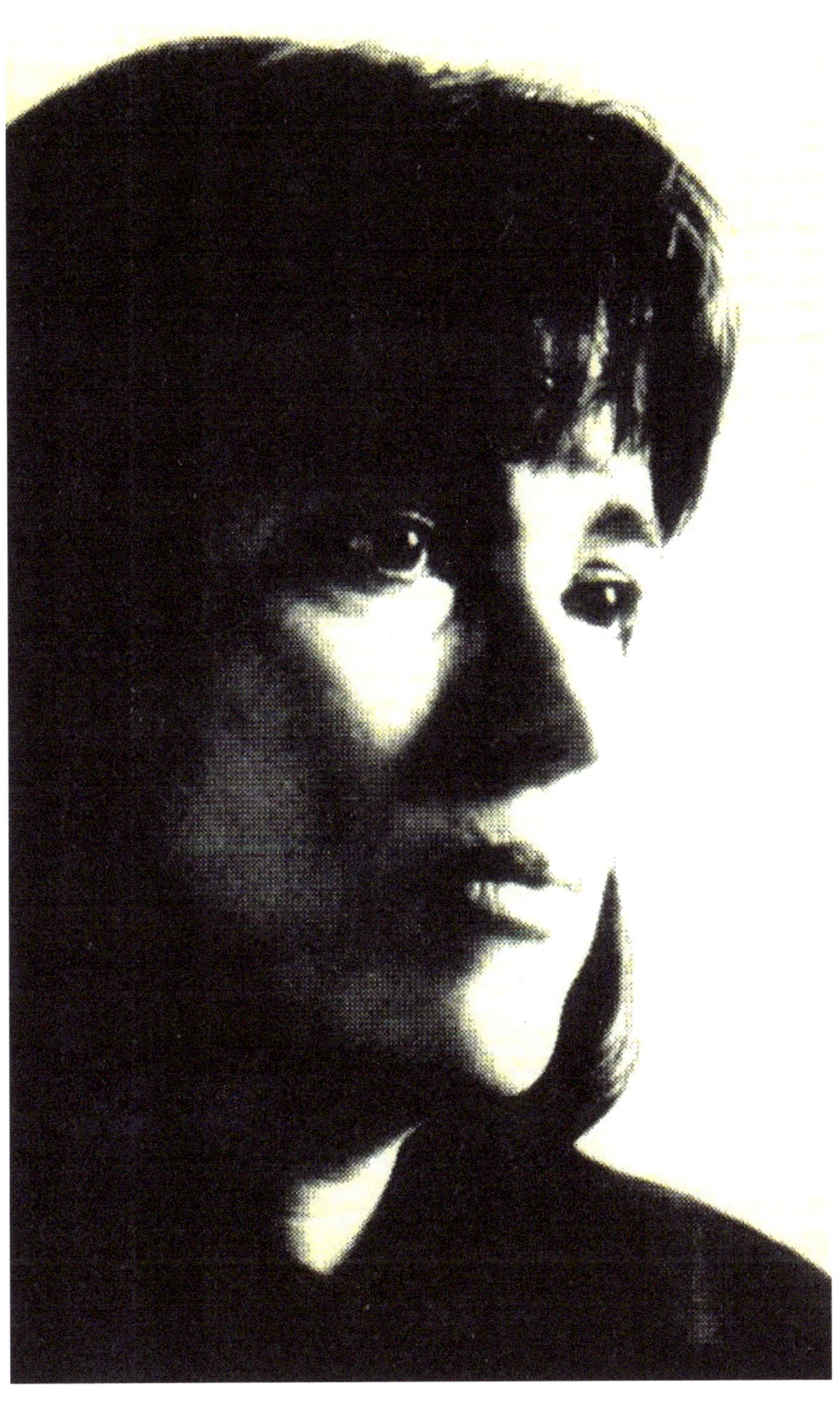

Again, if we add an "a" to the Levchev name we discover that Marta is a member of yet another famous artistic family in Bulgaria, that of Lyubomir Levchev. Marta is his daughter and Dora Boneva, his famous wife. Marta now lives in Vienna with her daughter. Her works tap into the subconscious with the sensitivity of Carl Jung who believed that the process of individuation was essential in order for a person to become whole and fully developed as a human being. He describes it as a process in which the various parts of a person, including the conscious and unconscious, become completely integrated so that the individual becomes his or her "true self." I do not know if she has achieved this "true self" in the dream-like visions she has, but they are arresting and touch us deeply the way dreams often do.

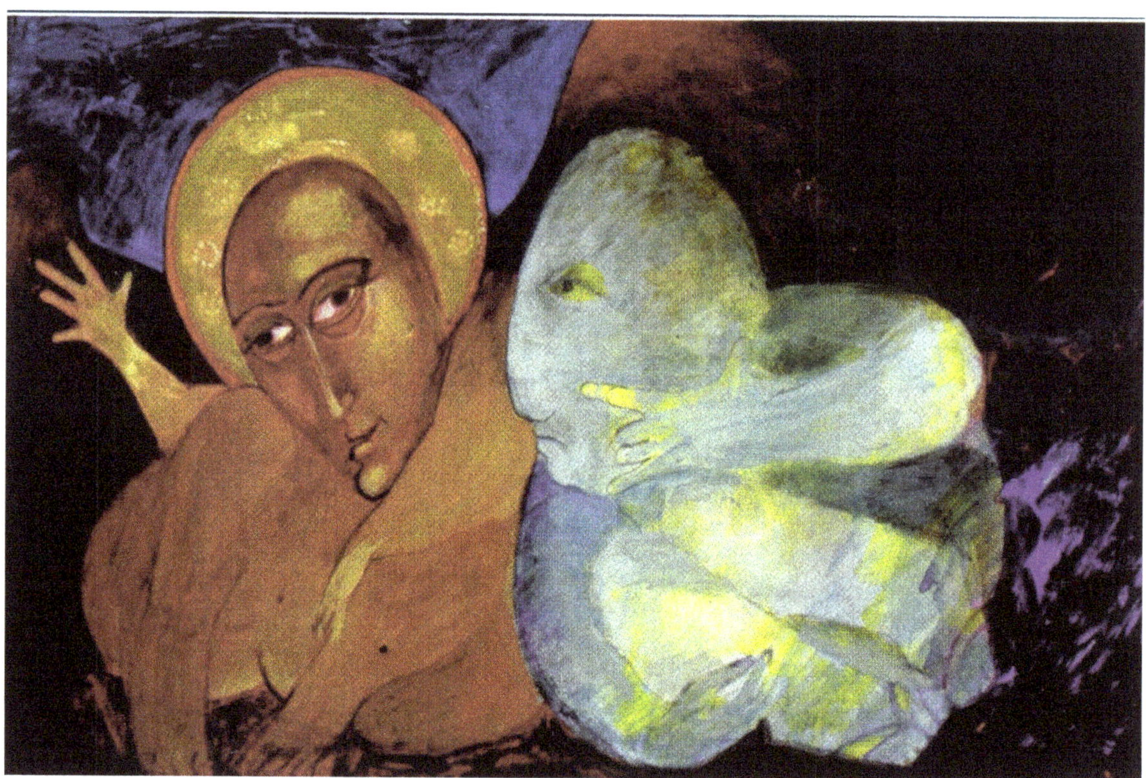

Marta Levcheva was born on June 1, 1960 in Sofia, Bulgaria. She has degrees from the School of Arts and the National Academy of Fine Arts in Sofia, where she graduated in 1985 in the class of the renowned Bulgarian artist Prof. Ivan Kirkov. She has worked as art director of "K&M" publishing complex, a graphic designer and book designer, and a creative director for a major advertising agency in Sofia. In 1988 she published "A Portrait", a book of poetry. She is a member of the Union of Bulgarian Artists, affiliated to the International Association of Art at UNESCO. In addition to some group shows, she has had the following individual exhibitions:

1988 – Newman gallery - Washington D.C., U.S.A.
1997 – Sozopol, Bulgaria, within the program of the National Day of Culture "Apolonia '97"
1997 – Draka Gallery, Sofia
1996 – Gallery 17, Varna, Bulgaria
1995 – Balabanova Kashta Gallery, Plovdiv, Bulgaria
1985 – Gallery 77, Sofia

Private collections in Bulgaria, Japan, USA, Cyprus, Austria, Switzerland own her works.

She graduated from the High School of Arts in Sofia, and then from the National Academy of Fine Arts in Sofia where she studied in the class of the renowned Bulgarian artist Ivan Kirkov and received her MA degree in 1985. She has worked as an art director for K&M Publishing Complex, as a graphic designer, a book designer, a creative director for a major advertising agency in Sofia, and a production manager for The Word Works publishing house in Washington, DC. In 1988 she published A Portrait, a book of poetry. She is a member of the Union of Bulgarian Artists, affiliated to the International Association of Arts with UNESCO

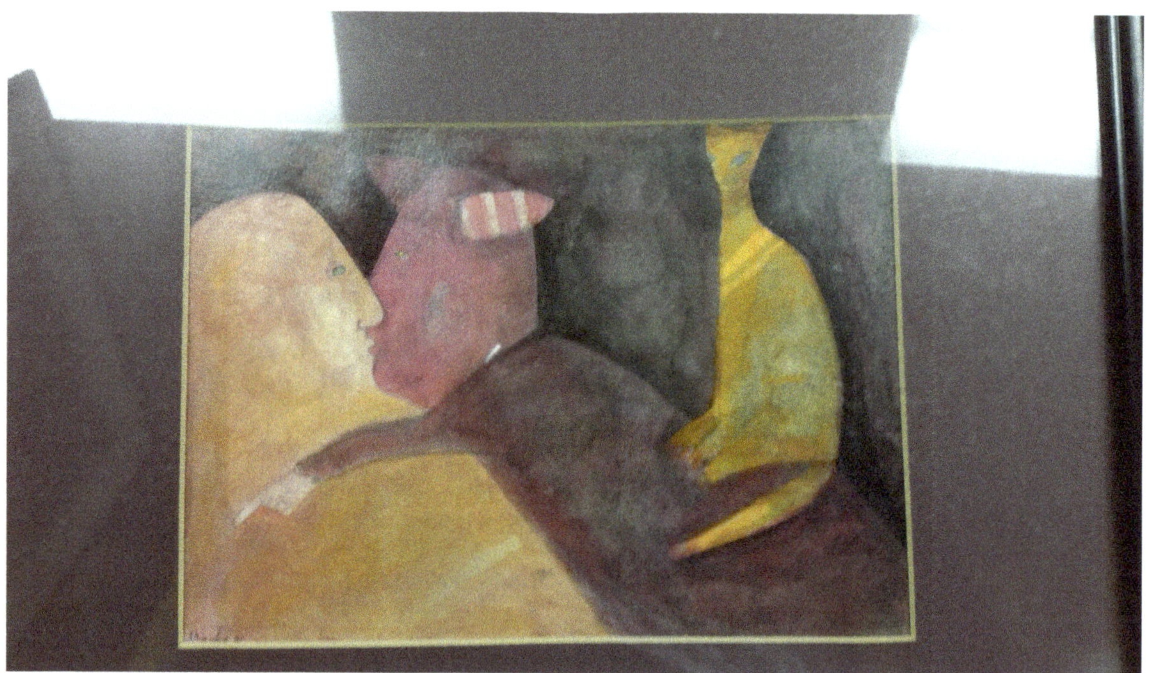

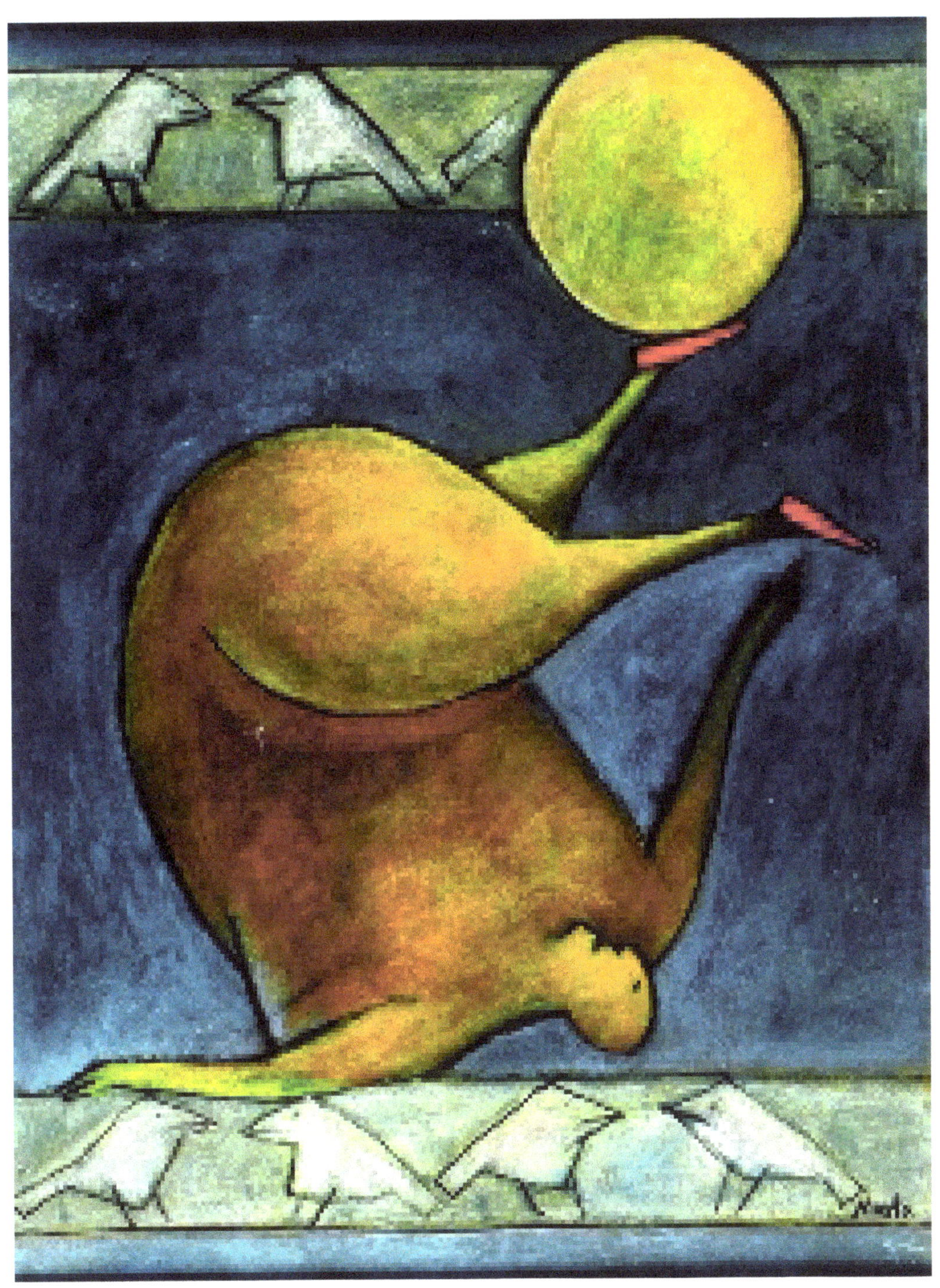

DORA BONEVA

Dora Boneva was born in 1936 and she received her Master's degree from the Academy of Fine Arts in Sofia. She studied painting under the guidance of the academician Denchko Uzunov. She took part in many national art exhibitions and in numerous Bulgarian art presentations in foreign countries.[1] She has won awards from the Union of Bulgarian Artists, from the government of Sofia, from the Institut Culturel de Solenzara in Paris, a silver medal from the French Academy of Fine Arts. Since 1981 she has been a corresponding member of the European Academy of Sciences, Art, and Literature, with head office in Paris. In 1989, 1990 and 1993, Boneva took part in the Autumn Salon in Paris. She was selected as artist-in-residence by the Griffis Arts Center in New London USA in 1994-1995. Here is a photo of Dora with her husband, Lurbomir Levchev. Shortly after residency in New London, William Meredith and I took her to Block Island for a week of plein air painting, one of which follows

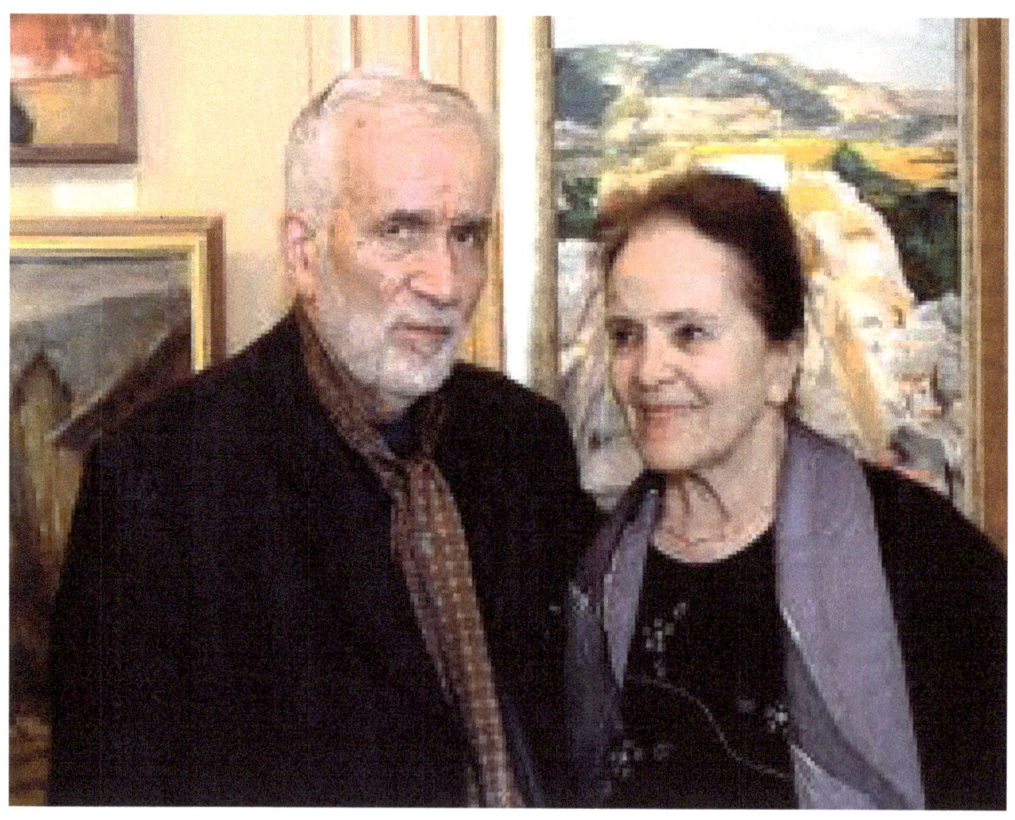

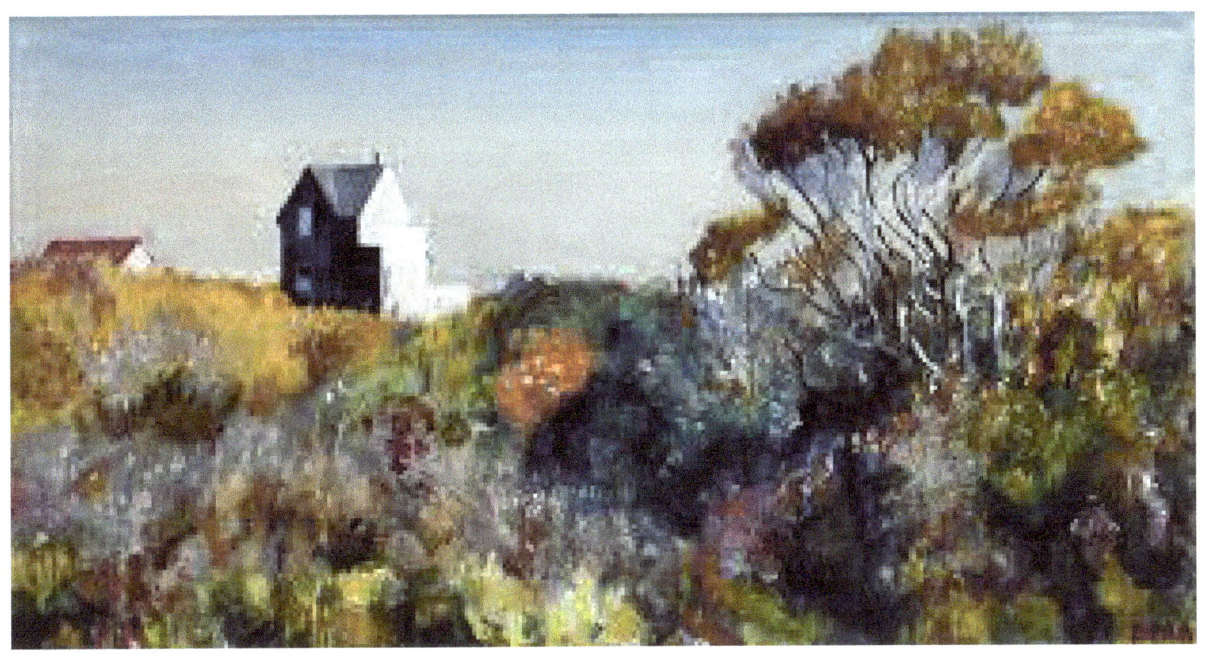

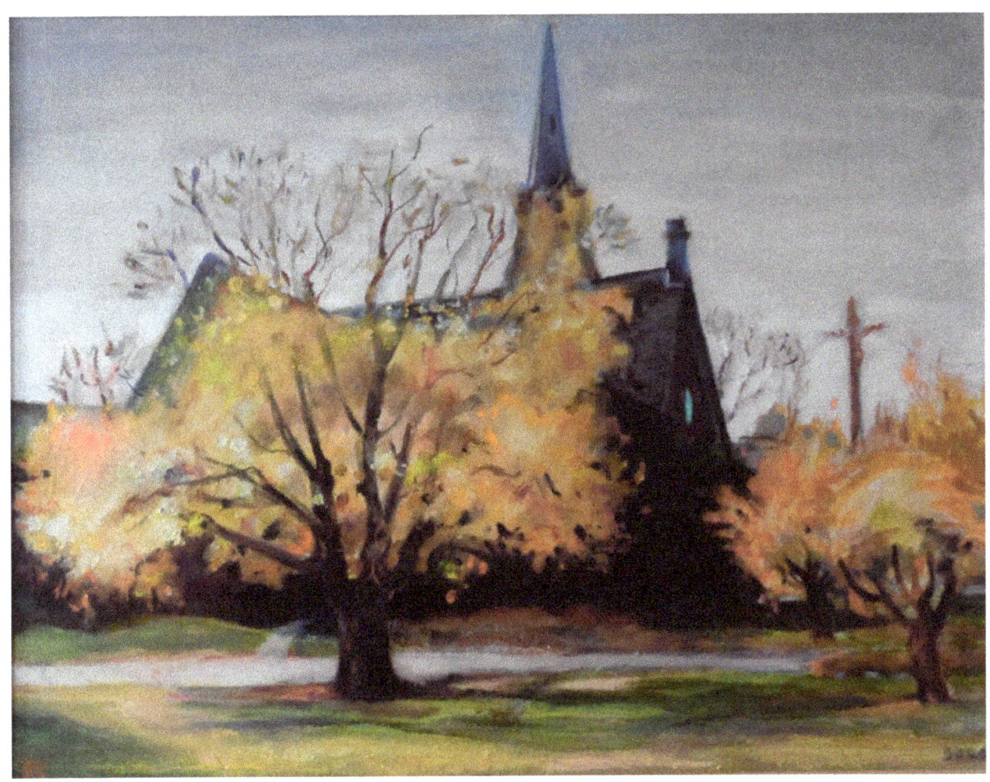

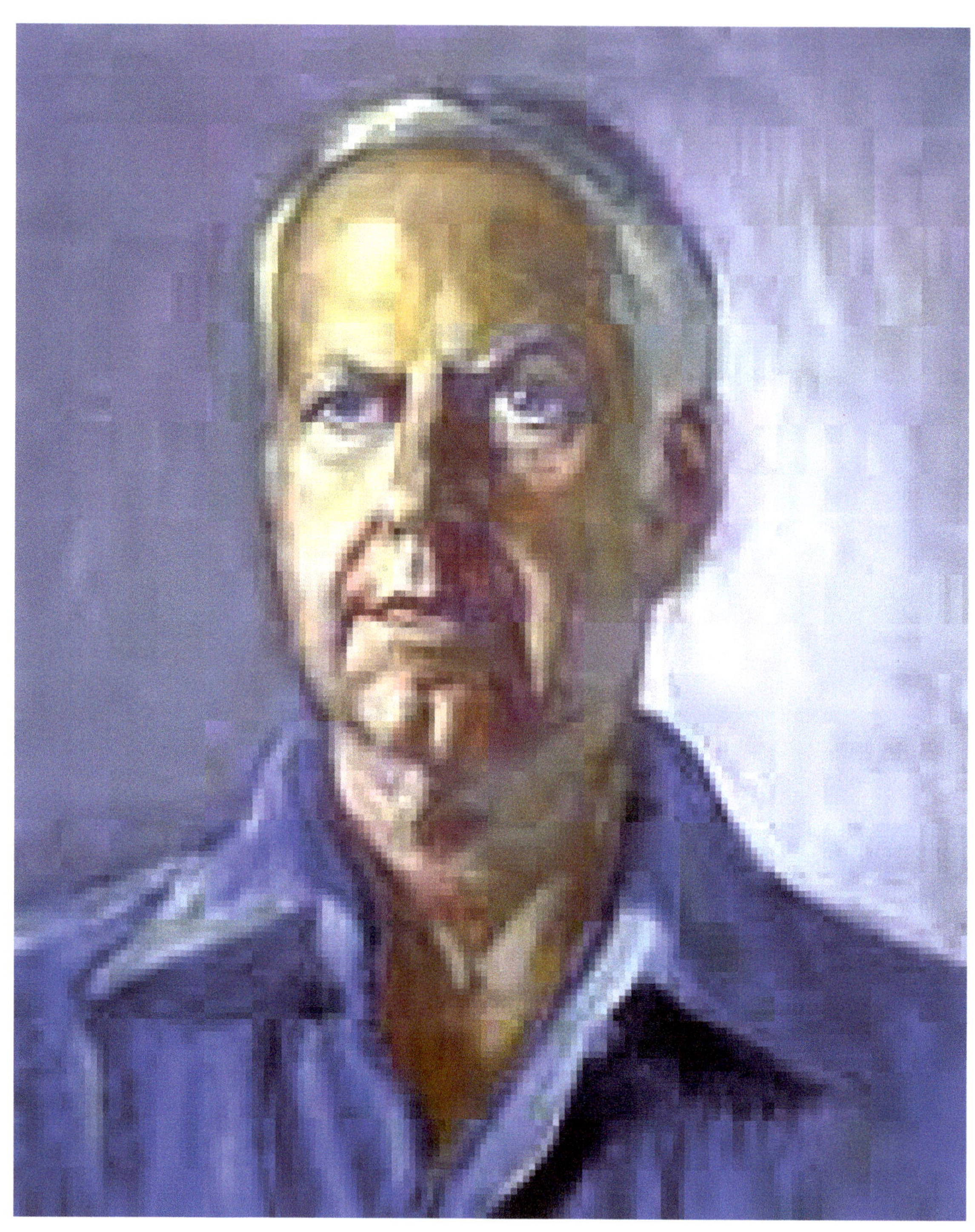

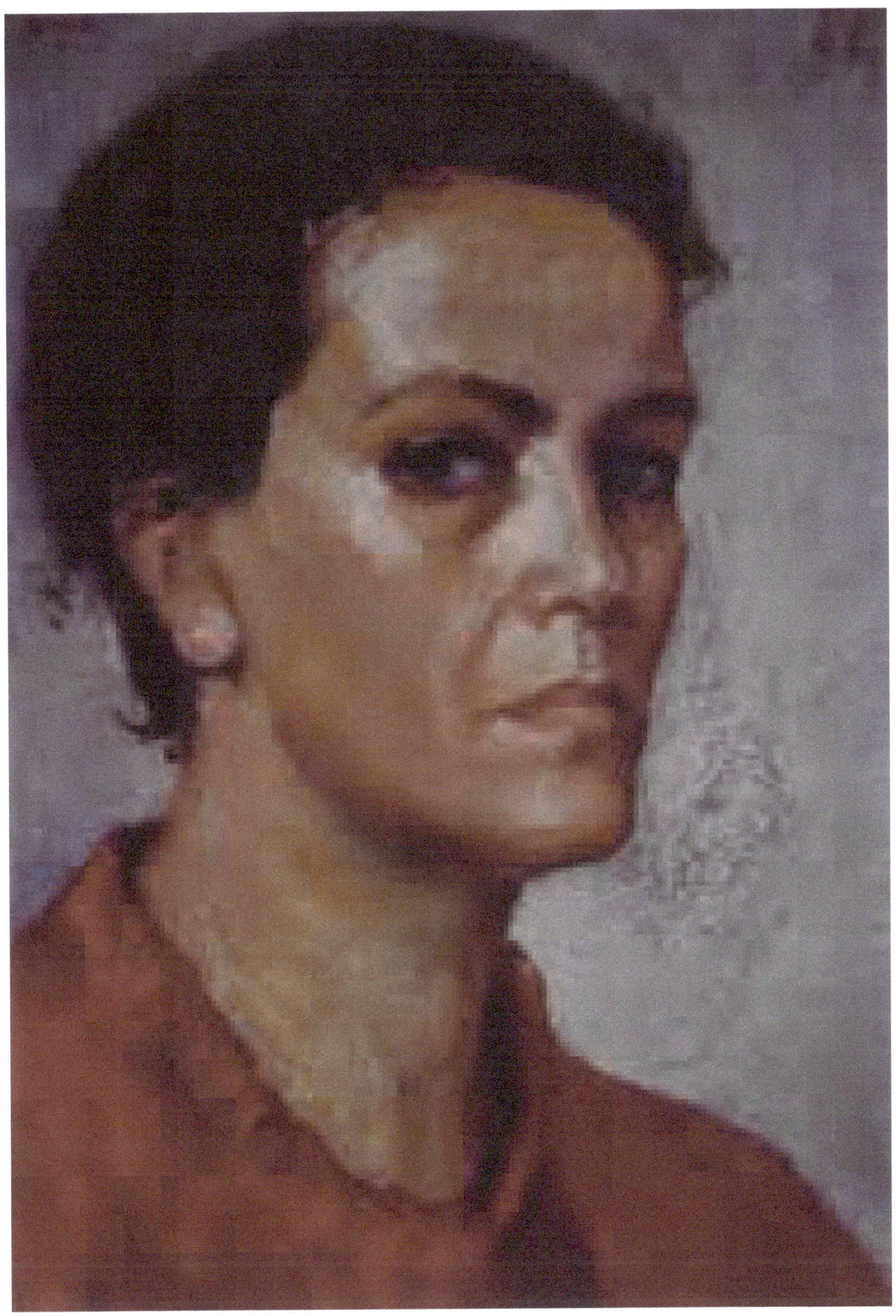

THE WILLIAM MEREDITH AWARD FOR POETRY

After Wiliam Meredith's death in 2007, his home of on the Thames River in Uncasville, Connecticut where he lived and worked for 60 years was declared an Historic Landmark by the State of Connecticut. That year a number of friends came together to establish the William Meredith Foundation who mission is to continue the legacy of this great American spirit. These friends wish never to forget this extraordinary human being and the impact he has hadon so many lives. Poet, pilot, arborist, beloved teacher and friend, his legacy is a treasure we wish to pass on to future generations. At the Meredith Center the flame of generosity and camaraderie continues to burn.

Though we feel his poetry will survive the test of time, in 2012, the board of directors decided to establish an award in his name to recognize and continue an appreciation of his work. The award includes publication of a volume of the awardee's poetry and a modest honorarium. The first award was presented to David Fisher, a poet William first brought to the Library of Congress in the late 70's to read his work. David was a remarkably talented and courageous poet who continued to write extraordinary poems, despite the great challenges he faced in his health and life circumstances. Sadly, this firest Meredith Awardee passed away in 2014. But we are so grateful to have had an opportunity to recognize this exquisite individual.
The following is the obituary which his family provided to the press in Sacramento where David spent the last years of his life.

DAVID FISHER

Sacramento, CA – David Lincoln Fisher, 72, internationally known, award-winning poet, died Feb. 2, 2015.

Fisher was a graduate of Rolesville, NC, high school and graduated summa cum laude from Duke University on an Angier B. Duke scholarship. He later completed course work for a doctorate at Yale University on a Woodrow Wilson Fellowship. He had further studies at the University of Tubingen and the Sorbonne.

Fisher taught college courses in English and poetry in the San Francisco Bay area for many years. He published several books of his poetry and received two National Foundation for the Arts fellowships. He was nominated for a Pulitzer Prize for "The Book of Madness" and won the first annual Poetry Society of America's William Carlos Williams award for the best book of poetry in America (1978) for his book "Teachings".

Fisher's last work, "I Hear Always the Dogs on the Hospital Roof", a collection of his poetry, was published in 2012 as the first William Meredith Award for Poetry.

He is survived by his brother Hugh Fisher (Serena Parks Fisher) of Winter Springs, FL and his niece Elizabeth Fisher Goad (Dean Goad) of Okinawa, Japan. He was predeceased by his father the Rev. Ben C. Fisher and mother Sara Gehman Fisher.

I traveled to California in 2012 to present him with the award which meant a great deal to him. I wrote about this meeting in a section in my recent book, WMD, A Memoir. Rita Dawley, a fine artist and neighbor at Riverrun illustrated David's book with wonderful paintings and provided the cover image. This first award was sponsored by Charles and Patricia Timberlake. Charlie, who is a board member for the foundation has been a great supporter of our projects.

I HEAR ALWAYS THE DOGS ON THE HOSPITAL ROOF

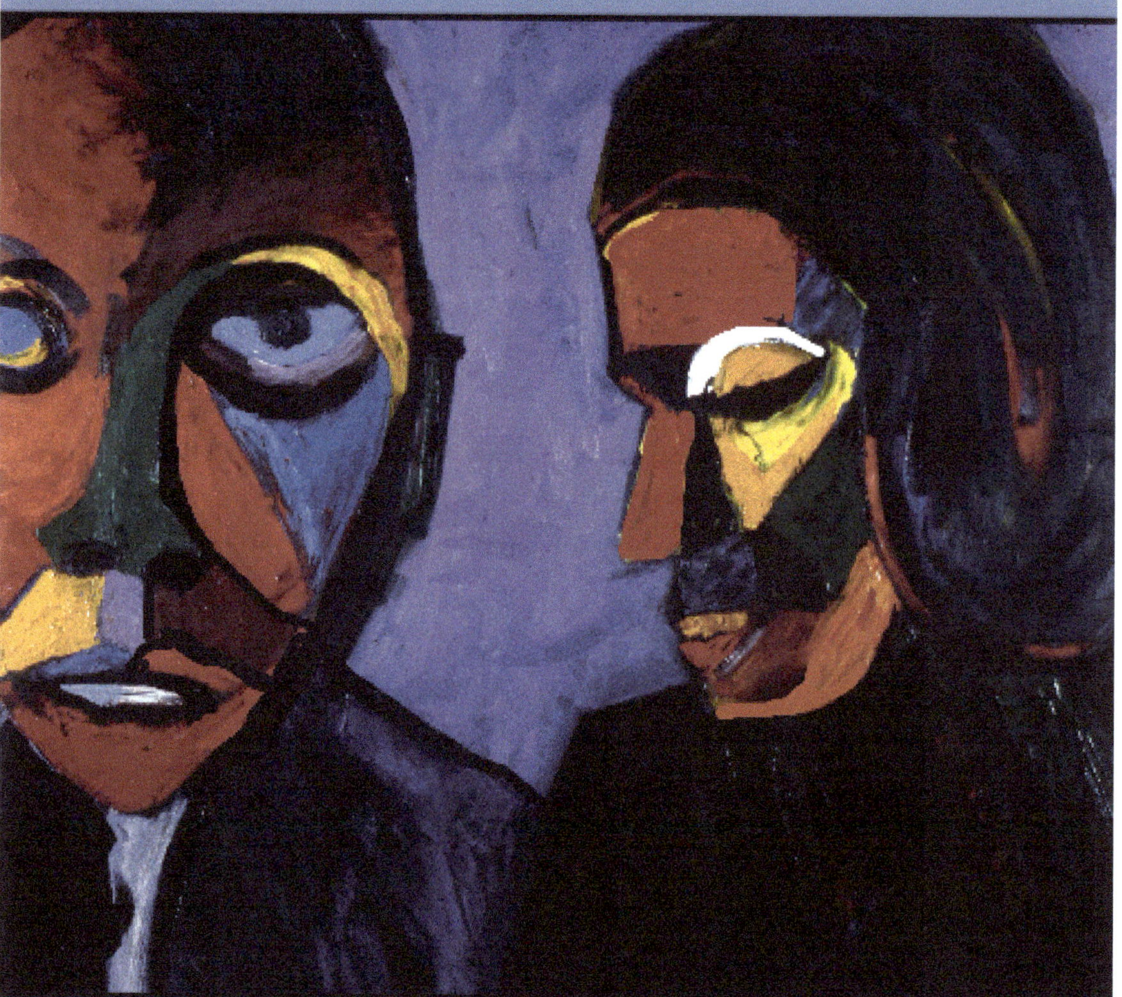

New and collected poems by

DAVID FISHER

California Dreaming Part Two: Visiting my Roomie

I made my long pilgrimage over the luminous mountains of California like the back of 'old geology's spotted hands' as William wrote of the high Atlas when we traveled in Morocco. Such extraordinary foothills, like a Georgia O'keef landscape as I descend on my way to visit David with lovely squares of green - orange groves, and lemon groves, melons and cherries, patches of Eden spread out like postage stamps across the valley floor. I could not have come this far west without visiting David after all these years to present him with copies of the book we have published as the first William Meredith Award for Poetry.

David liked the idea that he and I had become spiritual roommates and I became"Dear Roomie" in the scores of letters he began to send again. I hadn't seen him for decades, but occasional letters over the years let me know he was still writing. When we didn't hear from him, we knew he was "on vacation." I guess it was about the time I returned from Ireland that the foundation decided to present David with the William Meredith Award for Poetry. To potential sponsors we wrote:

"This is an award that has no application process, but comes to the author unsolicited in the spirit of generosity that informed William's interactions with the world of poetry when he judged competitions and supported new talent. For decades, David has continued to write remarkable work despite multiple hospitalizations and family tragedies such as the death of his children. He is a hero of large dimension, a poet of great tenderness, power and imagination. And humor is perhaps his most important life line as he sinks into the quicksand yet again. He wrote me recently, "I have been falling all over the place and they finally put me in a regular hospital where I belong. I have a terrific lady doctor testing my sharpness. She said, "what do you know about Viet Nam, and I said, quick as a wink, "the French got us into that, and Commander Nixon got us out in 1972." And I said, "I have been in mental hospitals scores and dozens of times and in Mexican jails where they check your sanity and let you out to starve, but I have never been in a nice regular hospital with room service."

I made my way to Sacramento and found him there in his home along with other clients who came to the door like timid deer to see who this mysterious editor was that David had been talking about. They treat him like a rock star now, and he relishes his newfound celebrity. He even gets his own desk as a special consideration from Nelson, the Filipino house manager who looks after the residents. On the front door I was greeted with various images of Jesus and the Virgin Mary, the Catholic motif running throughout the rooms inside. Clean, organized, it turned out to be quite a nice place as these things go, with a formal sitting room decorated in French porcelain lamps of shepherds and shepherdesses and more images of Jesus and his mother. But the garden was non denominational and a charming oasis where we sat and David read poems for me. I had hoped to take him to dinner, but all he wanted was a diet coke and a chocolate milkshake at a west coast eatery I'd never heard of called Carl Jr.'s. So we sat, David rambling on about how to promote the book, paging through so intently the binding was breaking down, like my heart as I watched him sip his chocolate milkshake, enthralled with the book which had brought him back, once again, from brink of hell.
I made my way back to San Diego the next day, like trying to check out of the Hotel California - hour after hour in a trance on the nightmare freeways, thinking they had no end, thinking they must end up in the Pacific Ocean. But finally I was able to rouse my host and hostess in the witching hour and fall into a real and mercifully dreamless sleep, in a bed as big as Lake Tahoe, and deep enough to put out the brush fire of my mind.

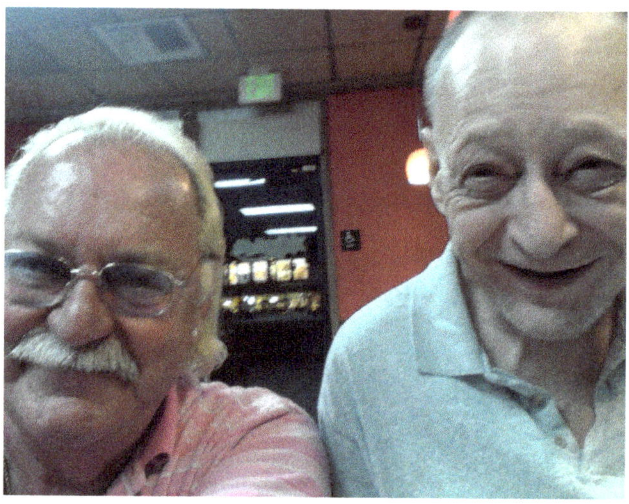

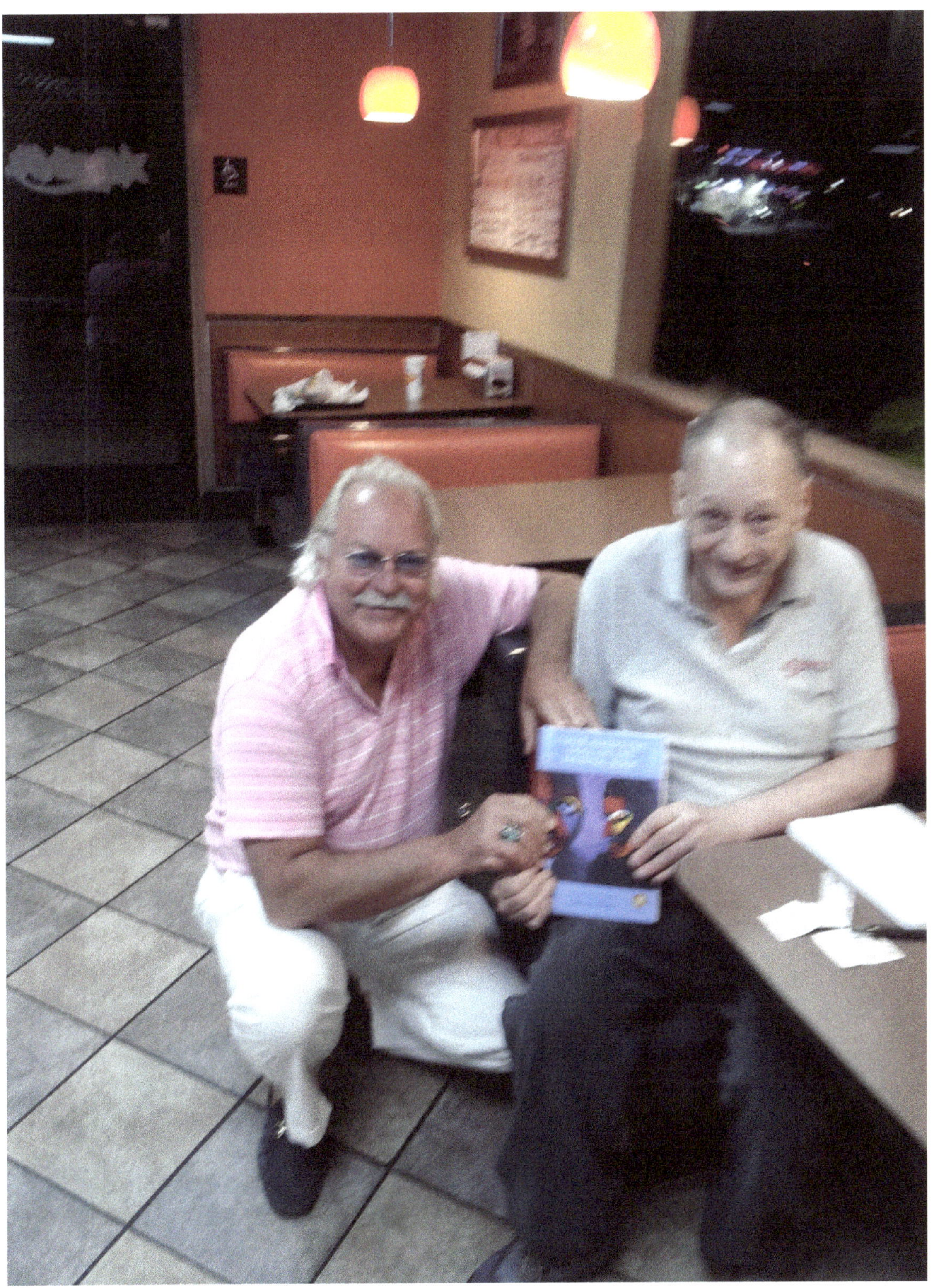

THE 2013 MEREDITH AWARD FOR POETRY TO LUYBMIR LEVCHEV

Lyubomir Levchev was born in Troyan, Bulgaria, on April 27, 1935 and is regarded as one of the great poets of Eastern Europe with international renown. He has a long and distinguished history of commitment and service to literature and culture. He served as Chairman of the Bulgarian Writers' Union (1979-1988), First Deputy Secretary of Culture of Bulgaria , and Editor-in-Chief of the literary weekly of the Bulgarian Writers' Union, "Literaturen Front". He is a member of the European Academy of Science, Art, and Culture, and the European Academy of Poetry. His many international awards include the Gold Medal for Poetry of the French Academy and the honorary title of 'Knight of Poetry' from the French Government (1985); the Medal of the Venezuela Writers' Association (1985); the Мбtй Zalka and Boris Polevoy awards, Russia (1986); the Grand Prize of the Alexander Pushkin Institute and the Sorbonne (1989); the Fernando Rielo World Prize for Mystical Poetry (1993); the Golden Wreath of the Struga Poetry Evenings, Macedonia (2010); the Bulgarian State Award Order of the Balkan Mountains 1st Class (2006) . Levchev is the founder and editor of the International Literary Magazine "Orpheus". He has over thirty poetry books and three novels published in Bulgarian. The latest two among those are the biographical novel Lament of the Dead Time (2011) and the collection of selected and new poems 77 Poems (2012). Over 58 of his books have been translated and published in 36 countries worldwide.

> Levchev's is a unique voice—a poet, like his native Bulgaria, caught between past and future, East and West, who ultimately transcends this polarity. At various times sad, bemused, giddy, mystified, awestruck, and wise, it is often a lonely voice; and when there is no audience, he is content to sing to the stars. Like Shelley or other great Romantics, he speaks to us directly, a lyrical leap out of space and time. In the East it is said that "between one person and another there is only light." The world is brighter for the light that shines in this work.
>
> —Richard Harteis and William Meredith

Levchev is a world-class poet of irony, historical depth, humor, and great compassion, watching with wistful amusement, as in his celebrated "Roofs," while the world shifts beneath his feet.

—John Balaban

People in the streets of Bulgaria greet their national poet "Lyubo" with love and respect. In him the words "poet" and "conscience" are twins.

—Yevgeny Yevtushenko

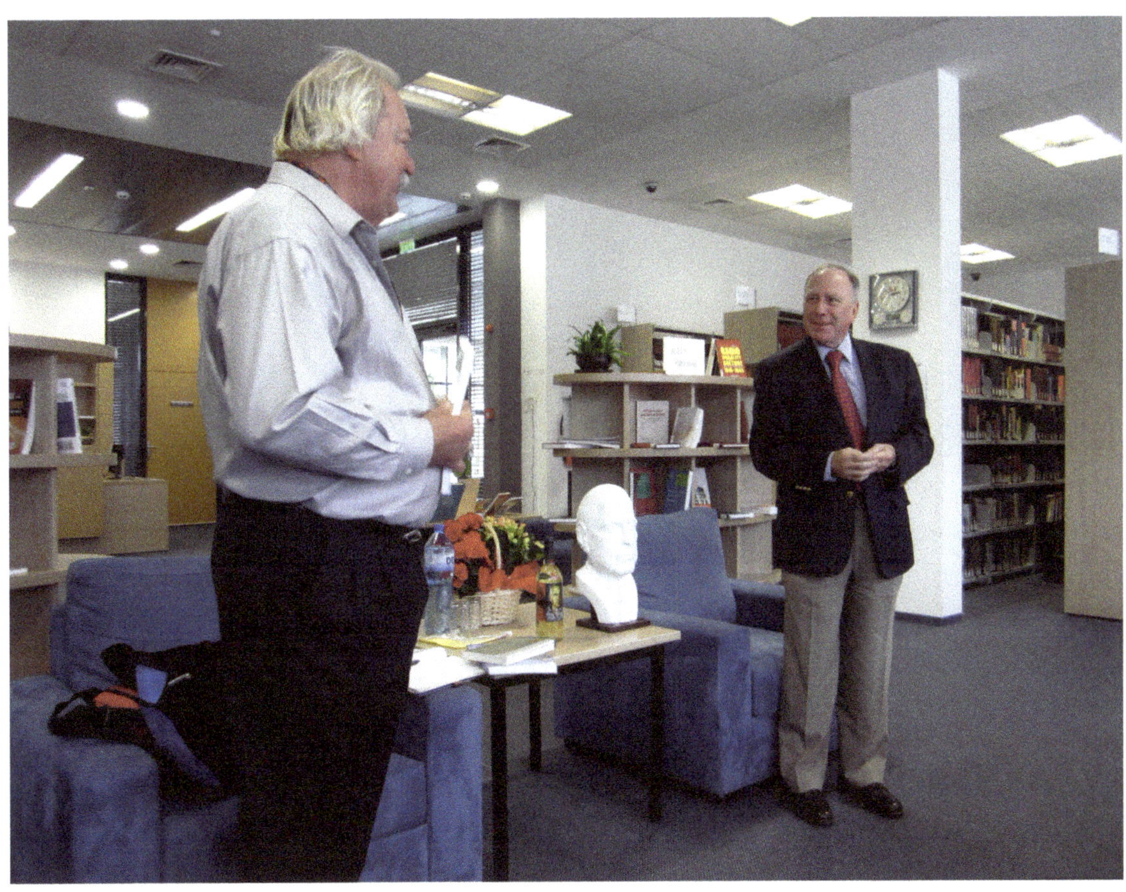

Richard and President Michael Easton launching Green-Winged Horse at the American University in Blagoevgrad

GREEN-WINGED HORSE

poems

Lyubomir Levchev

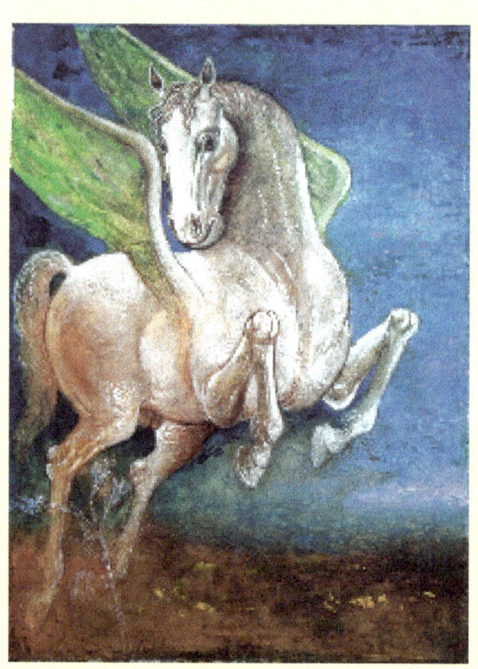

art

Stoimen Stoilov

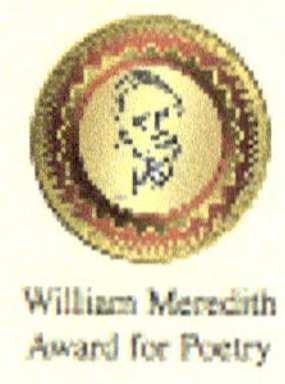

William Meredith Award for Poetry

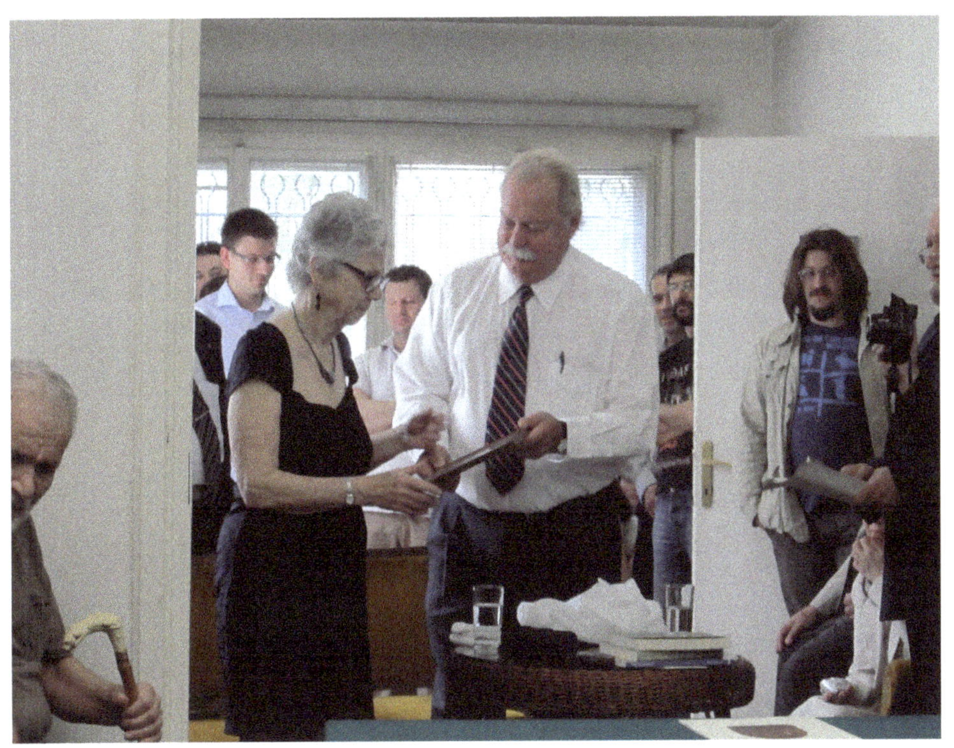

William Meredith Foundation Treasurer presents Poetry Award to Lyubomir Levchev at the Sts. Cyril and Methodious Foundation

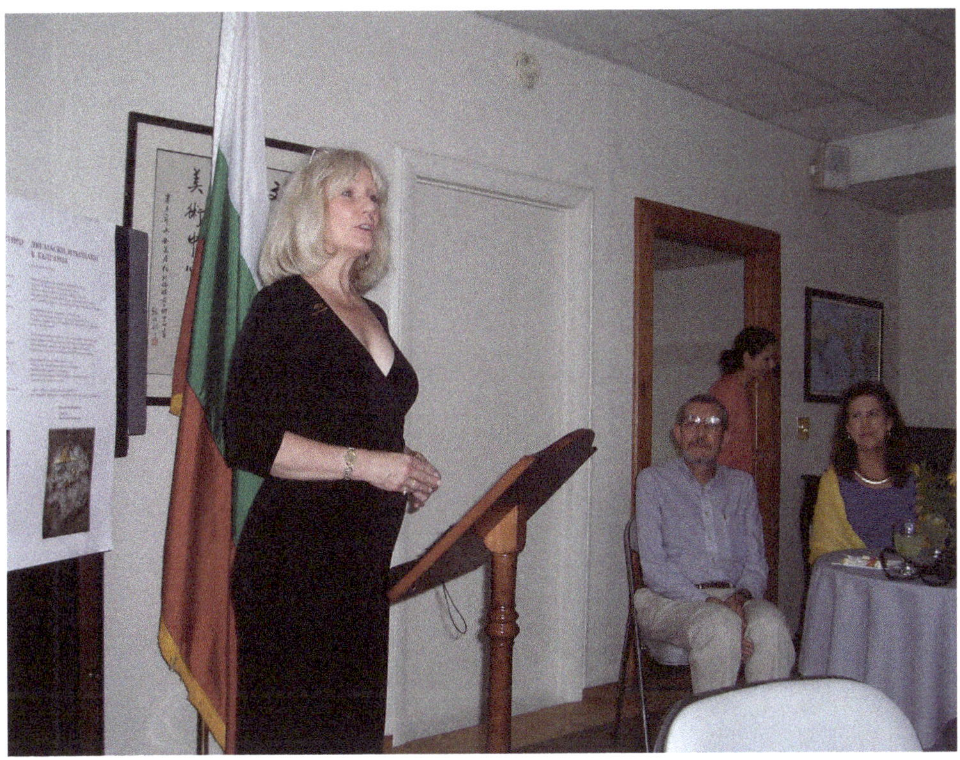

Sharon Griffis launches Green-Winged Horse at the Center

VALENTIN KRUSTEV

Valentin Krustev and Krassin Himmirski are perhaps William Meredith's oldest friends from Bulgaria. Krassin was the Cultrural Attache at the Blugarian embassy in Washington who got William interested in Bulgarian poetry in the first place. Valentin was the translator assigned to William when he first began visiting Bulgaria and has remained a close friend and colleague ever since. We worked on innumerable projects together including the 2013 award-winning GREEN-WINGED HORSE. It could be said that without his talents and that of Krassin, this friendship with Bulgaria could never have taken place or develop into the phenomenon it has become. He's a lovely guy and smart. He escorted Andrew Oerke around Bulgaria and arranged for presentations of his poetry several years before Andrew died. He translated the poems and has always been there when a letter, or an article or even a manuscript needed his expert translation ability. We'll always be grateful.

BIOGRAPHY

Valentin Krustev was born in Pazardzhik, Bulgaria, on April 26, 1949. Law graduate, he has worked mostly as a translator.
Valentin has translated extensively from and into English and from Russian, and has translated over fifty books of fiction and poetry by a number of authors, to name just a few: Alexander Taylor, Andrew Oerke, Jack Harte, Joseph Brodsky, Irwin Show, Richard Harteis, William Meredith, Bozhana Apostolova, Ekaterina Vitkova, Ekaterina Yossifova, Georgui Konstantinov, Lyubomir Levchev, Tanya Kolyovska, etc.

A book of his own poems titled *Between Heaven and Earth* was published by Orpheus Press, Sofia, in 2005. Some of his poems have been translated and published in literary magazines in Hungary, Russia and the USA.

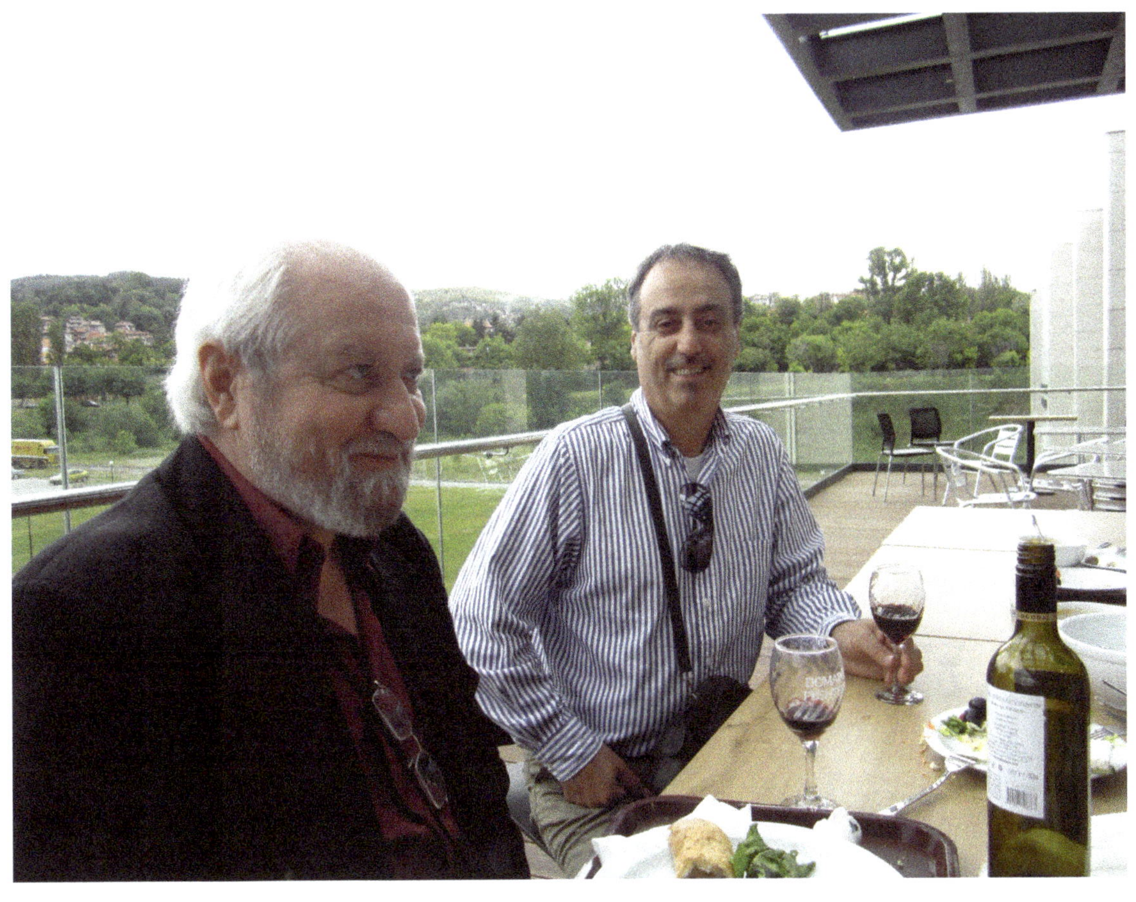

Valentin Krustev and Lucien Dimitrov having lunch at AUBG

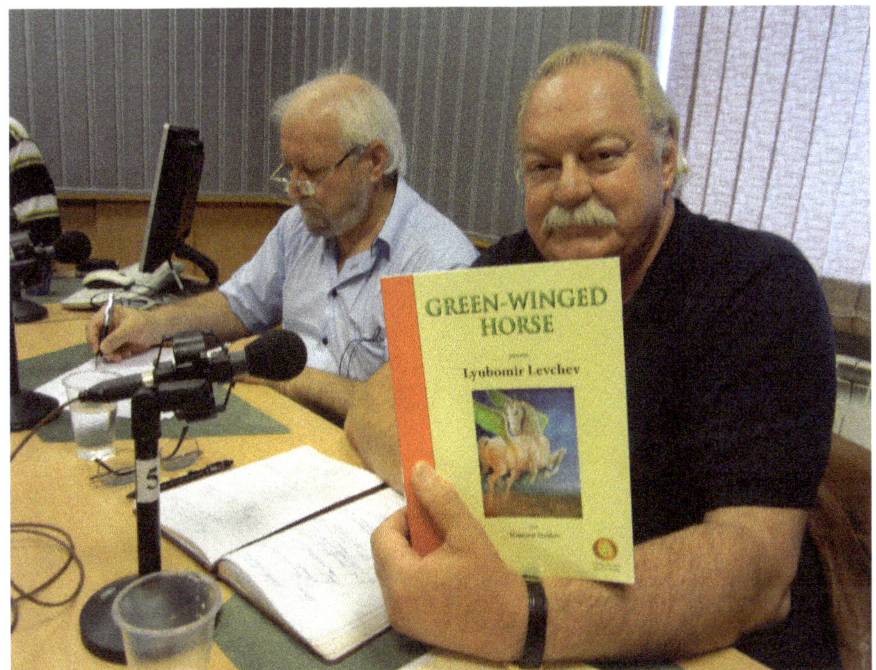

Launching Valentin's translation National Radio in Sof

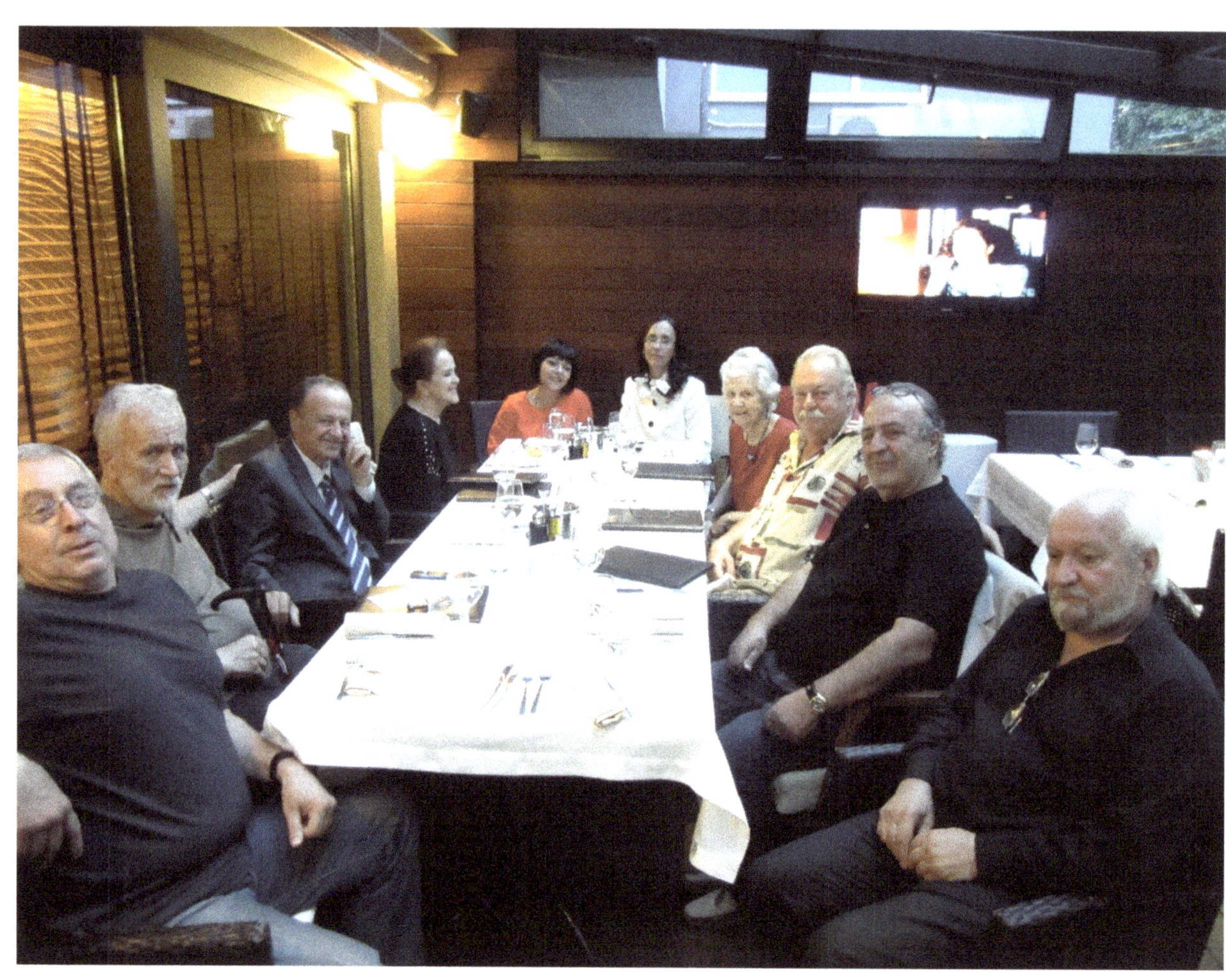

Dinner hosted by Nikolay Petev, Chairman of the Union of Bulgarian Writers in Sofia, 2013. Nikolay passed away the following year. Left to right: Slavi Georgiev, Luybomir Levchev, Nikolay Petev, Dora Boneva, Theodora Peteva, Mariana Licheva, Nancy Frankel, Richard Harteis, Stoimen Stoilov, and Valentin Krustev.

THE 2014 WILLIAM MEREDITH AWARD FOR POETRY

PRESENTED TO US POET LAUREATE NATASHA TRETHEWEY

The William Meredith Foundation presents the 2014 William Meredith Award for Poetry to US Poet Laureate Natasha Trethewey

The William Meredith Foundation invites writers, reporters, and press advocates to celebrate the 2014 William Meredith Award for Poetry presented to Natasha TretheweyUS Poet Laureate, in recognition of her talent as a poet and her work to promote poetry as an art form to American audiences. It carries a modest cash award along with the publication of a chap book by Ms. Trethewey, CONGREGATION, scheduled for publication during National Poetry Month in April, 2014.

HEADLINE:

The William Meredith Foundation presents the 2014 William Meredith Award for Poetry to US Poet Laureate Natasha Trethewey

BODY:

The William Meredith Foundation invites writers, reporters, and press advocates to celebrate the 2014 William Meredith Award for Poetry presented to Natasha Trethewey in recognition of her talent as a poet and her work to promote poetry as an art form to American audiences. The award has no application process, but comes to the author unsolicited in the spirit of generosity that informed William's interactions with the world of poetry when he judged competitions and supported new talent. It carries a modest cash award along with the publication of a chap book by Ms. Trethewey, Congregation, scheduled for publication during National Poetry Month in April, 2014.

When Natasha Trethewey was selected as the US Poet Laureate for a second term in 2014, Librarian of Congress James Billington writes in his citation "Her poems dig beneath the surface of history—personal or communal, from childhood or from a century ago—to explore the human struggles that we all face." She is, as Robert Casper has said, a poet of "reclamation and reckoning."

The Meredith Award to Ms. Trethewey recognizes in a personal way - as from one poet laureate to another - Meredith's belief that poetry's challenge is to be useful in the culture and that it reflect "the language of the tribe." "Morale is what I think about all the time now, what hopeful men and women can say and do," Meredith writes, and despite the darkness she often reports, it is the felt observation, "the exploration of the "human struggles we all face" that is the good news of Natasha Trethewey's poetry. Publishers Weekly describes Beyond Katrina, as a "hauntingly beautiful book, looking at "the vast devastation with sober and poetic eyes." Meredith's own assessment of Robert Lowell's poetry seems fitting as the foundation recognizes "one of our most indispensable poets."

The message you brought back again and again
from the dark brink had the glitter of truth.
From the beginning, you told it as memoir:
even though you didn't cause it,
the memoirs said of the trouble they recounted,
it was always your familiar when it came.

Born in Gulfport, Miss., in 1966, Trethewey earned a B.A. in English from the University of Georgia, an M.A. in poetry from Hollins University, and an M.F.A. from the University of Massachusetts, Amherst. She has had a distinguished teaching career and is presently the Robert W. Woodruff Professor of English and Creative Writing at Emory University.

She is the author of Thrall (2012), Native Guard (Houghton Mifflin), Bellocq's Ophelia (Graywolf, 2002), and Domestic Work (Graywolf, 2000). She is also the author of Beyond Kartina: A Meditation on the Mississippi Gulf Coast (University of Georgia Press). Her honors include the Pulitzer Prize and fellowships from the Guggenheim Foundation and the National Endowment for the Arts. In 2012, she was appointed the State Poet Laureate of Mississippi. Throughout 2013, she has joined Jeffrey Brown in a series of on-location broadcast reports for the NewsHour exploring issues that matter to Americans through the framework of poetry.

This award is being announced on the 95th anniversary of Mr. Meredith's birth.

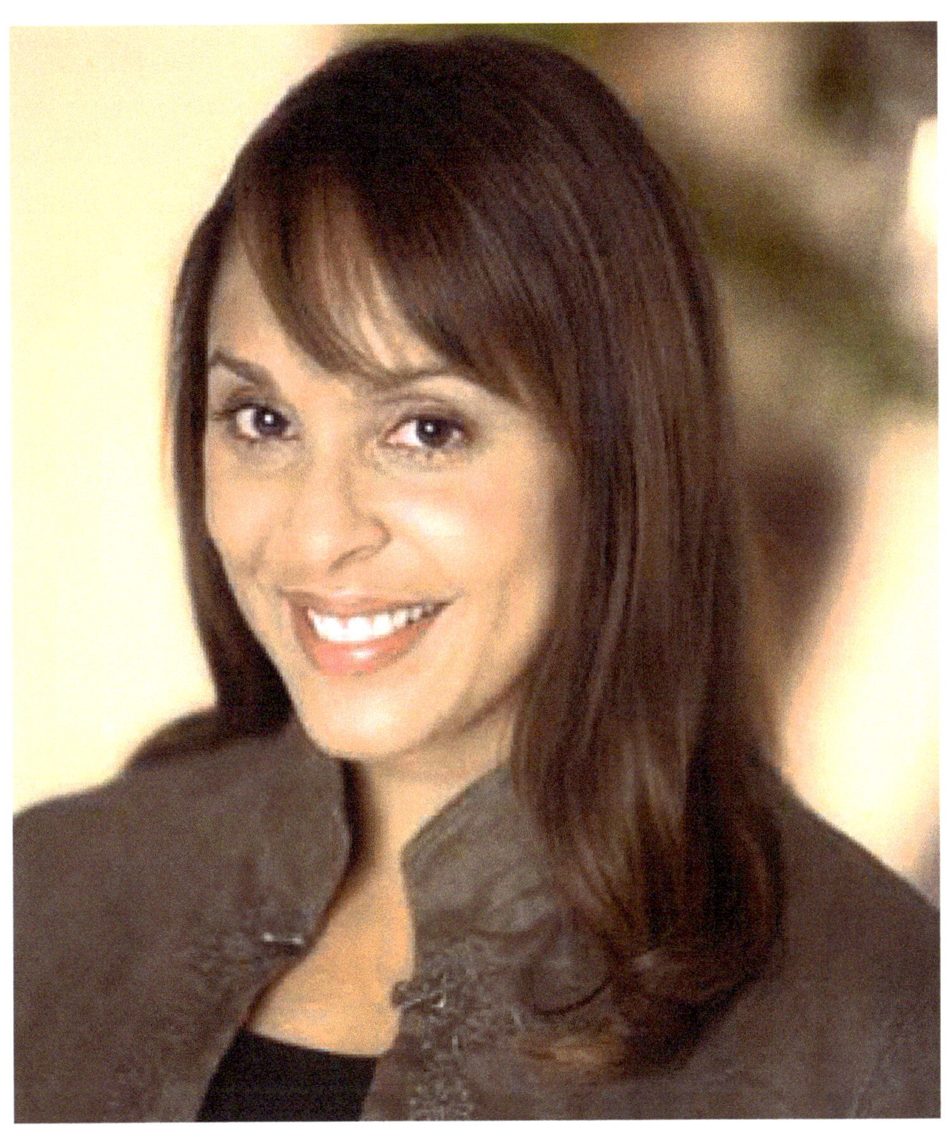

THE 2015 WILLIAM MEREDITH AWARD FOR POETRY PRESENTED DURING THE SLATER MEMORIAL MUSEUM EXHIBITION JUNE 21, 2015 TO

ANDREW OERKE

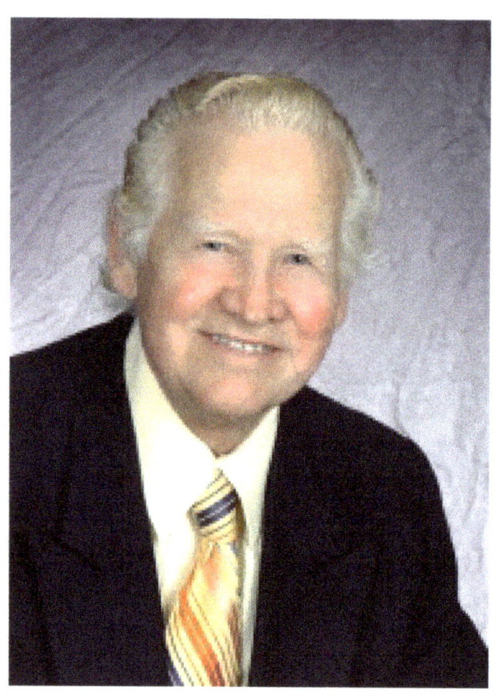

Uncasville, CT, January 09, 2015 --(PR.com)-- On January 9th, the anniversary of America's former US Poet Laureate, the 2015 poetry award named for William Meredith was be conferred on Andrew Oerke by the William Meredith Foundation. Oerke who died in 2014, was a true Renaissance man: CEO of an environmental foundation, president of a microfinance organization, Peace Corps Director, Golden Gloves boxing champion, and academic, he was a poet of great integrity and spiritual authority. "The poet has to write from the real stuff of life, the major concerns of the heart, and of life today," he has said. Like Meredith, a friend and colleague, Oerke believed that poetry was more than just words on a page, that it is a way of living and perceiving and relating to other people. For them, poetry can be useful in bringing about social justice and serve as a solution for changing the mind and spirit of mankind. "Hunger's grip is cold stone," Oerke has written of famine in Africa. "It does not forgive good intentions and tonic by the pool." In his extraordinarily rich and varied career, Oreke has given us an example of a life lived purposely and fully and well.

Harold Bloom has said of Oerke, "...his eye is shrewd, his mind capacious, and his generosity toward mankind is endless. He is very much a person who lives out in the world, aiding other men and women to live better lives." Literary critic Jewel Spears Brooker believes, "Andrew Oerke writes with enormous depth of feeling and mastery of form. His poems are an American treasure." William Meredith himself, writing with his partner several years ago, has said, "Andrew Oerke's work is a window on the world, a world seen through the compassionate eye of a fellow pilgrim. In the exquisite particulars of Africa, he sings the human condition, 'in the heart's duress, on the heart's behalf.'"

Please see the attached biography for a full description of Oerke's many awards, publications, and achievements. Oerke's New and Selected Poems, THE WALL will be published by Poets's Choice Press and launched at a major retrospective of Bulgarian Art at the Slater Museum in Norwich Connecticut, June 21st 2015. The award also carries a cash prize and promotional events scheduled throughout the year. For more information, please visit the foundation website: WilliamMeredithFoundation.org

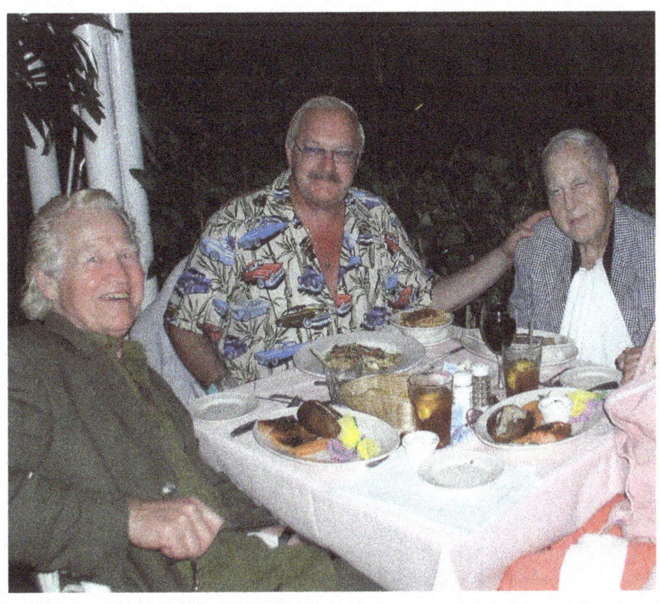

ANDREW OERKE, RICHARD HARTEIS, WILLIAM MEREDITH IN WEST PALM

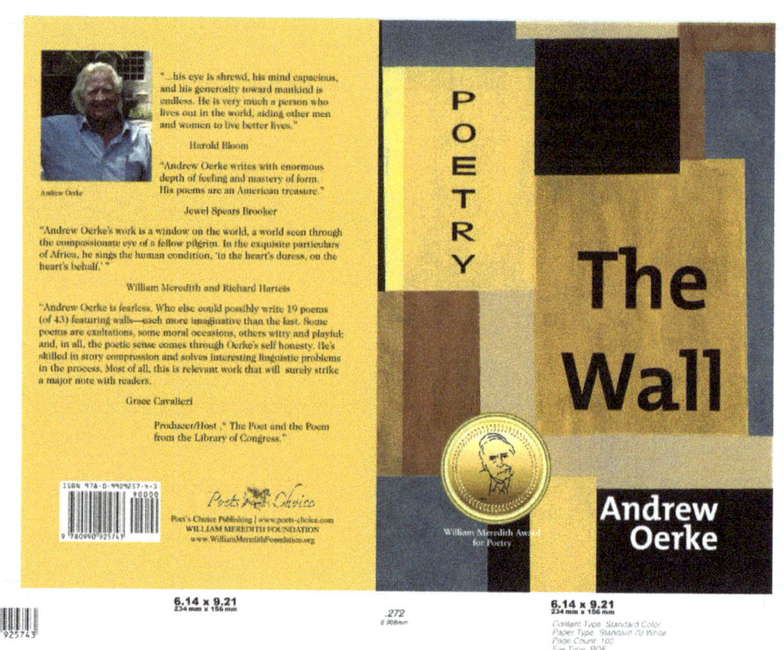

Perfect Bound Cover Template

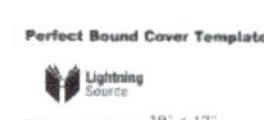

Document Size: 19" x 12"
306 x 483mm

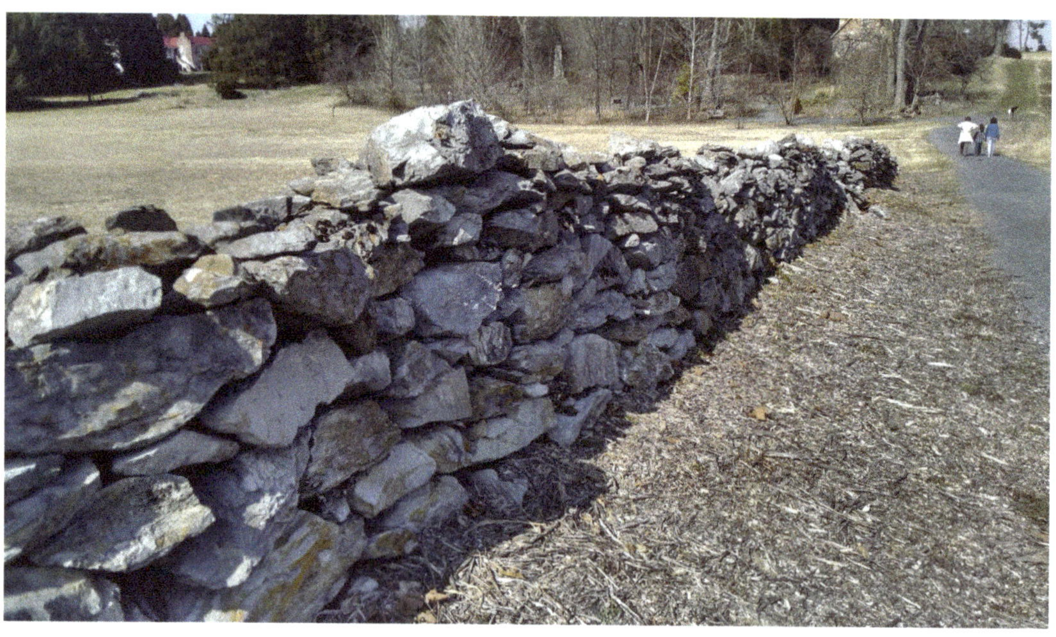

Introduction to THE WALL

Something there is that doesn't love a wall,
That sends the frozen-ground-swell under it,
And spills the upper boulders in the sun,
And makes gaps even two can pass abreast.

Robert Frost from "Mending Wall"

In an oft mis-quoted line by Robert Frost, the owner of the pine grove on the other side of Frost's apple orchard insists that, "Good fences make good neighbors." Frost's apple trees will never get across and eat the cones under his pines, Frost tells him. But the thick-headed neighbor repeats the line passed down from his father as though it were God handing out the ten commandments. Frost would playfully suggest that perhaps it is elves who go about knocking down walls, but Frost realizes who he is dealing with. The neighbor "moves in darkness" as he repairs the wall, and it is more than forest shade Frost implies, rather a kind of ignorance or bull headedness or non critical thinking on the neighbor's part: there are no cows or other farm animals to fence in or out here.

In this year's 2015 William Meredith Award for poetry, Andrew Oerke writes what must be the definitive analysis of walls with his own elf-like wit and magic. There is no freedom without discipline, form gives rise to structure. A child that does not respect boundaries will never grow into a adult, "no means no," boys are trained when they are courting. Walls are barriers, walls limit us, walls constrain us like time, holding us "green and dying," yet we are able to "sing in our chains like the sea," as Dylan Thomas tells us.

Oerke's collection, THE WALL examines every aspect of separation that walls imply from to the limitations of love to those of language itself ("Words be a window, Words be a Wall") It is a tour de force by a master poet writing at the height of his powers. The nineteen meditations on "wall ness" in Section One take on the weight of philosophy at times like theologians pre-occupied with "the other," or psychologists speculating on the nature of the id, ego and superego. But the saving grace in poems that risk verging on the pedantic is how they incorporate humor: many of these poems are extremely funny, at least to my funny bone. He takes a character called Harley Davidson and rides the metaphor right up to the "God" Wall.

"Then the letters started chirping again,
each in its own way in a babble in which,
however, individual sounds blended to a harmony
the way all colors combine to make white.
It was all so absolute it utterly made sense
--when, in a lightning flash and a thunder clap
the frozen wall boiled away like hot ice and, Zounds!
the smoke thinned off, and behind and before him
was exactly the same scene: nothing but green grass
and a river running in perfect balance towards
each end of the self-justifying horizon."

And at the "Wall Surrounding the Chapel Perilous,"

"Now, raindrops hand down plumblines that resemble
harpstrings strung on elbow-shaped clouds plucked by
the wind's fickle fingers; so Harley's hearing device
turns the volume up on Celtic arpeggios.
Thunder shake-rattle-n-rolls through some tom-toms.

Next, a rainbow-crested fortress staved with sunbeams:
Horizon hangs around like a lovesick hound
since once in a while you see a cloud in the shape of a dog.
Harley's the pupil in Horizon's point of view
that runs around his vision like puppy dogs do."

The power of the poems derives from the speed and agility in which the poet shifts from the profound to the absurd. The mixed tone is shocking, part vaudeville, part St. Augustine. The pun, it is said, is the lowest form of humor, but in the hands of a wit like Oerke the poems become a kind of wild carnival ride for the intellect. He really likes to play, and that finally, is the charm of this poet. He takes his lack of seriousness very seriously!

Oerke's parody of Henry Vaughan's "A Circular Wall" ends with a line that is well-earned and hits like a proverbial brick.

"A CIRCULAR WALL, Henry Vaughan Speaking

(A ring is a circular wall enclosing a
space. Whatever its diameter, a circle is endless
but open enough to marry your finger.)

I saw Eternity the other night
Like a great ring of endless light
All calm as it was bright;
And round beneath it, Time in hours, days, years,
Driven by the spheres
Like a vast shadow moved; in which the world
And all her train were hurled. –Henry Vaughan

I saw Eternity the other night.
I had collapsed in a puff of ashes
on the living room floor at the end
of the spherical world when my veiled vision
was rent and a great ring of endless light
unfurled itself and what I saw I was,
which was an endless ring of light,
and round beneath it a vast shadow moved
through which the world and all her train were
hurled.

I saw Eternity the other night.
I went to bed and couldn't get up for two days."

Section Two of The Wall expands into ruminations of everything from contemporary culture to African geography to the great wall of China, but always in the context of language.

"Let's face it, a sentence <u>is</u> a piece of architecture.
It strings words together as if they were bricks made of breath.
So the Great Wall was one helluva long sentence then?
Yes, he answered; you could think of it in that way, as a
culture laying down fence like a monumentally long sentence.
So fence, defense and offence are language's intents.
Poetry is starfire; prose is ashes to ashes, dust to dust."

Andew Oerke died unexpectedly in 2013, the sort of instant passing we all hope for at the end. As he says in Section One of THE WALL, "I will always love the wall for its other side." But he was writing poems right up to the end and living the life of philanthropist, scientist, political activist, and entrepreneur he had created in a long distinguished career. He and William Meredith were friends and met in Florida and New England occasionally to take the lay of the land in contemporary poetry and just enjoy a good dinner together

We can imagine them scrutinizing the scene over a glass of wine somewhere "upstairs," as William used to say, Andrew's eyes sparkling like their Dom Perignon, each man taking pleasure in the other, language restored to William, Andrew delighting in the spoken word, time, like history holding them green and live in the palm of its hand.

Richard Harteis
April 21, 2015
Kensington, Md.

MEET THE ARTISTS: WEST

KAT MURPHY

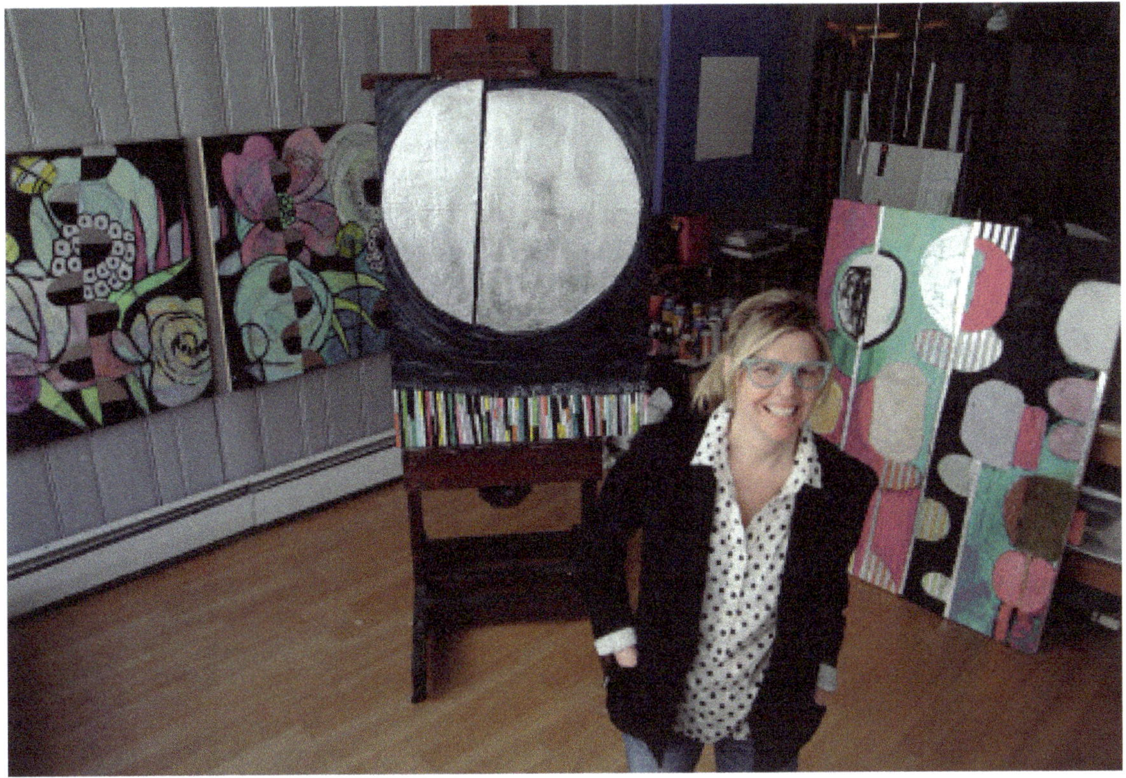

Contemporary artist Kat Murphy lives and works in New London, CT. For nearly two decades, Kat has worked in the art and design industry. She started honing her skills as a professional decorative painter and venetian plaster artist in London. She has collaborated with artists and professionals along the way, near and far, in window display design, installation art, prop sculpture, custom murals and interior design. Her design sense and quality of craft is revealed in her artwork where she creates intricate, color-rich, multilayered surfaces with vibrant color. Pop culture, repetitive pattern, and line drawing inform her paintings.
Art studies include RISD, Print Design, the International Institute Madrid Spain, School of Fine Art at Boston University, founding member and former Artist in Residence at Hygienic Art, New London, CT and a fellowship at Griffis and Orpheus Foundation, Bulgaria. In addition, she was a draftsman on the Sol LeWitt "Wall Drawing #1196" at the New Britain Museum of American Art.

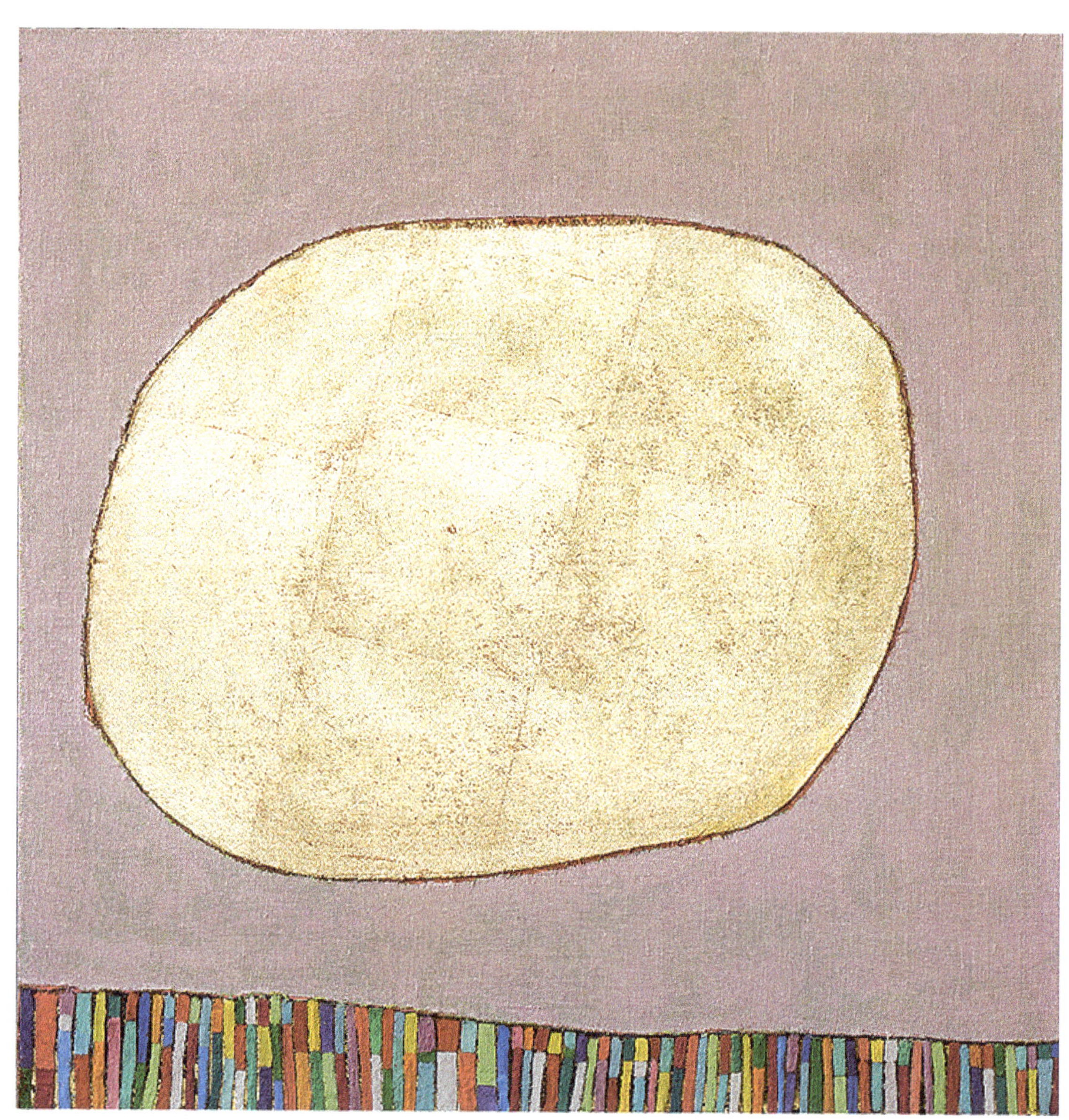

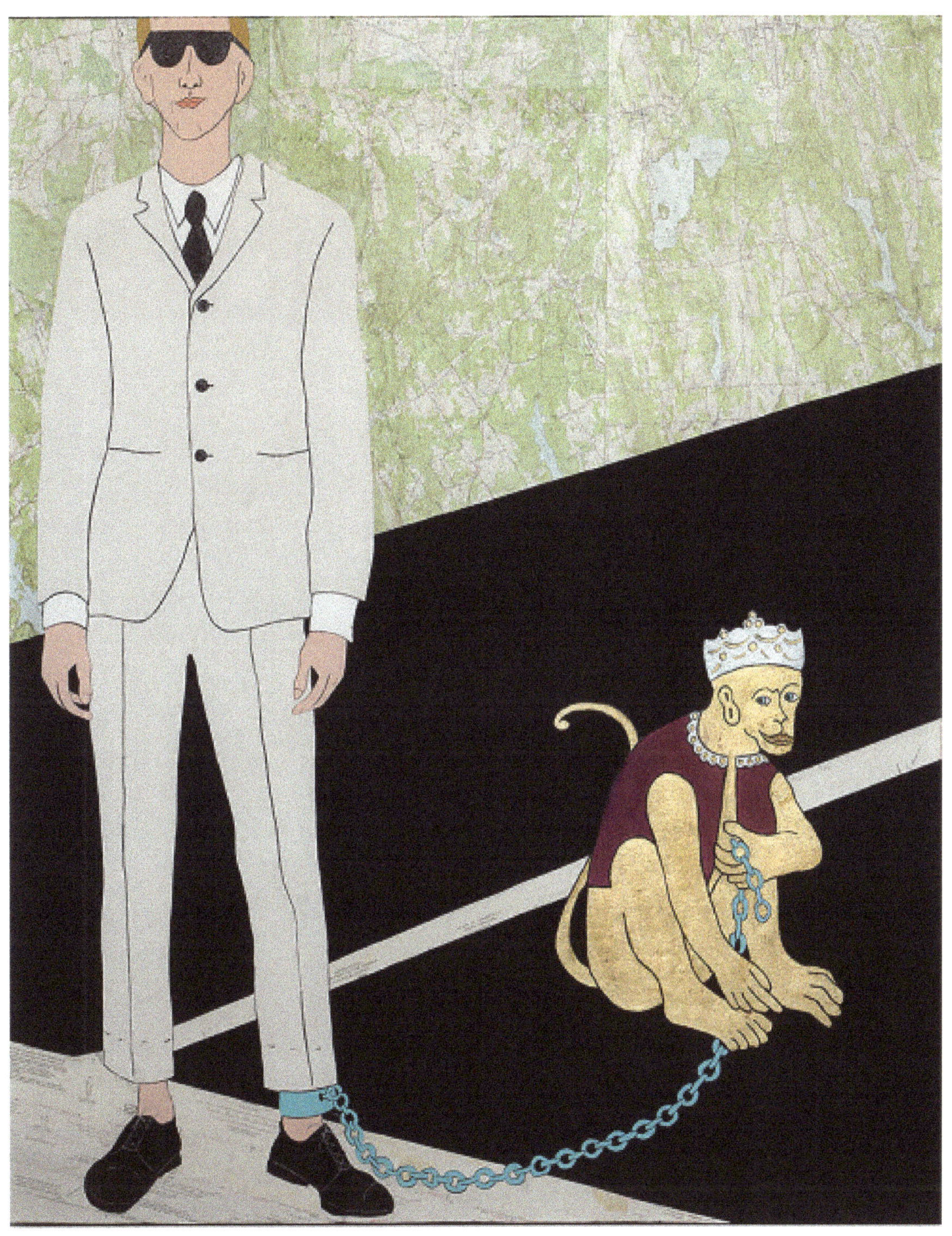

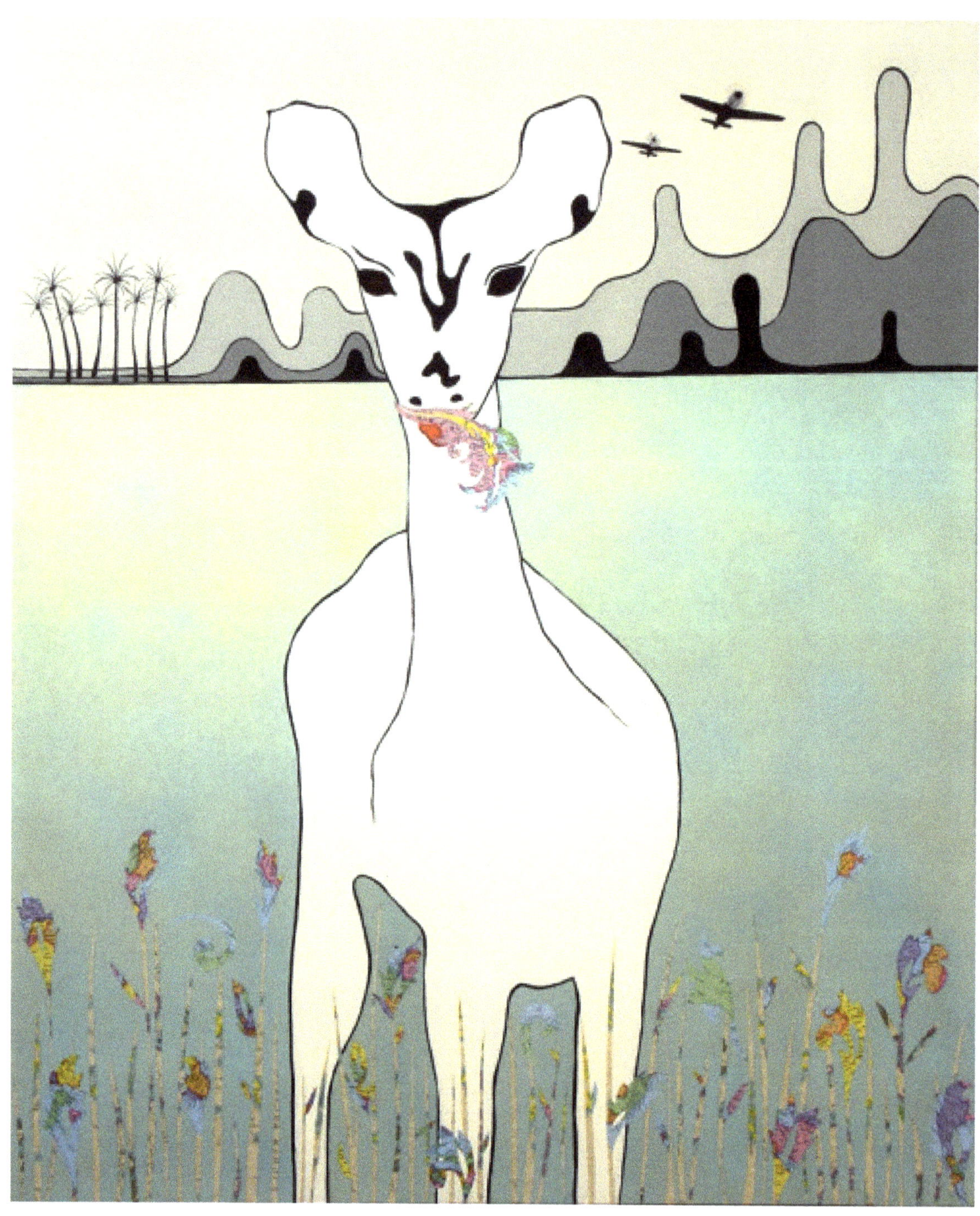

MARK MCKEE

Mark McKee was the first American artist to visit Bulgaria on the Griffis exahange program. As it was beginning, Mark visited me and William at Riverrun and we discussed the program in Bulgaria. I agreed to take his portfolio to Sofia and present it to Lyubomir Lecvhev whose Orpheus Foudation would be his host. Here is a shot of Mark and Migdalia and family, that summer afternoon when we met to discuss all this. Mark is a very talented artist as his work and resume show. He has progressed exponentially since those early days.

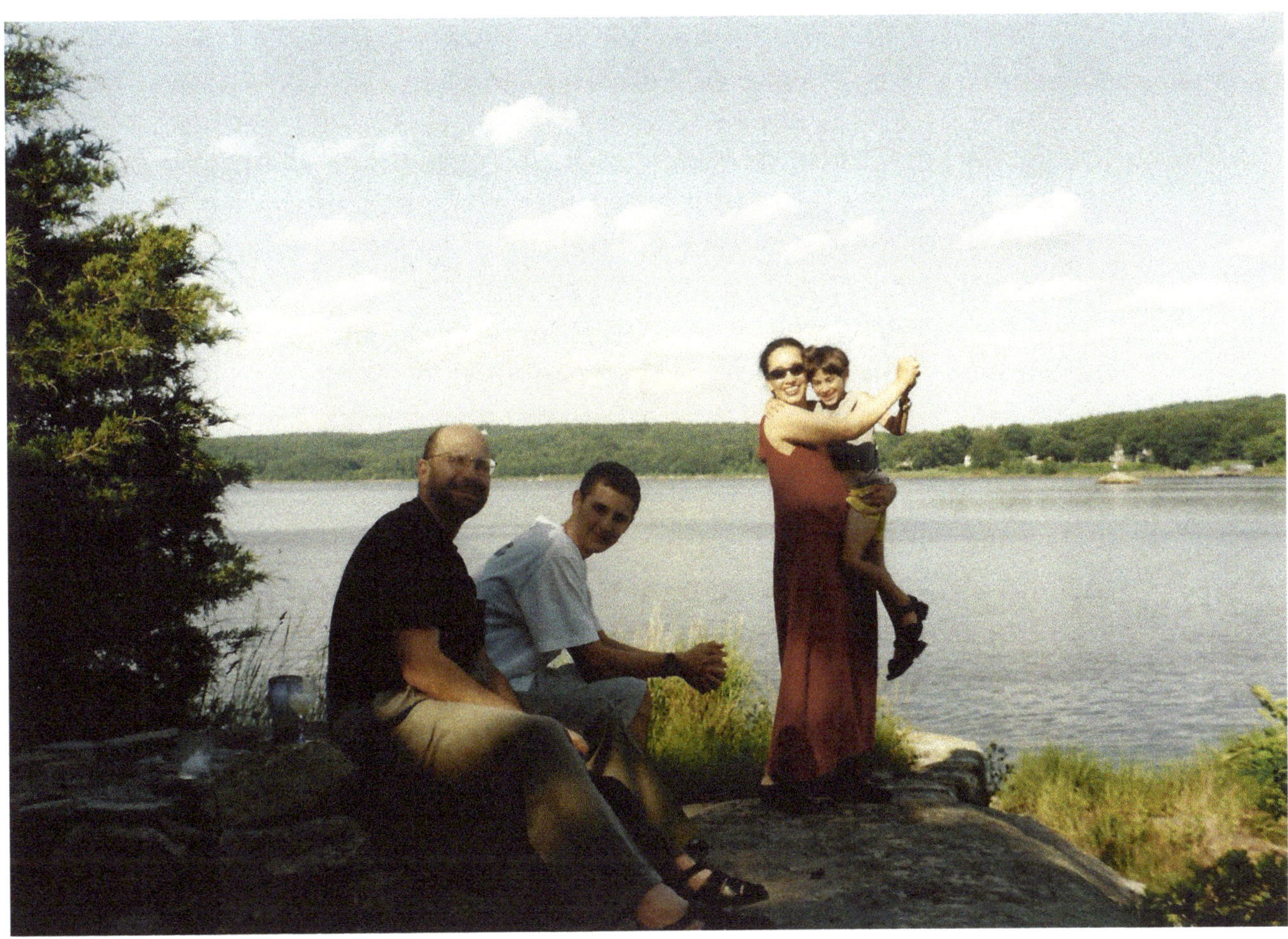

MARK GERARD MCKEE

August 2009 Written on the occasion of the exhibit, Bulgaria Then / Now at the Hygienic Art Inc., New London, Connecticut

I cannot truly lay claim to being first artist from the United States to travel to Bulgaria as a participant in the Bulgarian American Exchange, it was William Meredith's own bold journey to Bulgaria as poet laureate of the United States that spearheaded this exchange; his and that of fellow poet Richard Harteis that laid the foundation of what would become an enduring bond between New London, Connecticut and Polkovnik Serafimovo, Bulgaria. I am forever indebted to their foresight and the help that they so unselfishly provided; without which my journey to Bulgaria would not have been possible.

My own journey began with a romantic fascination with the Balkans, a part of the world where East intersects with the West.
This fascination was piqued upon my meeting Sharon Tripp Griffis and Toby Griffis in the 1995. In the course of that fortuitous encounter, I was to discover that not only were they the founders of the Griffis Art Center of New London Connecticut, but that they had expanded the program to include an artist's exchange with a sister organization, the Orpheus Foundation, in Bulgaria, which was headed by the esteemed poet Lyubomir Levchev. I vowed on the spot to travel to Bulgaria, and entreated Sharon and Toby to permit me to participate in the exchange. Until that time no American visual artist had taken advantage of their program, and, understandably, they felt it crucial that the initial artist- participant be an individual possessing the maturity and cultural competence needed to function as envoy of the Griffis Art Center. To this day, I am grateful for their trust and respect in selecting me to be the first. My three-year preparation for the journey to Bulgaria was extensive and included considerable research into its history, culture, and customs. This research revealed a people whose Thracian origins predate the Trojan War, and that the specific site of the residency, the Rhodope Mountains, was none other than the birthplace of the Orpheus himself.
I would be remiss in not acknowledging the help given to me by Sharon and Toby Griffis. Not only did they provide the vehicle for this international exchange, they also generously proffered the moral, financial, and logistical support necessary to bring it to fruition. Even

more important than their material support, is their sense of vision and dedication to the arts and artists. In addition to them however was the encouragement and cultural and historical preparation provided to me by Pamela and Niles Bond, as well as US Ambassador Kenneth Hill. Clearly, this was not only my journey, but also that of a community of individuals who made it possible.

However extensive my preparation, nothing truly prepared me for the actuality of Bulgaria, and in particular, the magic of the Rhodope Mountains. Here Orpheus, that tragic figure from ancient mythology, still roams the high meadows and dark alpine forests. His music echoes through the steep valleys. As for Bulgaria as a whole, it can truly be described not only as a cultural crossroads, but a historical nexus as well. Here mosques stand next to orthodox churches, and donkey carts share the road with sleek new automobiles.

Of my host, Lyubomir Levchev, Poet Laureate of Bulgaria and founder of the Orpheus Foundation, I can say that his is a fitting presence in such a romantic and enigmatic land. He speaks little English, and I no Bulgarian. Yet, this has never prevented our communicating. Often our time together was spent either in silent "manly" companionship, or, if a translator was at hand, we'd discuss the nature of art and poetry, or the persistent presence of Orpheus; anything but the trivial or day to day banalities of the rest of the world. We have become fast friends and share a kinship that transcends nationality and language.

The exchange would not have come this far without the commitment and support of Toby Griffis and the Griffis Foundation whose generosity made it possible for me to return to Bulgaria a second time. It is said that the second time is never the same as the first. While this may be true in some ways, nevertheless, my second journey to Bulgaria revealed cultural nuances that in my naïveté were lost in the novelty of that initial experience. Much the way a long friendship reveals a dear comrade's depth of character, my subsequent return to Bulgaria uncovered even more layers of the magic of that wonderful nation and its people.

During one of our many long walks together my host Lyubomir Levchev once asked, "Why do you keep coming to Bulgaria?" I could only respond that "I do not know quite why, maybe it is because it feels as if it is where I belong." His acknowledging smile told me the perhaps that is reason enough

Artist Statement

A pigment loaded brush is dragged across the void of the empty canvas. Beginning with loose transparent colors and values the surface is eventually covered. This is followed by subsequent layers of varying opacity and texture. There is no particular purpose or end product other than the act itself. Yet patterns do emerge suggesting forms in space. Certain propensities, such as a fascination with the human form and visual representation assert themselves. Nebulous figures coalesce from the co-mingling swirls, smears and splatters of paint and re-submerge in much the same way that buried memories emerge from the labyrinths of the psyche. Some forms are re-enforced while others may be wiped down or covered. This is not necessarily to eradicate them but rather to see them with fresh eyes, to postpone the urge to render. Remnants of these previous patterns often reassert themselves in unexpected ways, either becoming the foundation for new images or creating a dialogue between the old marks and the more recent. At some point the random patterns suggest an image too obvious to be ignored. Whether it is from remote or recent memory, it is as if this image was waiting for this particular moment, for these particular patterns of paint. Pulling these forms from the patterns is a juggling act, a fine balance to preserve the inherent beauty of the random while realizing the emergent image. It is only when the pattern and its potential becomes irresistible that the image is brought to a level resembling completion.

To paint, that is to render in a manner that has a relationship to visual experience, is not simply the transcription of that visual experience. The painter does not exist in isolation, an impartial observer of that which is rendered. They inhabit a corporeal "lived body" through which the world is experienced and interpreted. As such, that body, as a sensing and thinking organism, is subject to certain conditions, i.e. the capacities and limitations of physiology, the effects of time, the vicissitudes of history and memory as well as the processes of painting. The painter's awareness of those conditions is ultimately manifested in their work and is as much its subject.

My work resides at the intersection of seeing and perceiving, where the experiences of painting meet those of lived body and memory. As a painter, that is, to see as a painter, the element of paint, and its qualities are now mirrored in the qualities of things; things which,

along with the processes of painting must also include the artist's memories and the events which give rise to those memories. Likewise, seeing and memory take on the qualities of the paint, just as seeing and memory are realized through that medium.

Each painting is an evolving and expanding process, and as such is a means of negotiating and engaging with the world. Seeing and memory are elements of that means. These elements fit into the structure of a greater realm of inquiry - one that both explores and marvels at those capacities, perceptions, conditions and events that identify us as thinking and experiencing entities.

Biography - http://www.mckeestudio.com/

A native of Pittsburgh, Pennsylvania, McKee studied at the School of Visual Arts in New York and earned his graduate degree in fine art from the Art Institute of Boston/Lesley University. His bachelor of fine arts degree from the Lyme Academy College of Fine Arts in Old Lyme, Connecticut.

McKee has travelled and exhibited extensively both nationally and internationally, participating in teaching and artist residencies at the National Academy of Art in Dublin, Ireland, Master Artist Residency of the School of Visual Arts in New York, Vermont Studios and the Bulgarian/American Exchange Program Residency in Polkovniv, Serafimovo, Bulgaria, a program of the Griffis Foundation and the Orpheus Foundation.The artist is an adjunct professor of art at Eastern Connecticut State University, Willimantic, CT and an adjunct professor of art history at Mitchell College, New London, CT. As an advocate for the arts, McKee has served on many arts boards of directors including, the San Diego Art Institute, the Latin Network for the Visual Arts and presently serves on the board of the Griffis Arts Center, International Artist Residency Program in New London, Connecticut and his works are in national, corporate and university collections.

McKee served in the United States Army as a combat illustrator and senior infantry medic, he lives and works in Connecticut and is represented by Tony Carreta, Director/Founder of the New Arts Gallery, Litchfield, Connecticut.

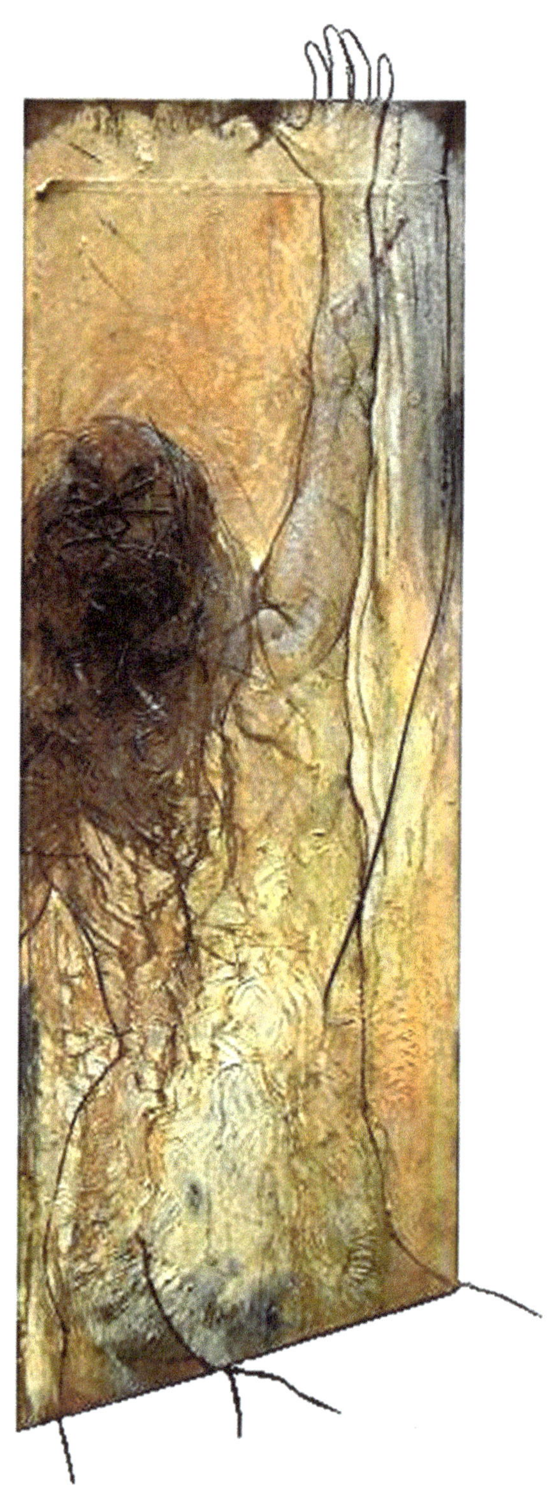

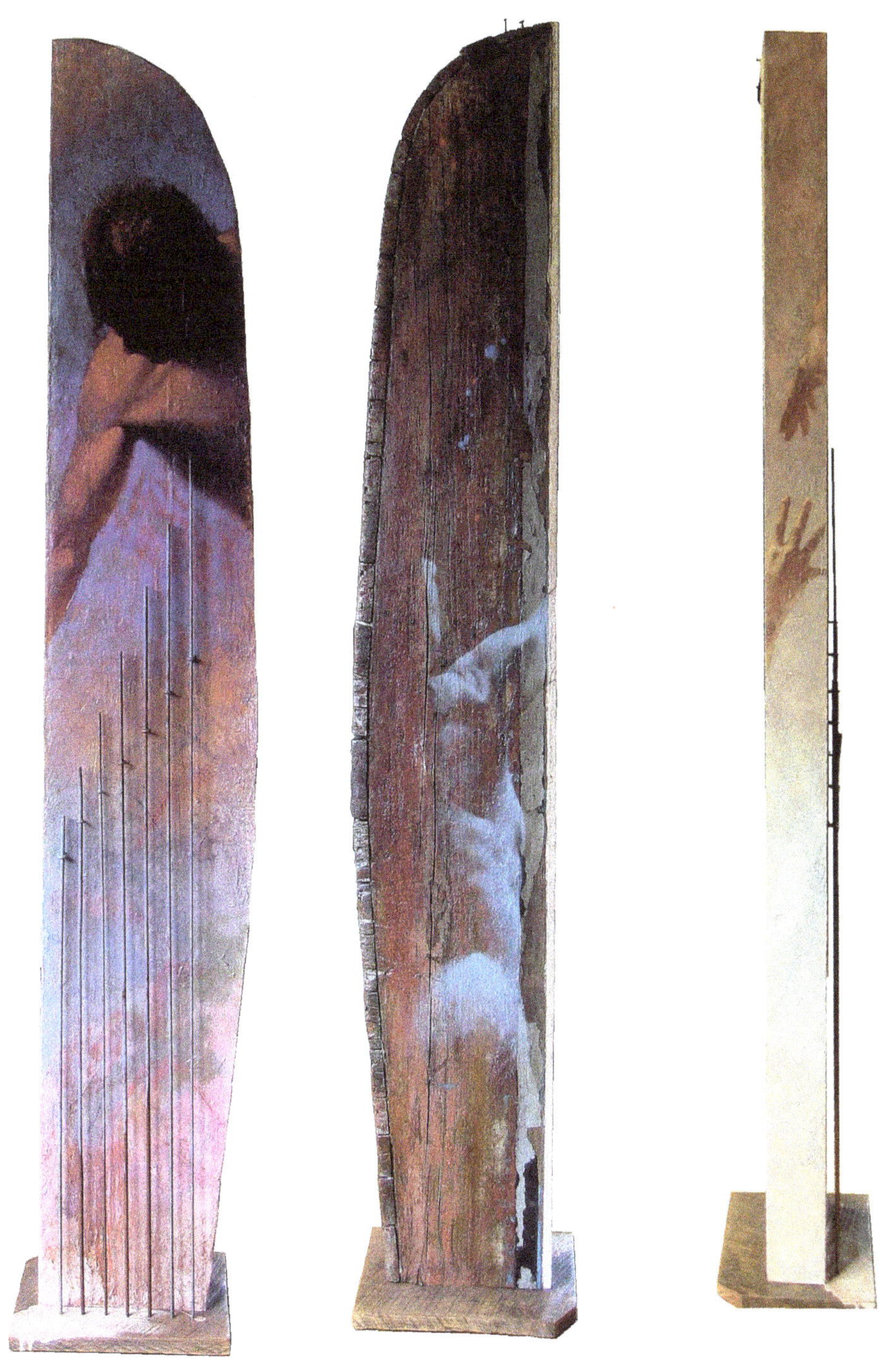

DONNA MARTELL

Artist Statement – Bridges of Light

In my career of surprising twists and turns, by far the most life-changing gift was the Griffis Foundation's invitation to spend a month painting abroad in 2005 as part of a cultural exchange with Bulgaria. It was a discovery of breathtaking landscapes, fascinating culture, and beautiful, generous people, all while I was wrapped in the warm hospitality of Lyubomir Levchev and Dora Boneva, their family, and their friends.

Just being included in the Griffis-Orpheus cultural exchange made me see my own self in a new light. I was deeply grateful, and at the same time terrified, that the Griffis Foundation was trusting me to represent American art and artists. I walked a little taller, and I worked a lot harder.

Sometimes a bridge can be built over time, without anyone being aware that it is being built. The first exhibition of my career was held at the Starcutters hair salon in New London, in 1999. We held an annual exhibition over the next four years, and that was when I met Toby Griffis for the first time. He stuck out , first because he passed by the food table, and second because he was the one walking around slowly, spending time at every painting. He seemed like a nice man, and he was very encouraging. At the next, and last, exhibition there, Toby attended again. This time he told me that his foundation sent artists to Bulgaria as part of a cultural exchange, and that he would like to invite me to participate. As I said, it has been a career of surprising twists and turns. Thank you, Toby, for taking that walk around the Starcutters gallery and for sending me over that Bridge of Light.

Biographical Information

Donna Martell began painting in 1990 at the age of 36, and has continued for 24 years. She fell in love with the pastel medium, and she now paints exclusively using soft pastels. After several years of hard work, Ms. Martell became a professional artist. Her first solo exhibition was in 1999 in New London, when the hair salon Starcutters was transformed into an art gallery to show her work. Since then, invitations to show bodies of her work have led to over 20 exhibitions. She won the first of 14 awards and prizes in 2000, about a third of which were awarded at national competitions. Her most recent has been an Honorable Mention at the first Chamard Vineyard exhibition, sponsored by the Six Summit Gallery in 2013. By far, the greatest impact on her career has been from her participation in the Griffis Foundation's cultural exchange program in partnership with the Orpheus Foundation in Bulgaria. The results of that experience have been far reaching with respect to her growth as a professional and her connection with the eastern CT arts community.

Commissioned work includes professional buildings, homes, people, dogs in Santa hats and a guinea pig. Her pastel Keeney Cove, was the cover image for the DEP Connecticut Boater's Guide: issue 2000. Early Start was published in Pastel Artist International: issue May/June 2001. Work has appeared on program covers and posters for five Eastern CT Symphony Chorus winter concerts. Sharma Howard interviewed her for a two-page article in the New London Day, and Ms. Martell appeared in the Pastel Journal: issue Dec 2005 article, The Master's Hand, a discussion among several Master Artists, including Foster Caddell, on the importance of becoming a mentor to rising artists like Donna Martell. In 2013 Polly Seip interviewed her for the popular online series, Artist to Artist.
Since Ms. Martell's move in 2014, she resides in Windsor, CT. She has already held Hartford area exhibitions at the Integrative Medicine Clinic at St. Francis Hospital and The Hartford Club. Her acceptance into the 2014 International Association of Pastel Societies' exhibition at the Vose Gallery in Boston is the beginning of her next adventure – submitting work to exhibitions and galleries across the US.

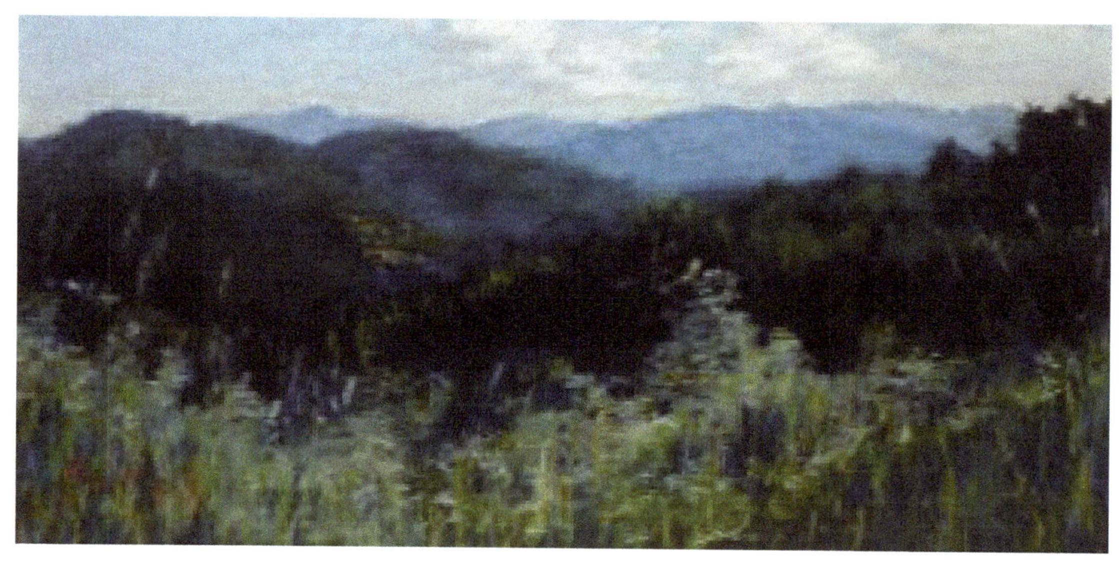

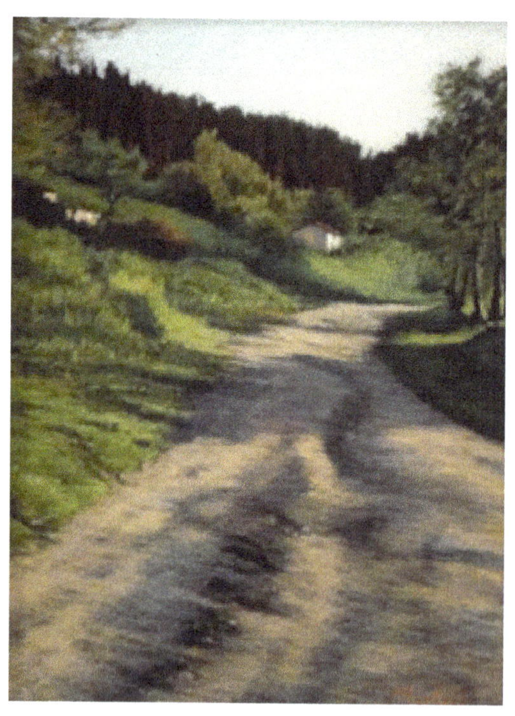

MARK PATNODE

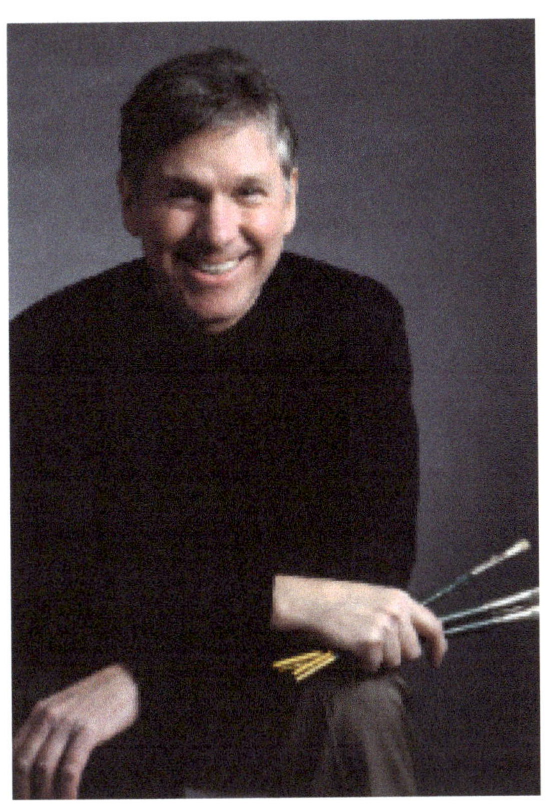

Artist Statement

The goal with all my artwork is powerful visual simplicity. The first strokes establish a relationship with the subject and it becomes a dialog as I develop the work. In creating artwork, the more I study nature the more I arrive at a language of form and color.

Working quickly and with great intensity, I create the poetry of the inspired moment. I want to feel free with paint and don't want to be constrained with convention. Why not throw it, sling it, splash it? It's the artist's mark - it's Mark-Making™

Biography

Mark Patnode received his Bachelor of Fine Arts from Purchase College and is a Fellow of the Urban Artists Initiative (UAI) Hartford, CT, funded by the National Endowment for the Arts (NEA) and the Connecticut Office of the Arts (COA), in partnership with the Institute for Community Research (ICR). Mark has received numerous fellowships, residencies, and grants, including two all-inclusive COA awards to Vermont Studio Center where he worked with William Beckman, Michael Gitlin, David Kapp, and Carol Robb. Mark has also received two all-inclusive Residencies to I-Park Artists' Enclave. A Silver Rose recipient from Bulgaria's Preeminent Poet, Lyubomir Levchev, Mark was sponsored by the Griffis & Orpheus Foundations for a summer 2006 Artist Residency at the Sharon House in the village of Polkovnik Serafimovo, Smolyan, Bulgaria. Mark's work has been featured internationally in galleries and museums, including The White House, National Mall, National Palace of Culture, Bulgaria, Neuberger Museum, Wadsworth Atheneum Gallery at Connecticut Convention Center, Connecticut Commission on Culture & Tourism Office, Lyman Allyn Art Museum, Four Faber Birren National Color Award Shows, Real Art Ways, Ezra and Cecile Zilkha Gallery at Wesleyan College, ALVA Gallery, Fuller Gallery, Left Bank Gallery Essex. Mark's work is in the permanent collection of The Smithsonian Institution and private collections internationally. He has been interviewed by American, African, Bulgarian, Cape Verde, and Portuguese press and appears in the 2008 Orpheus Art Album Ford / Brod, St. Klinent Ohridski University Press, Lyubomir Levchev, Editor. Mark received publicity in the January 2003 edition of American Artist magazine for his large-scale paintings project of urban New London. Mark's work has also been featured in Jack Richeson & Co. catalog. Mark was commissioned by CT Governor M. Jodi Rell to create a painting of the Charter Oak for Connecticut's Tercentennial. The painting resides in the Governor's Residence Conservancy. Mark was sponsored by COA Arts in Education to represent Higher Order Thinking (HOT) Schools in 2010 at the Ellipse in the National Mall for the Connecticut Tree at the National Christmas Tree lighting. Mark was selected by Senator Joseph Lieberman as Connecticut's Designated Artist for the 2008 White House Christmas Tree

Ornament Design. Mark attended an Artist's Reception at the White House on December 2, 2008 (his ornament is in the permanent collection of the Smithsonian Institution). Mark's work was also featured in Senator Lieberman's Washington, D.C. from 2006-12 at the Hart Building office as part of CT Art in Public Spaces Program. Juried into the COA Teaching Artist Directory, a reflection of excellence in both teaching and artistry, Mark conducts residencies through COA Arts in Education HOT Schools and public and private organizations seeking to fulfill Federal, State, and local curricular mandates. Mark is a Presenter for COA HOT Schools Summer Institute and invited panelist. Mark served in 2007 & 2008 as the USA Professional Visual Artist Instructor for Center for Creative Youth Cape Verde Visual Arts Program in Africa. Mark is a member of the Bulgarian-American Exchange Program, CREC CCY CulturArte, Elected Member of Mystic Arts Center and Norwich Arts Center, Executive Board of Directors, Purchase College Alumni Association, Inc., Rotary International and is listed in Who's Who in American Art. Mark shares a Studio with five other Artists in New London and resides at the Griffis Art Center, New London, CT. Solo Exhibitions

SOLO EXHIBITIONS

2013 Illuminations – Norwich Arts Center Gallery, Norwich, CT – Apr 5 - 27 2012
A Live Retrospective of Mark Patnode – Tsetse Gallery, New London, CT - Feb 2011
Trees – Norwich Arts Center Gallery, Norwich, CT - Jan 5 - 29 2010

Created official State of Connecticut Charter Oak Painting 2009
Images of Cape Verde – Norwich Arts Center Gallery, Norwich, CT - Jan - Feb 2007

Scenes from Bulgaria – 3rd Rail Studio, New Rochelle, NY - Feb 24 - Mar 24 2006

Bulgarian Paintings – National Palace of Culture, Sofia, Bulgaria - Sep 25 - 28 2006 Bulgarian

Paintings – Smolyan Art Gallery, Smolyan, Bulgaria - Sep 22 - 25 2006

Selected Works – Windham Theatre Guild, Willimantic, CT - Feb 20 - Mar 5 2006

Selected Works – Wood Memorial Library, S. Windsor, CT - Feb 18 - Mar 15 2005

Unseen America – Mitchell College Library, New London, CT - Aug - Sep 2005
Selected Works – Gallery 121, Boston, MA - Jun 13 - Jul 9 2003

Painting on the Beach – Mitchell College, New London, CT - Oct 20 - Nov 26

FOR MORE DETAILED INFORMATION PLEASE VISIT:

www.marktheartist.com

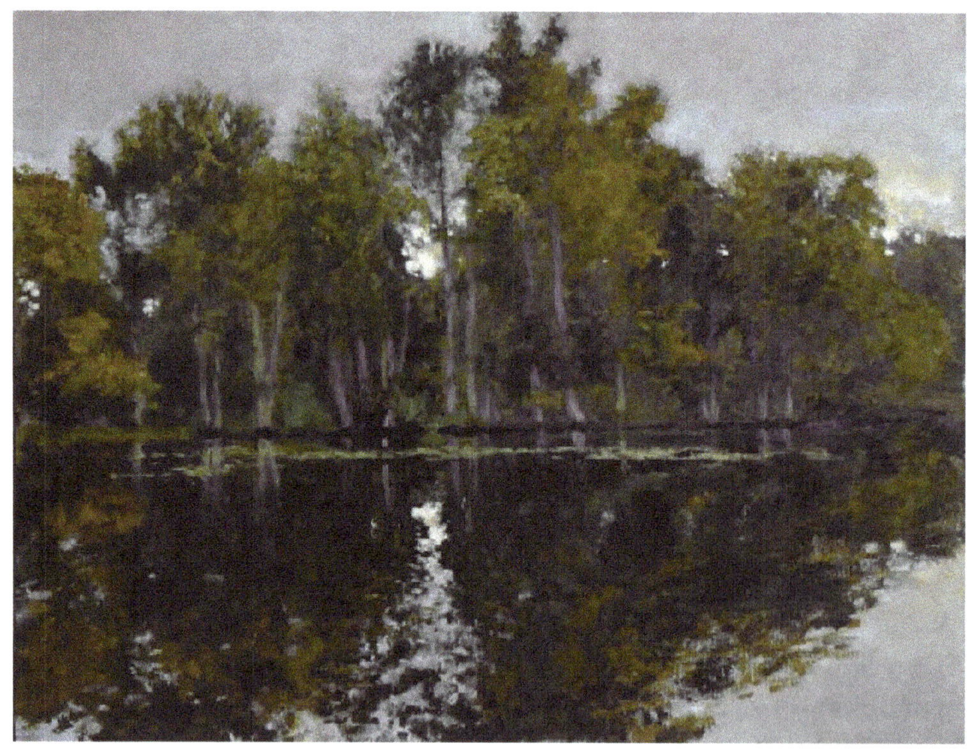

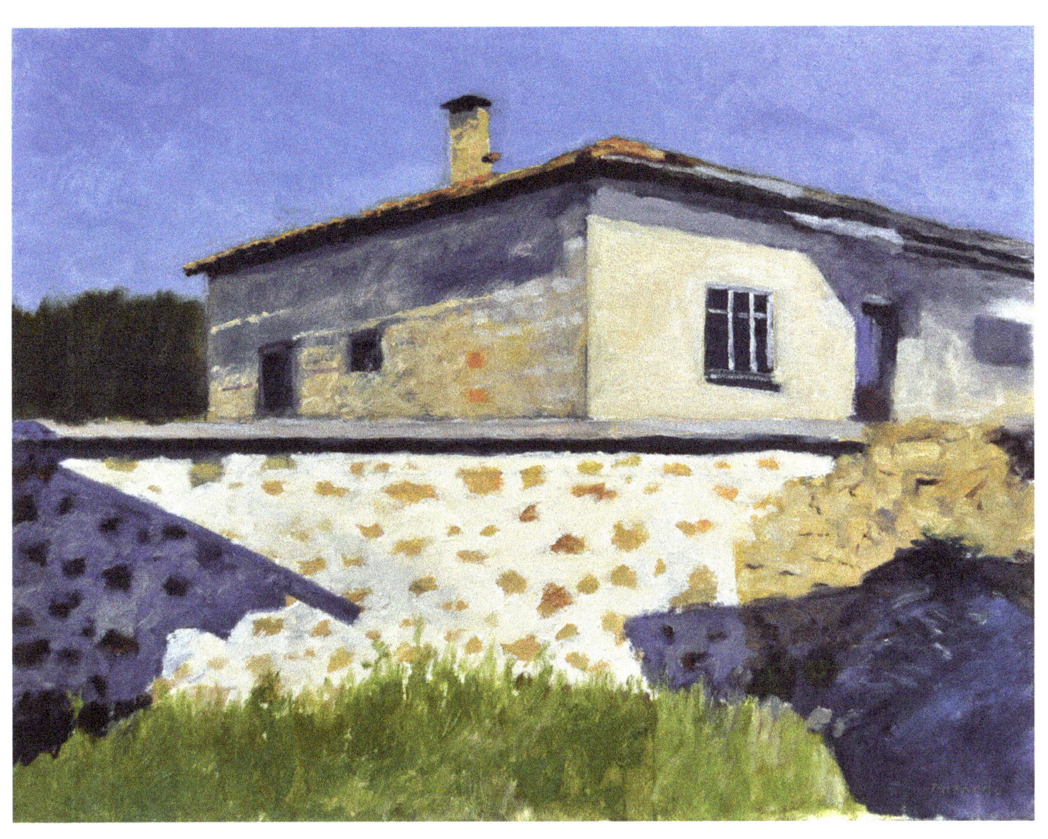

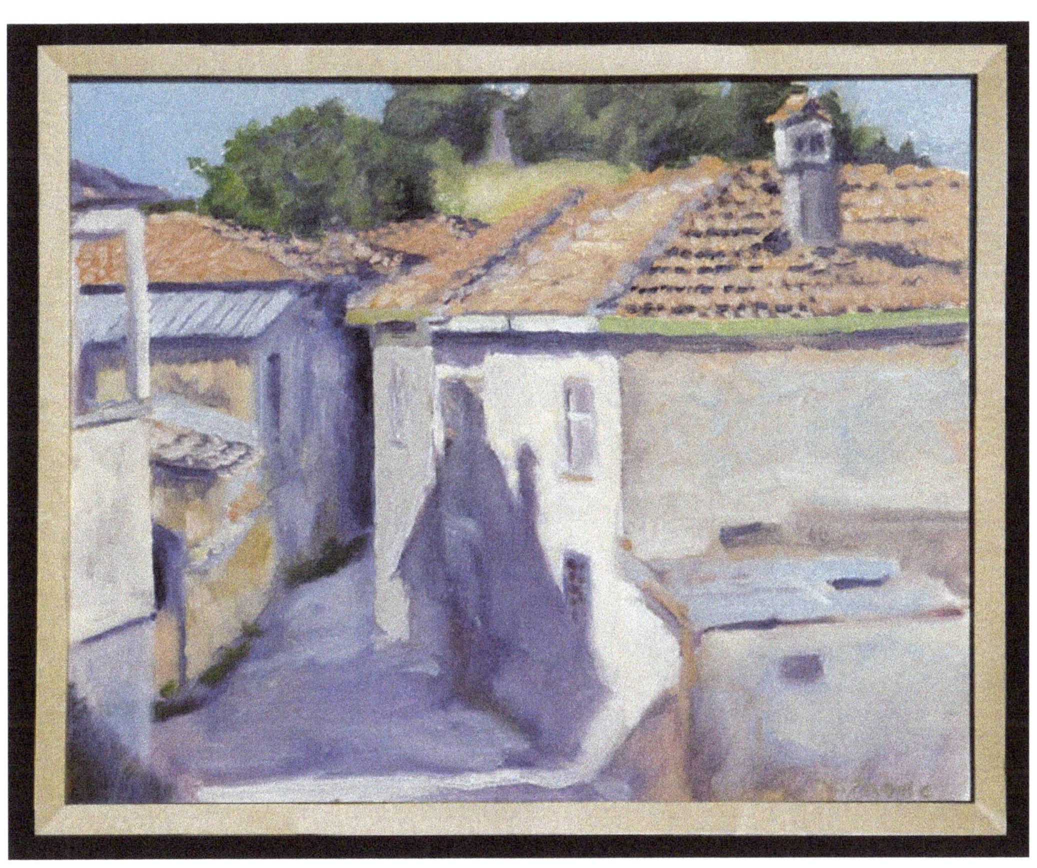

DEBI PENDELL

Biography

Born in Connecticut, Debi Pendell currently lives and works in the Eclipse Mill in North Adams MA (www.eclipsemill.com). She holds a B.A. from Central Connecticut State University and an M.A.L.S from Wesleyan University in Connecticut. Pendell is a 1999 recipient of an Individual Artist Fellowship Grant from the Greater Hartford Arts Council. She participated in CowParade 2000 in New York City, an event in which more than 500 life-sized fiberglass cows, painted by various artists, were displayed throughout the 5 boroughs; Pendell's was on Broadway. In 2007 Pendell was granted a 5-week artist residency in Bulgaria by the Griffis Foundation of New London CT and the Orpheus Foundation of Sofia, Bulgaria.

Pendell's work is in the permanent collections of The District Art Gallery and Museum, Smolyan, Bulgaria; OppenheimerFunds Inc., New York, NY, Sheppard Pratt Health System in Baltimore MD, The D'Amour Center for Cancer Care in Springfield, MA, and, in Connecticut, St. Francis Hospital, Hartford Hospital, Naugatuck Valley Technical Community College, Hamilton Sundstrand and West Woods School, along with several private collectors in the United States, Canada, Bulgaria, Switzerland, Germany, France, and London, England.

Pendell's work has been exhibited in Bulgaria at the Palace of Culture in the capital city of Sofia and The District Art Gallery & Museum in Smolyan; as well as in many galleries in the Northeast United States, including: Coohaus Art Gallery on 27th St, New York NY, The Gallery at the Pen & Brush, New York NY; Mass Mutual in Springfield MA; Young & Constantin Gallery in Wilmington VT; The Eclipse Gallery, NAACO Gallery, Gallery 51, and Kolok Gallery, all in North Adams MA; Ferrin Gallery in Pittsfield MA; Gallery 100, Saratoga Springs

NY; and, in Connecticut, SmallSpace Gallery at the Arts Council of Greater New Haven, The Promenade Gallery at The Bushnell in Hartford, 100 Pearl Street Gallery in Hartford, The Norman Stevens Gallery at the University of Connecticut in Storrs, and the Zilkha Gallery at Wesleyan University in Middletown.

Pendell's work is pictured and discussed in the books Rethinking Acrylic: Radical Solutions For Exploiting The World's Most Versatile Medium by Patti Brady, and Acrylic Innovation: Styles & Techniques Featuring 64 Visionary Artists by Nancy Reyner.

Debi Pendell's work can be viewed on her website, and in her Eclipse Mill studio by appointment.

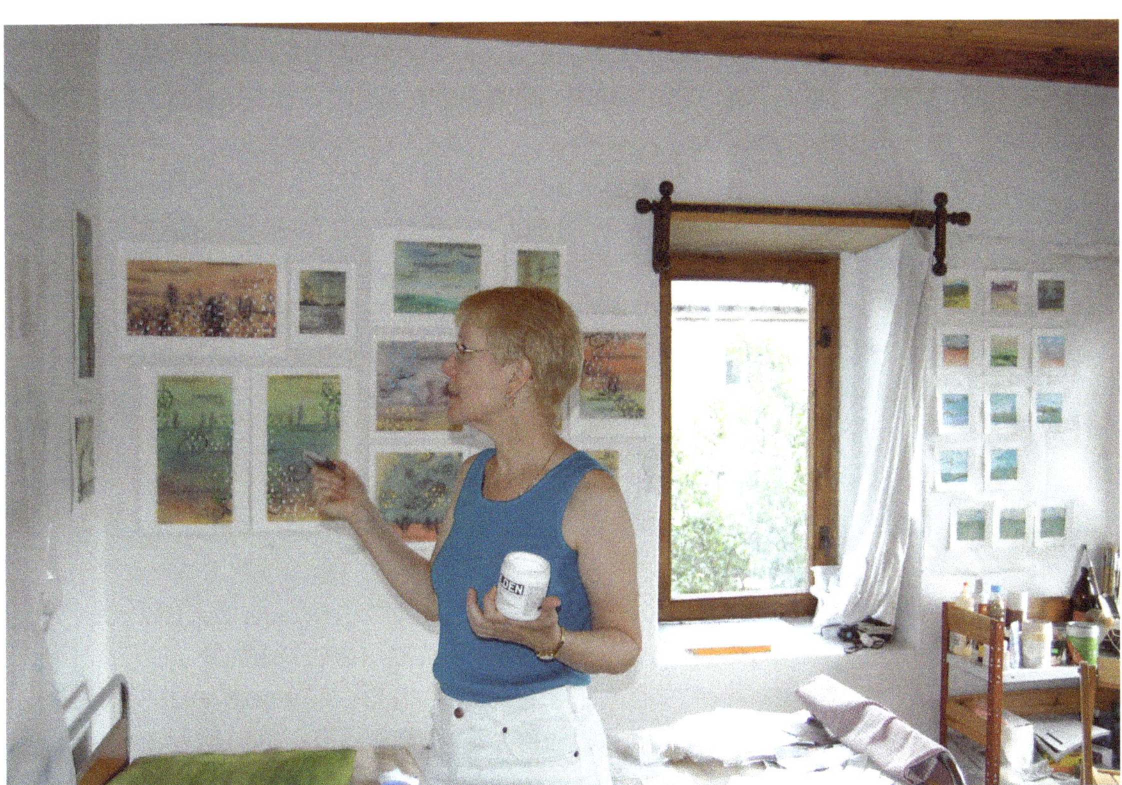

Debi Pendell at work in her studio in Sharon House, Bulgaria

Artist Statement

Artists create lexicons – brushstrokes, marks, scrapings, drips, motifs – and use them to create nonverbal "stories". Viewers take pleasure in "reading" these visual art works.

Most of Debi Pendell's works are investigations of semiotics, language, and meaning based in the format of landscape painting. Concentrating on abstract elements of recognizable shapes and characters in combination with materials and processes, Pendell plays with symbols of both visual art and language and how people "read" them and make meaning from them.

Letters, numbers, math equations and such are used abstractly, serving as value, texture, pattern and spatial indicators. Trees, birds, circles, and other images are also symbols. Actual space and the illusion of space are explored; created and thwarted. Viewers successfully combine the disparate imagery and find meaning in the gestalt of the combination.

Many viewers mistake these works for encaustic. But no wax is used, only acrylic gels and mediums. The main process of these works is collage, along with painting, drawing, and mixed media. Often viewers don't recognize the collage because the process embeds the elements within layers of acrylic.

Not always landscape and not always thickly layered, Pendell's work includes collage done in a more traditional fashion; the gluing of paper to paper, canvas or board, and the "thingness" of everyday objects are clearly evident. The process of collage has a definite, unique impact. In her latest works, done in the first half of 2015, the letters, numbers, trees, birds, and other symbols are left out. The acrylic encaustic is missing, or is much thinner. The landscape format is still in play, the collage process is plainly evident, and the physicality of the materials and textures is paramount. In some, rectangles and triangles suggest the possibility of dwellings. In others, there is no recognizable imagery at all. Even the landscape format begins to disappear. Pendell is playing with the line where abstraction and representation merge and diverge.

Pendell states, “My work evolves from the spontaneous and unconscious convergence of several experimental directions. Only after the creation and exhibition of the works do I begin to understand what they might be about. Making art is wordless and viewing art is wordless. Once one talks or writes about a visual image it is changed into something else, and perhaps becomes locked in. Any absolute conclusion about an image robs it of its changeable aliveness and its power to continue to inform.

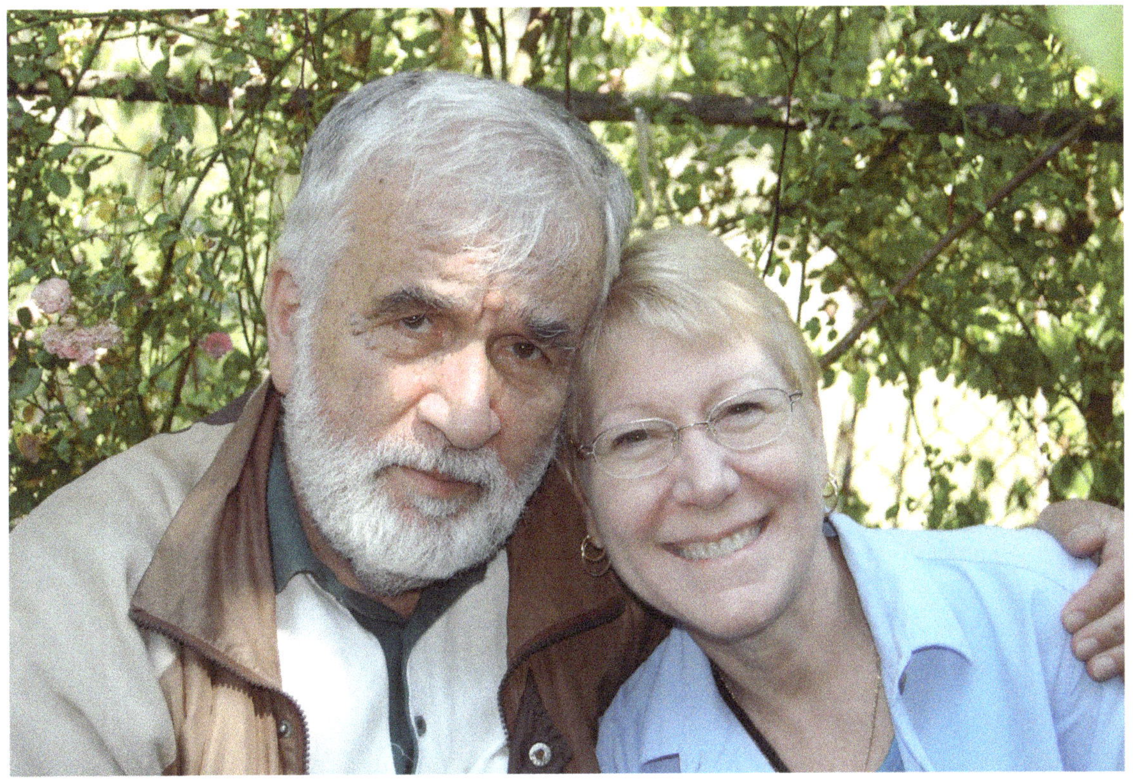

Debi and her host in Bulgaria, Luybomir Levchev

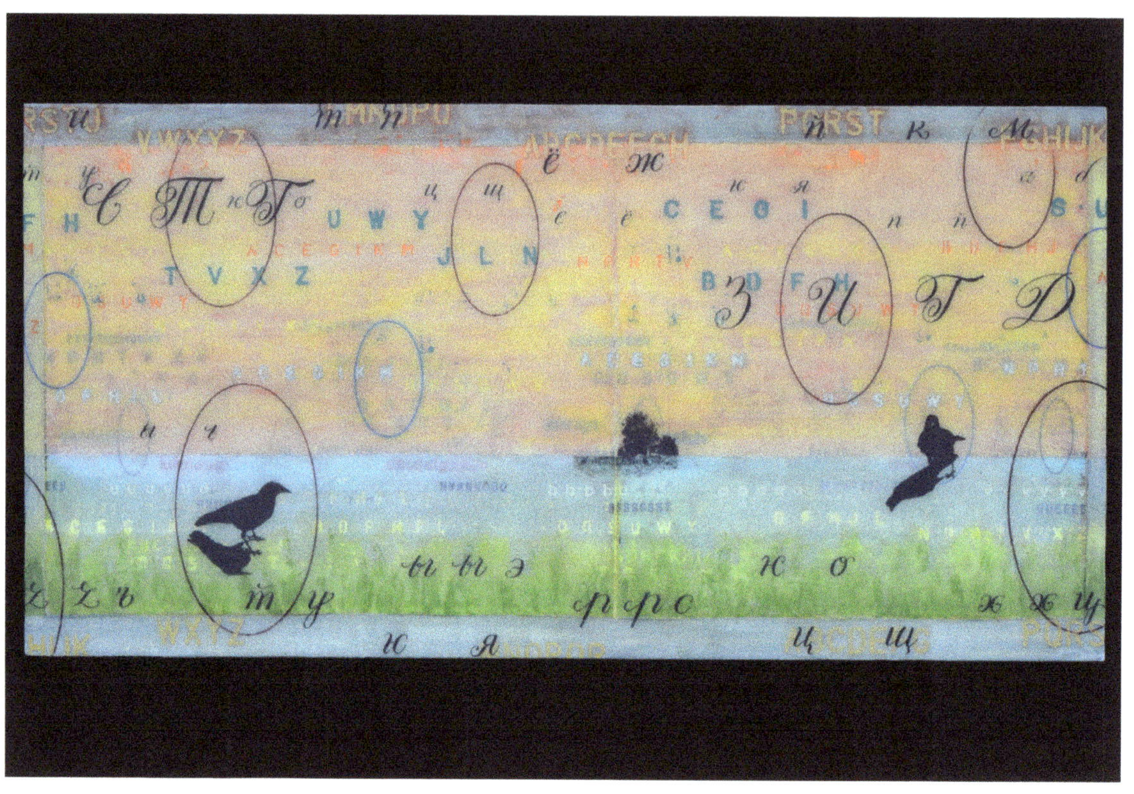

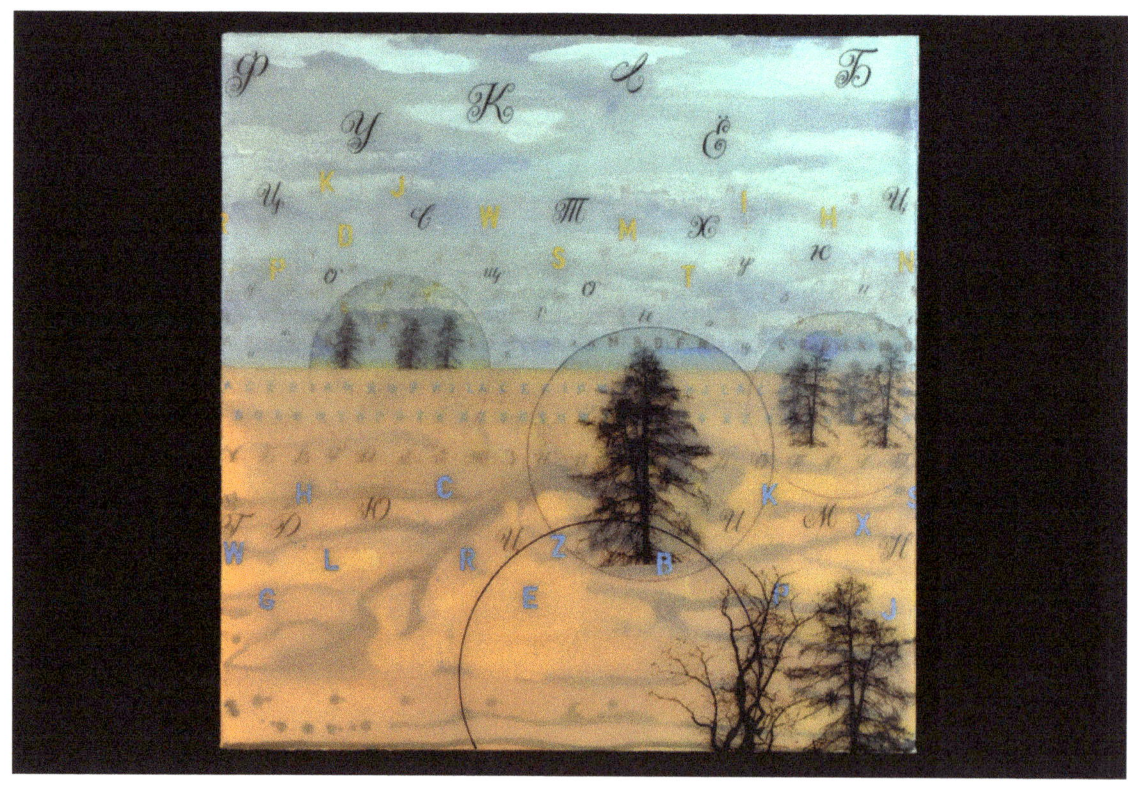

BRIAN STEPHENS

Brian keith Stephens

How to capture the past, present and future at the same time; this is at the center of my work as an artist and as a father, son, friend and lover. As we navigating our daily lives, we must face thoughts, anxieties, joys and emotions from all three of these tenses, and often at the same time. Seemingly opposite emotions -- lust, hatred, desire, love, pride, inhibition -- exists simultaneously between these moments in time. For some of us, some emotions out weigh others, grabbing our attention and transfixing our minds, sometimes taking over the way we live and breath. For myself, the emotions that occupy my mind and capture my energy are that of love, desire, and the fear of hurt or disappointment. And so, at the center of my work are these forceful emotions--they guide my hand to paint and my heart and mind to live. My work explores the emotions that guide us, that pull us and push us and ultimately define who we are, in relation to others and to ourselves.

Lately, what I have been most interested in capturing is how alternative perceptions of ones identity can affect these daily emotions. My work speaks to this in two mediums: oil pantings and collage/installation. With the first medium, I do this primarily through mystical imagery juxtaposed with figurative technique. I am using oil paints to create this mystical alter-reality where the human is the animal and the animal is the human.

I am captivated by the power of my own emotions, the playful desires and the sometimes dangerous energy that is the essence of the human spirit. We love, we hurt, we laugh and we cry -- it's this fantastic and sometimes frightful spectrum. The 'contemporary soldier', a motif represented in my work through oil on canvas, is my own conception of this power we have to love and to hurt, to build and to break. For me the contemporary soldier is child freed from the gaze of the parent or society, it is the spirit, freed. But also faced with the challenge of the future, even as it moves freely from its past.

At the center of my work and life are these fascinations with myth, the spectrum of human passion, our kinship to the spirit of the wild animal, and challenge of balancing the real with the fanciful. We must balance all of this while also navigating the spectrum of time, the web of past, present and future. My art has been and continues to be my outlet for exploring these themes and conjuring up new ones.

Briankeithstephens.com

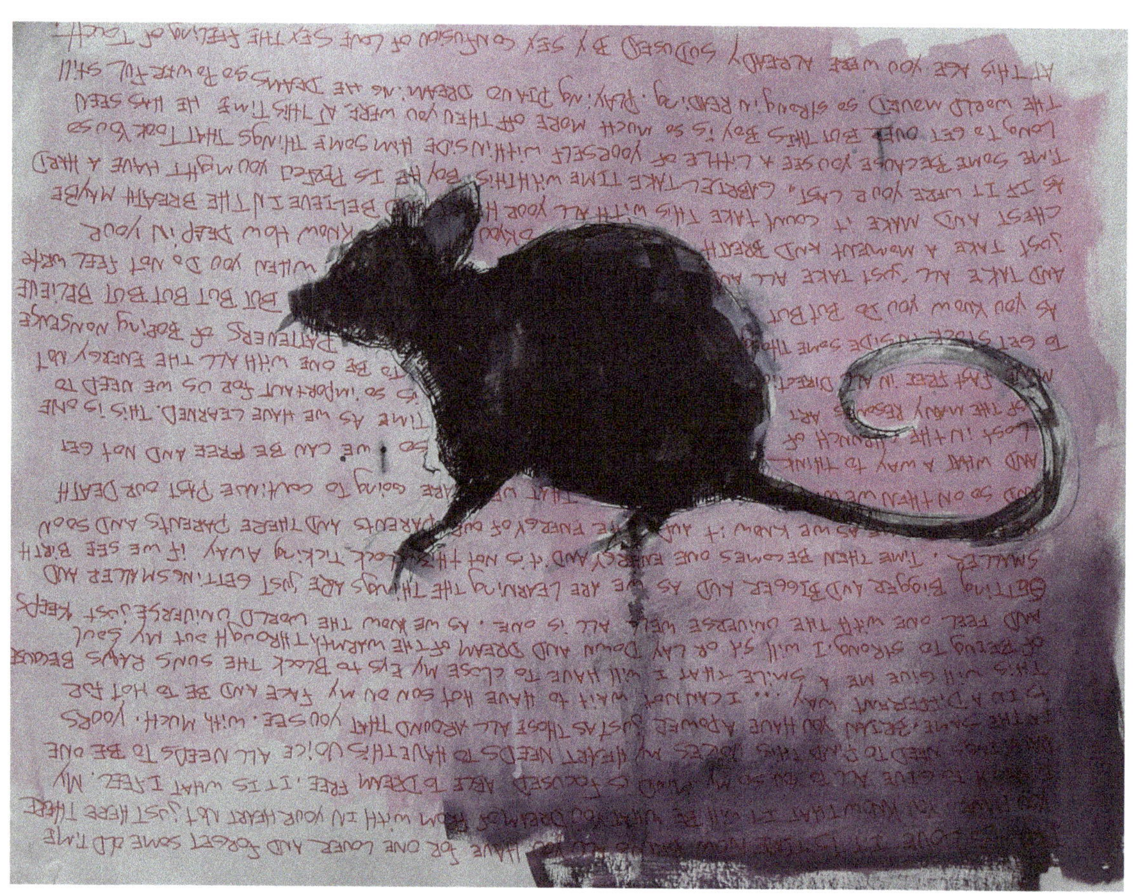

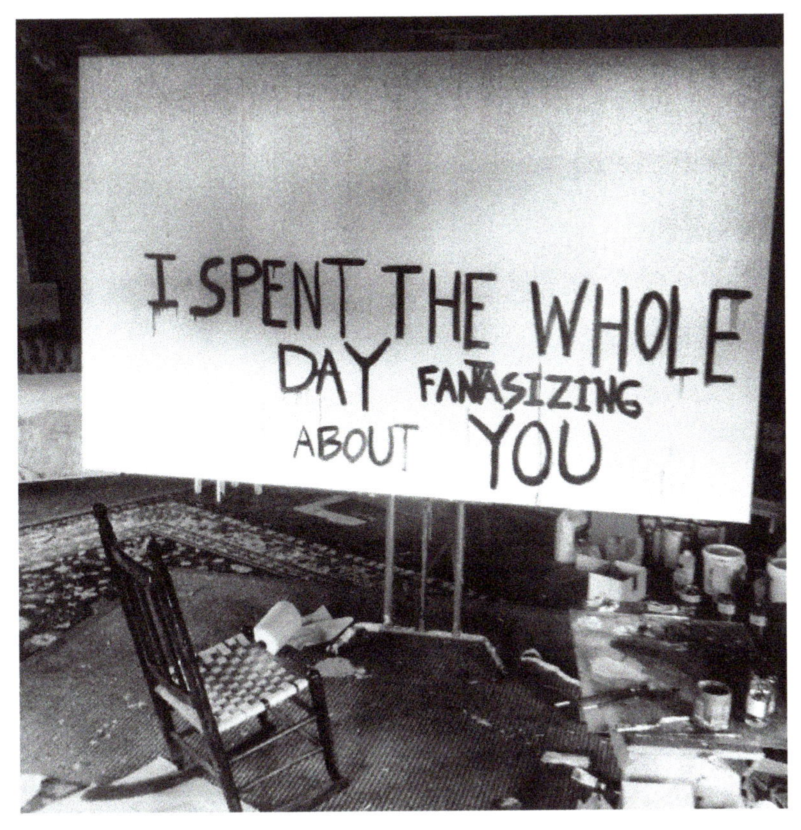
I SPENT THE WHOLE
DAY FANTASIZING
ABOUT YOU

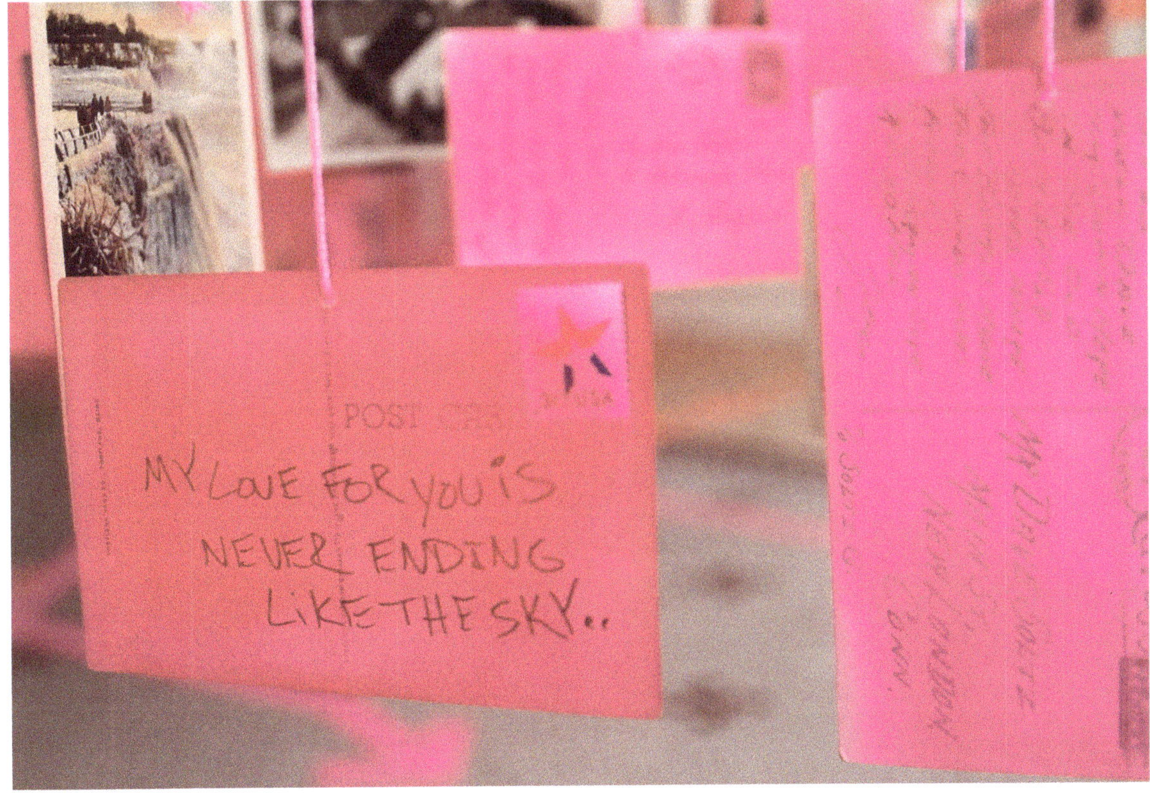
MY LOVE FOR YOU IS
NEVER ENDING
LIKE THE SKY..

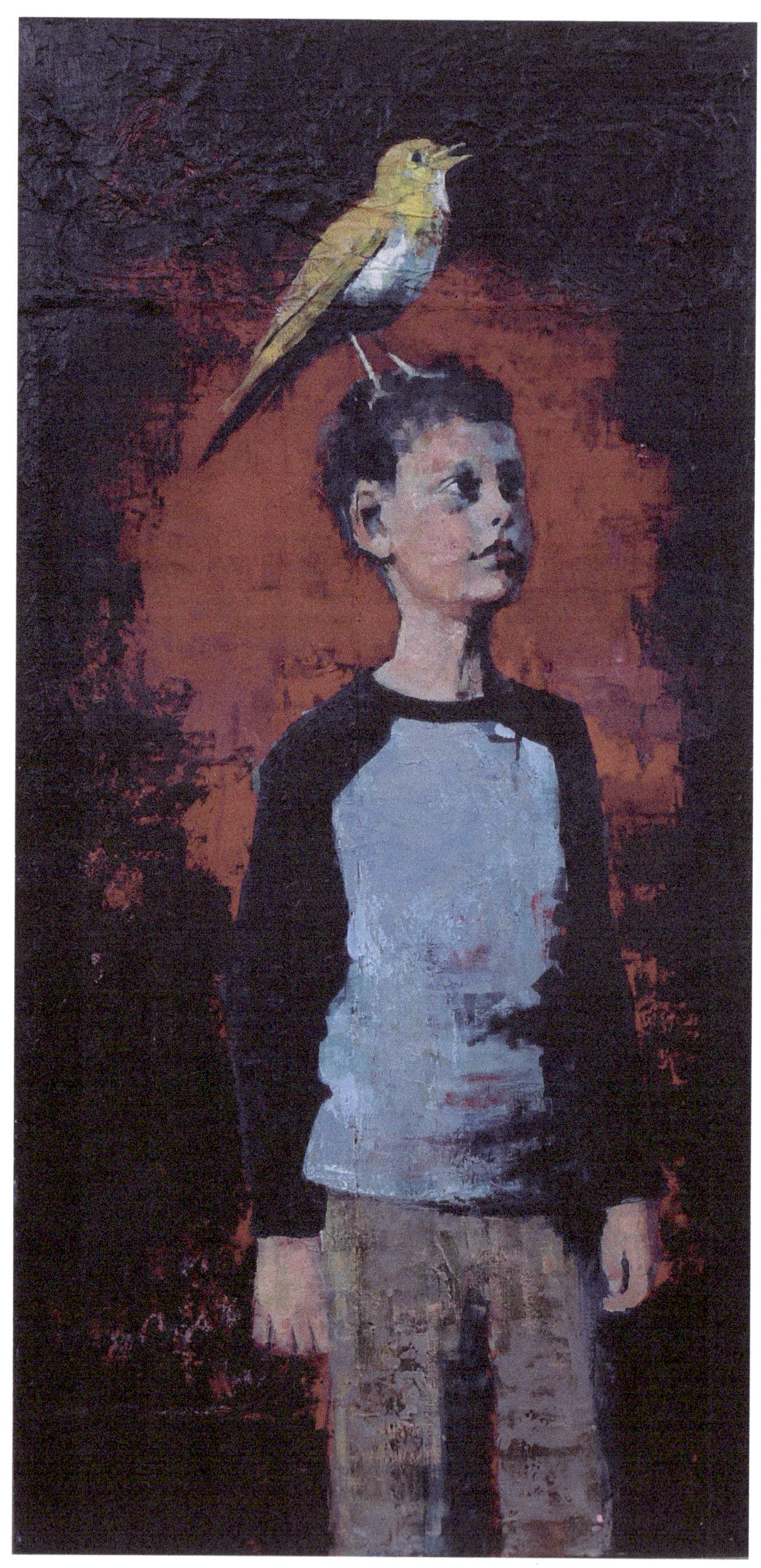

ANNE SEELBACH

Art Statement

www.anneseelbach.com

Patterns of Nature, a new series in my work, expresses my observations of the essential shapes and rhythms of nature and how they are repeated in different ways. “Rhodope Strata” is inspired by the hills surrounding Polkovnik Serafimovo, Bulgaria and my vision of the underlying rock strata - layers and layers of rock sediment built up over millennia. In “Rhodope Strata/Island Waters” this curving contiguous form is also in the movement of water currents in nearby bays and ocean around eastern Long Island, NY.

Tidal waters and the shoreline have inspired my art. The question “What is happening?” interests me far more than what a scene looks like. I look for the unseen physical laws of nature that create each visual element of a particular moment. Changing tides and the rich colors of each season are effects of the earth’s gradual rotation around the sun. Green shoots pierce frozen ground in early spring. Sheets of ice fracture and melt on the bay. Horseshoe crabs mate at the summer solstice. Water, plants, birds and marine life all follow the dictates of the planetary shift.

I am interested in the tension between opposing elements of representation and abstraction: illustrative delineation versus gestural marking; line versus free-form washes; mechanical and geometric shapes versus atmospheric color fields. I use these oppositions to create a tension between three dimensional illusion and a flattening of space. Gestural brushwork and many washes of paint create rich color and texture.

Beginning with an understanding of the physical forces of nature that create a visual landscape or seascape, the paintings evolve out of a complex layering of the painting process.

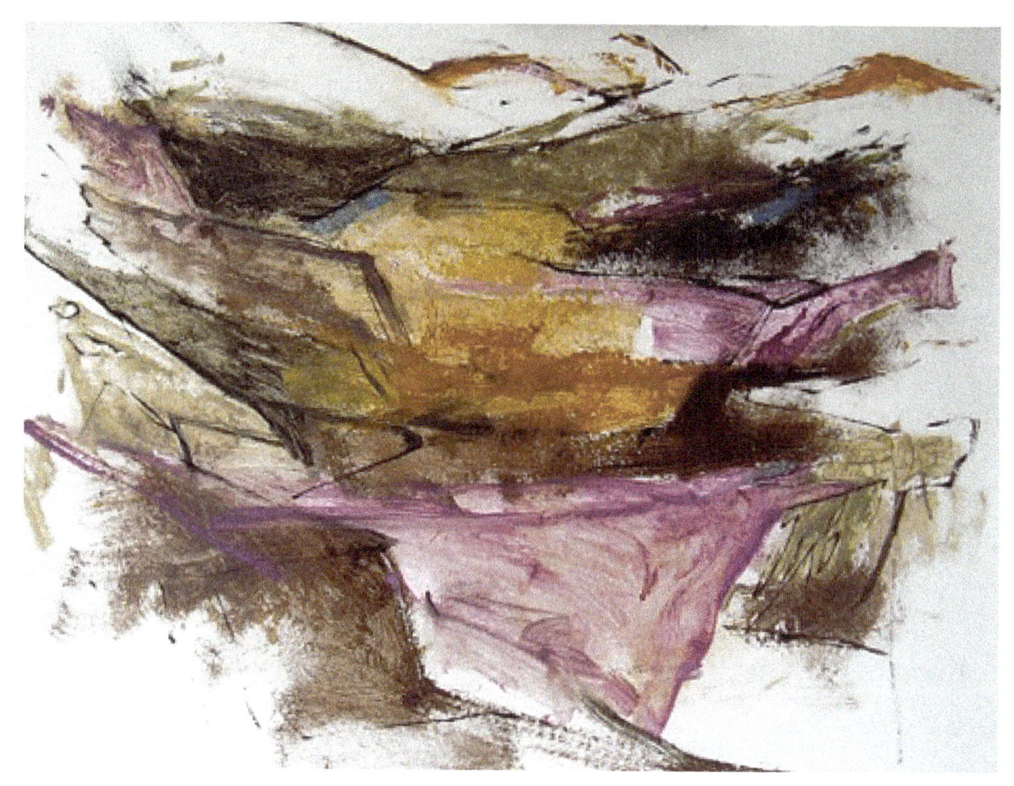

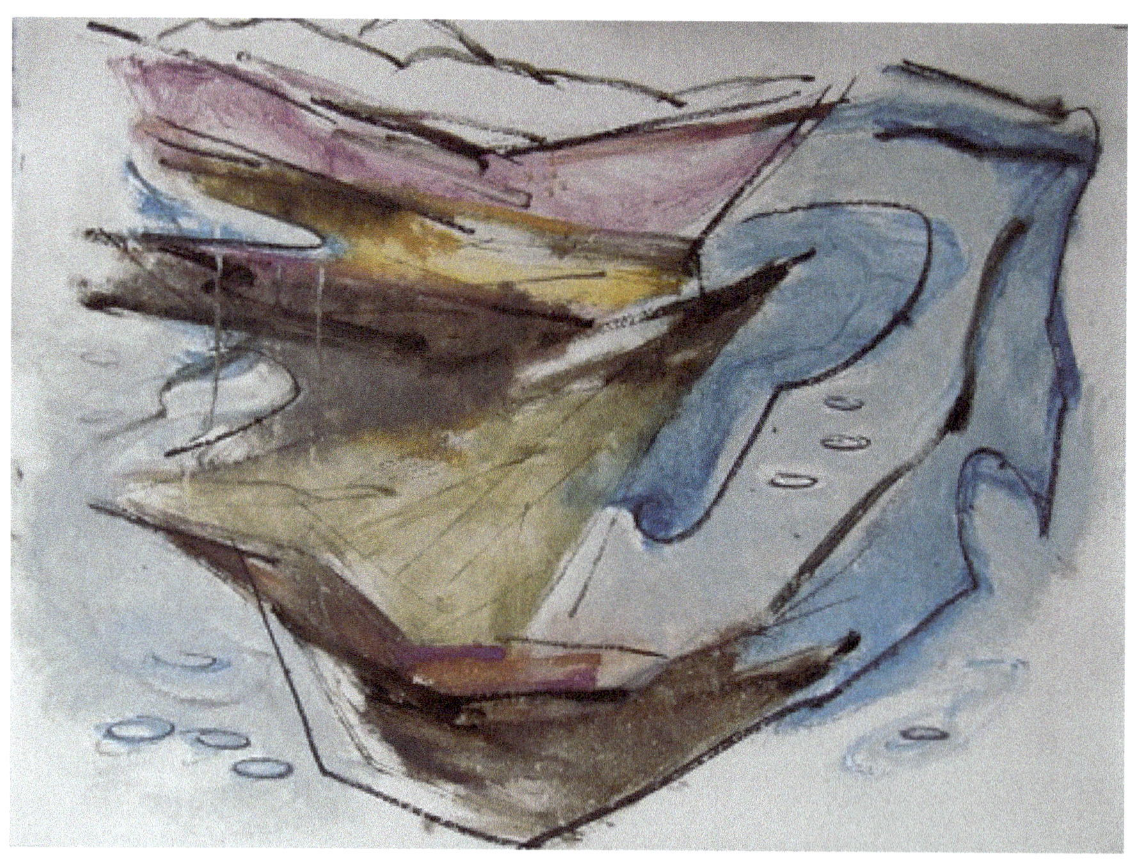

CATHERINE DOOCY

Artist Statement

Representation & Illusion

In my work, the representation of a "landscape" is not the final goal. Instead, I use the vernacular of landscape painting as a method for exploring composition and color; attempting to evoke the feeling of the landscape rather than documenting the landscape's actual forms.

Yet I marvel at how easily a line can transform itself into a tree, a simple stain of blue becomes sky, and wind is created with a brushstroke. If a work seems "unfinished", it may be that I have chosen to stop just as the paint begins its magic.

EXHIBITIONS

Solo Exhibitions

October 2014 • "To Each Her Own", Eclipse Mill Gallery, North Adams, MA
May 2014 • "Transitions", Green Street Arte, Middletown, CT
April - June 2014 • "Stops Along the Way", Good News Cafe, Woodbury, CT
August-Sept 2013 • "Blue Variations", NAACO. Gallery, North Adams, MA
July-Sept 2010 • The Alexey von Schlippe Gallery of Art. UCONN's Avery Point Campus, Groton, CT
Summer 2009 • Hartford Fine Art & Framing Co. Gallery, East Hartford, CT
July-Sept 2008 • "365 - a year of everyday", EBK Gallery, West Hartford, CT
June 2008 • "Bulgaria Revisited", EBK Gallery, West Hartford, CT
March - May 2008 • "Transitions", Good News Cafe, Woodbury, CT
June-August 2007 • "Other Worlds: Fact & Fiction", Mattatuck Museum, Waterbury, CT

May-June 2007 • “Landscape”, Washington Art Assoc., Washington Depot, CT
Sept-Oct 2005 • The Alexey von Schlippe Gallery of Art. UCONN's Avery Point Campus, Groton, CT
July-August 2005 • “And Skies”, Seven Knots Gallery, Isleboro, ME
June-July 2005• “Director's Choice”, Clark Gallery, Lincoln, MA
Dec-Jan 2005 • “Panoramas”, The Sue & Eugene Mercy, Jr. Gallery, The Loomis Chaffee School, CT
Sept-Oct 2004 • Hartford Fine Art & Framing Co. Gallery, East Hartford, CT
June 2004 • “Stops Along the Way”, Town & County Club, Hartford, CT
May-July 2004 • Mass Mutual Headquarters, Hartford, CT
Jan-April 2004 • “Horizons /Transitions”, The John Bryan Gallery, Farmington, CT
Sept-Oct 2003 • Promenade Gallery, The Bushnell, Hartford, CT
Jan-Feb 2003 • Weir Farm Visiting Artists 2002, UCONN Stamford Gallery, CT
April 2003 • Renana Gallery, Middletown, CT
Jan-March 2002 • EBK Gallery, West Hartford, CT
Dec 2001 - Jan 2002 • Ventana Capital, LLC Headquarters New York, NY
Sept 2001 - Nov 2001 • Mass Mutual Corp Headquarters, Springfield, MA
Nov 2000 • “Landscapes: No Boundaries”, Artworks Gallery, Hartford, CT
Nov-Feb 2000 • “Canton Artists Guild: Member Artists”, Krasdale Gallery, Bronx, NY
Jan-March 1999 • “Passing Through”, Norman Stevens Gallery, Babbidge Library, UCONN, Storrs, CT
Dec 1998-Jan 1999 • “Landscape Suite”, The Pump House Gallery, Hartford, CT
Sept-Nov 1998 • “Stops along the way”, Gallery in the Wood, South Windsor, CT
January 1998 • “Horizons & Transitions”, Small Walls Gallery, Hartford, CT
Jan-March 1997 • “Eclectic Landscapes”, Jorgenson Gallery, UCONN, Storrs, CT
October-Nov 1996 • Three artist show, 100 Pearl Gallery, Hartford, CT

March-April 1996 • Two artist show "Earth & Sky". Artworks Gallery, Hartford, CT

March 1996 • "Looking at the Land", The Equity Bank Contemporary Art Series. Wethersfield, CT

July 1991 • Graduate Show, "Night Drives". Zilka Gallery, Wesleyan University, Middletown, CT

July 1990 •Normandy Painting, group show. Zilka Gallery, Wesleyan Univ.

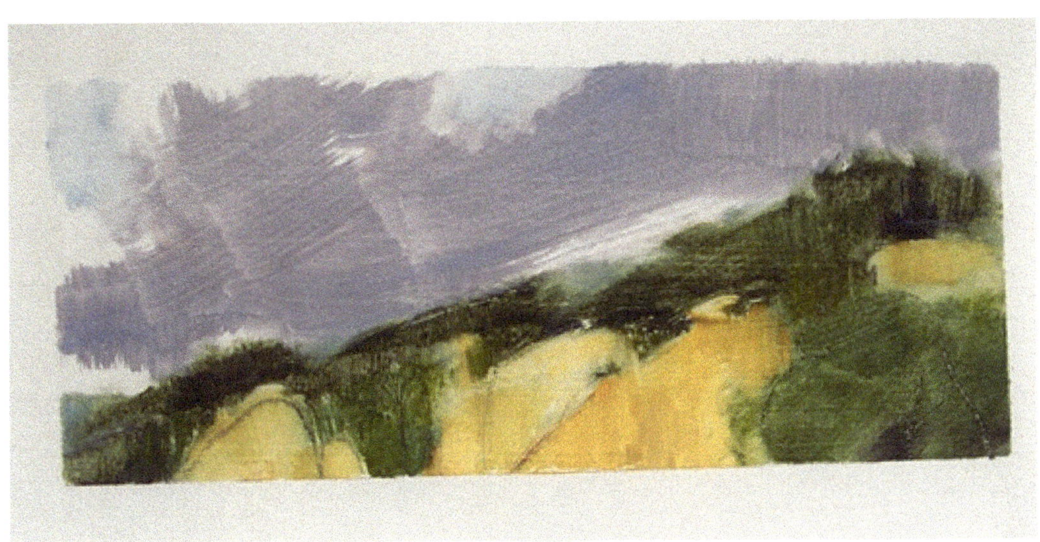

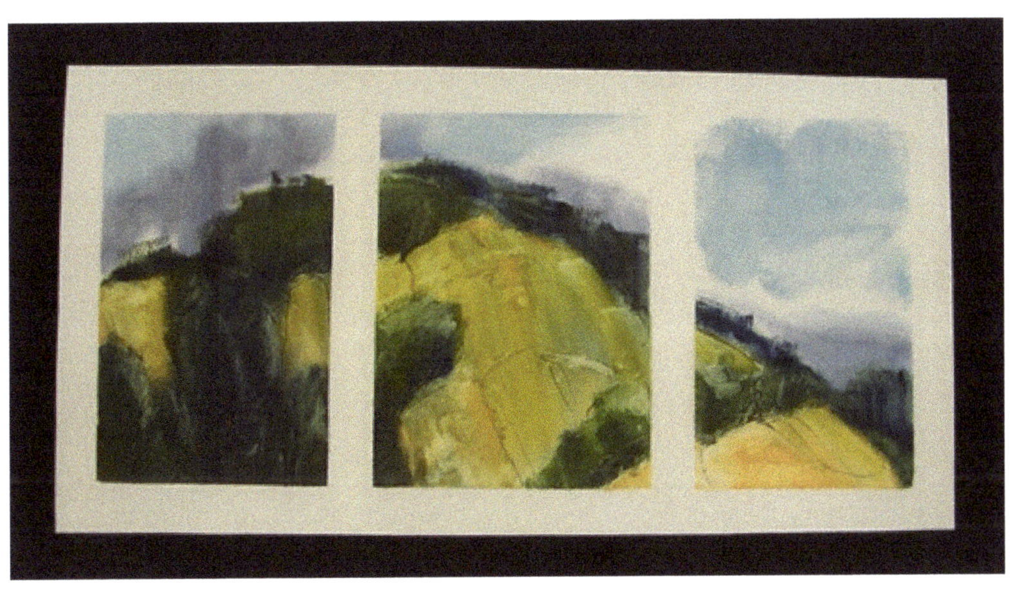

POLA ESTER

PHOTOGRAPHER, INSTALLATION ARTIST

Born in Poland, based in the US. http://polaesther.com/

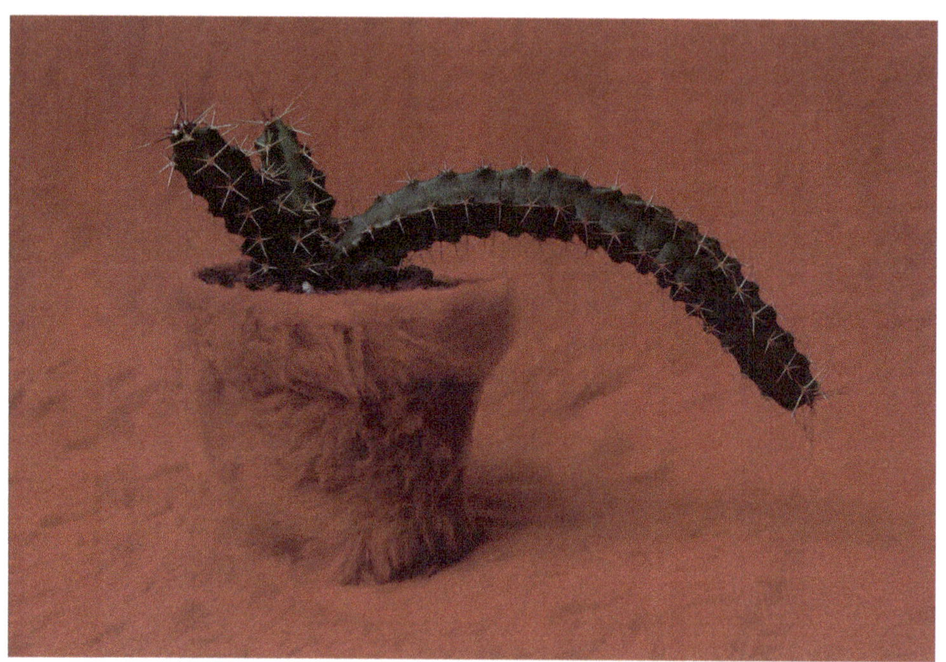

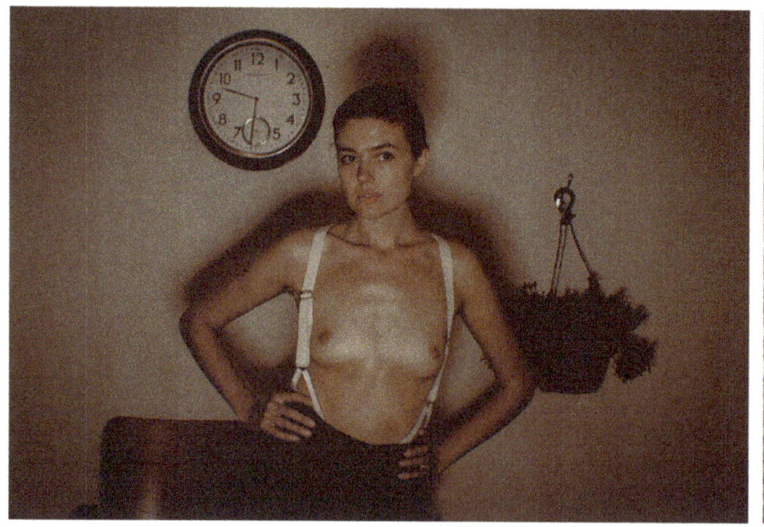

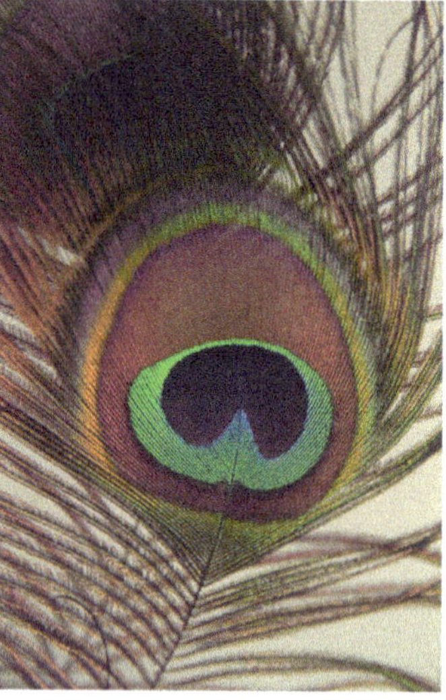

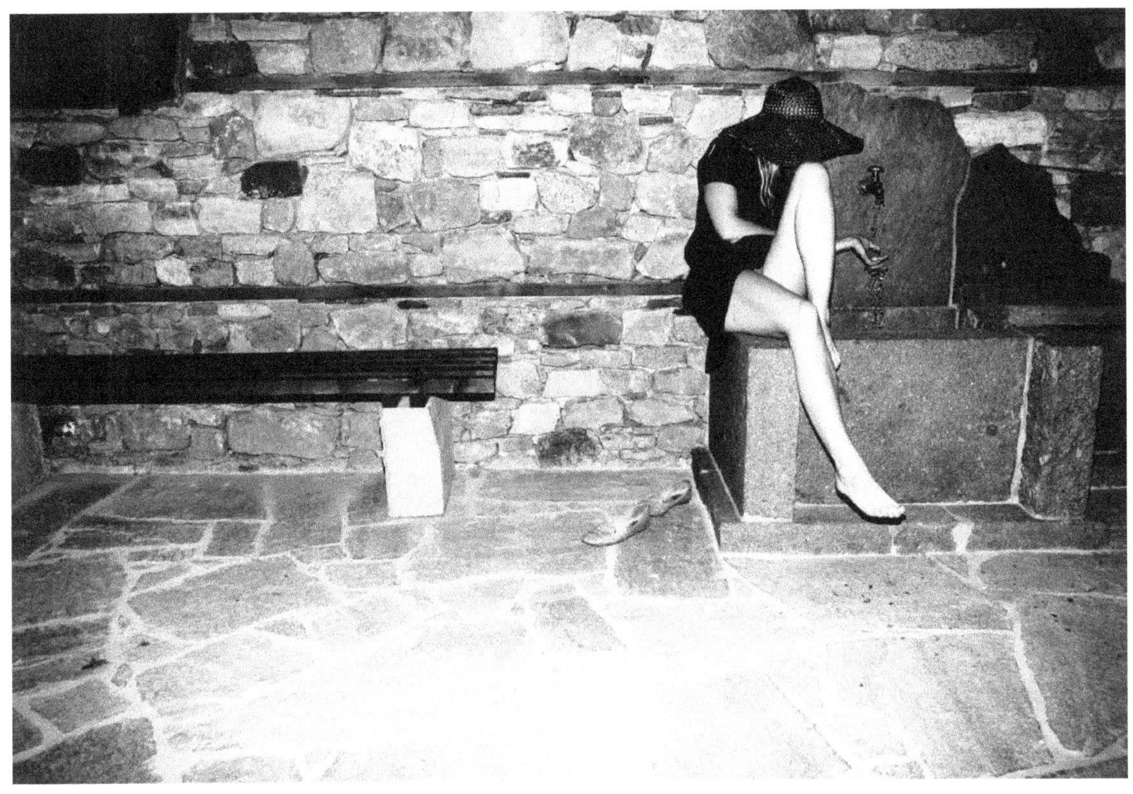

My name is Pola Esther. I was born in Poland. The legend says I was kissed by the Pope and that event made me who I'm. As an artist I use photography as main platform for expression. I like to photograph nature, mostly human. In my work I reflect upon my intimacy, femininity and sexuality. I respond intensely to my close surroundings, approaching it with poetic, eager and sometimes ironic eye. I'm constantly looking for visual fantasy in commodities. I'm not only searching for beauty in its given form but also in its peculiar dimensions. I often challenge my subjects to reach towards extraordinary aspects of their personality to achieve certain social commentary and reaction in a personal way. I have a background in theater and use its action and dynamic energy in my concepts and presentations. I'm always ready to play and experiment with these endless variations of people, places and things - this is the spirit which drives my creativity.

Art is fun

ARIEL MITCHELL

ABOUT THE ARTIST

Ariel's work spans graphic design, installation, painting, makeup, garment construction, and photography. She is a working artist in marketing as well as her own practice, and is consistently fascinated by what makes an image turn heads.

She has had solo and group exhibitions internationally and in the US, as well choreographed fashion shows, directed videos, styled lookbooks, and collaborated with other artists. She has a small fashion line called American Qi, and she lives and works in Brooklyn, NY.

Artist's Statement

Ariel makes work that reflects dichotomies and uses materials that represent those dichotomies. Feminine and masculine are represented by fabric and and by hardware, growth and decay are represented by scale and gravity. Simultaneously referencing relationships and the body, Ariel's work uses everyday materials and takes them out of their usual context.

She lives and works in Brooklyn, New York, and also runs a fashion brand.

www.arielmitchell.com
www.americanqi.com

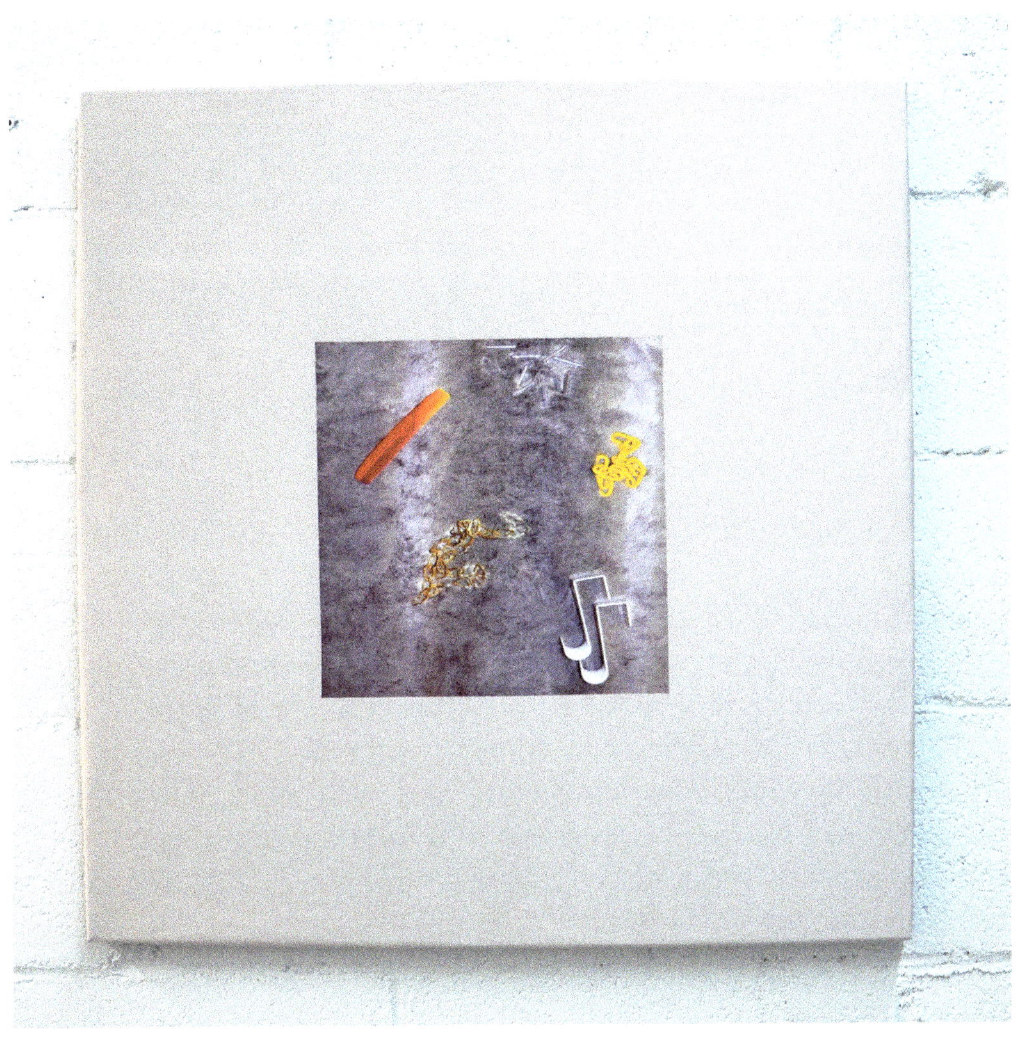

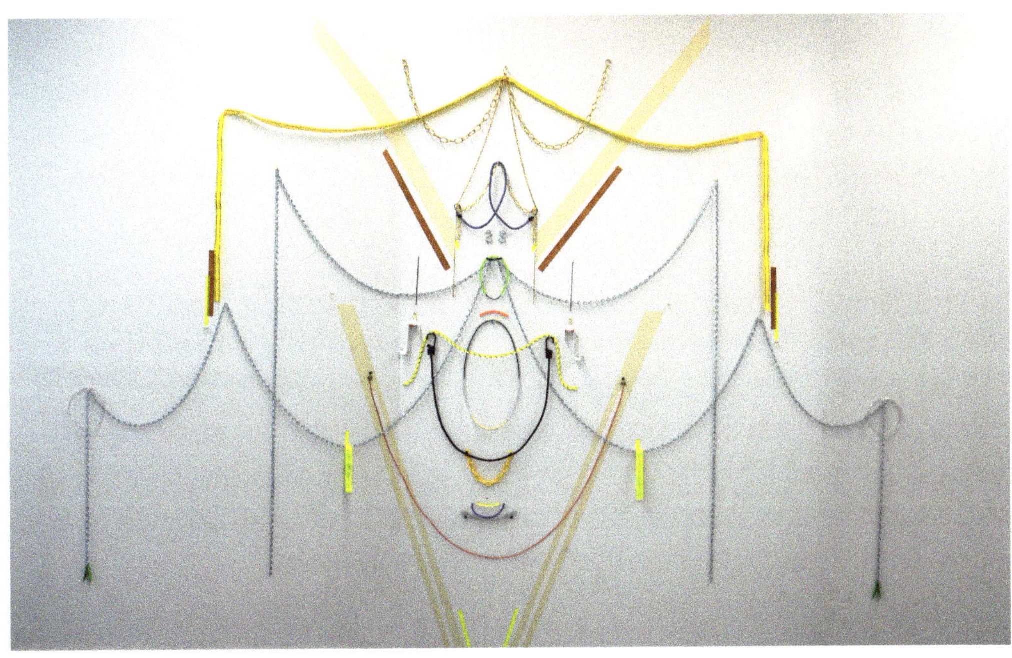

BRAD GUARINO

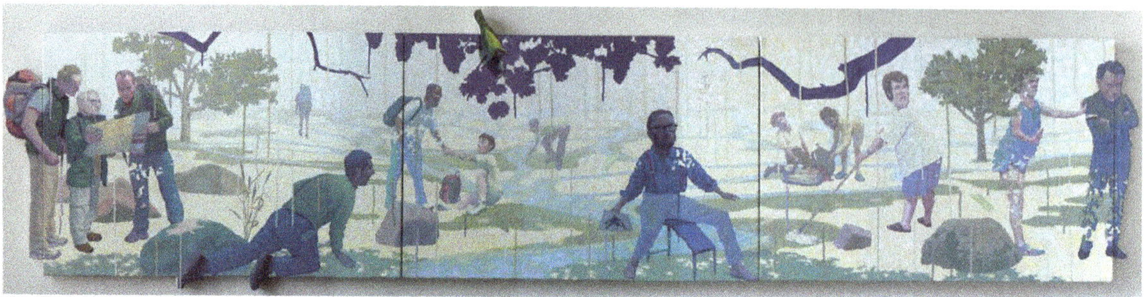

Statement

The tension between who we are now and what we want to become is a fundamental motivating force in our lives. Most of us strive to be something better. To do this requires a certain fluidity of identity; we must willingly open our minds to new ideas and ways of thinking, and we must continually challenge our beliefs and behaviors. Based on new information, we try to rid ourselves of things we deem outdated or harmful and replace them with those we consider better or more consistent with who we want to be.

For a boy, the prospect of becoming a man is a significant driving force. Boys look around them to find male role models and then try to assemble from these various sources a masculine ideal that they hope to live up to. They imitate behaviors and attitudes that conform to this ideal and suppress those that do not. Long before they are of age, they begin to "act" like men. This act continues to evolve but never ends, even long after the boy has become a man.

In my paintings and drawings, I contrive fictional worlds populated exclusively by men. The figures in my compositions are drawn or painted from photo-based collages made by recombining parts from various images of men. The collage process refers the constructed nature of gender and how boys form their concept of male roles, i.e. by piecing together the perceived characteristics of cultural icons and stereotypes with those of influential men in their lives.

My figures exist in awkward relationship with one another, and their activities suggest unresolved narratives. My work explores how boys are socialized and how this socialization affects both their identity as adults and their interactions with other men. I use the illusionism of representational art as a metaphor for the artificiality of gender. Incompletely rendered forms, along with evidence of erasure, correction, obfuscation, and expressive processes refer to the actual art-making as well as to the mutability of gender constructs, and the struggle boys face in their efforts to forge a masculine identity.

Brad Guarino: Bio

Brad Guarino is a figurative artist who lives and works in New London, CT. He currently is adjunct faculty at the University of Connecticut, Eastern Connecticut State University, and Manchester Community College. Guarino did postgraduate study at Bulgaria's National Academy of Art on a Fulbright Fellowship, and was twice an artist-in-residence in southern Bulgaria on Griffis and Orpheus foundation fellowships. Guarino holds an MFA from the University of Connecticut School of Fine Arts and a BFA from Lyme Academy College of Fine Arts.

brad@bradguarino.com

www.bradguarino.com

Solo Exhibitions

Recent Work
Alexey von Schlippe Gallery, University of Connecticut, Groton, CT Real Art Ways, Hartford, CT Southern Vermont Art Center, Manchester, VT Galllery Gray, online gallery, www.gallery- gray.com Jorgensen Gallery, Univ. of CT, Storrs Mitchell College, New London, CT Middlesex Community College, Middletown, CT NOMAS Conference: Men and Masculinity 31: Creating Connections for Gender Justice, Ramapo College, Mahwah, NJ National Palace of Culture, Sofia, Bulgaria and Open Society Gallery, Smolyan, Bulgaria The Atrium Gallery at Quinebaug Valley Community College,

Danielson, CT and Alexey von Schlippe Gallery, University of Connecticut, Groton, CT Norwich Arts Council, Norwich, CT Mitchell College, New London, CT
Naked City Gallery, Wichita, KS Silo Gallery, New Milford, CT Smolyan City Gallery, Smolyan, Bulgaria and National Palace of Culture, Sofia, Bulgaria European Cultural Center, Rousse, Bulgaria and Serdika Gallery, Sofia, Bulgaria
Golden Street Gallery, New London, CT Stonington Vineyards Gallery, Stonington, CT Pfizer Central Research, Groton, CT Nexus Gallery, New York, NY

What Manner of Men

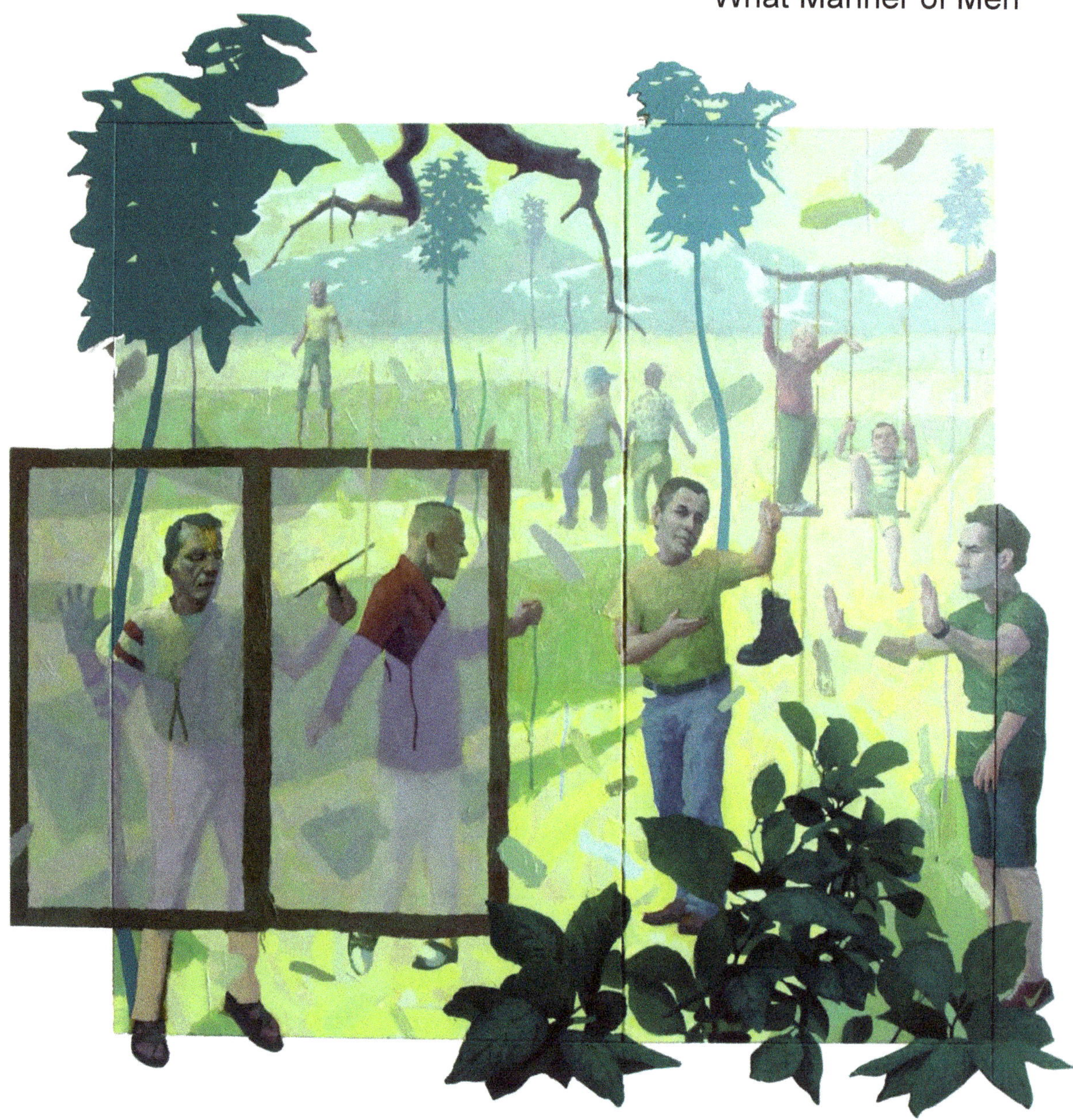

TED EFREMOFF

Ted Efremoff, born in Moscow, Russia, is a cross-disciplinary artist engaged with performance, video, installation and social practice. Spurred by his personal interest in social justice, he envisions collaborative activity as an instrument that builds critical relationships between people. His art explores the personal and cultural constraints ingrained within prevailing political, economic, and social power structures.
He has spent time in Polkovnik-Serafimovo, Bulgaria through the Bulgarian-American Creative society residency program as well as a year in Sofia, Bulgaria through the Fulbright program.
He is an Assistant Professor at Greensboro College where he teaches Art, administers The Citizen Scholar Lecture Series and directs LIFT Gallery.

KUKER-MUKER
Street action East Haddam, CT / New Britain, CT / NYC

A Kuker is a Bulgarian beast who comes out in late winter to chase away evil spirits. No one truly knows how this Kuker-Muker wound up on this side of the pond. Researchers into this episode have debated the possibility of transport through some sort of primeval magic. His first sighting was at I-Park, a retreat for artists in East Haddam, CT, and subsequently he was sighted again in New Britain CT and NYC. Eyewitnesses and Kuker sighting researchers have speculated that his dances around NYC power sights might have been performed as some sort of Shamanistic antidote to the ultra material culture that America stands for. This video is the only document of his visit.

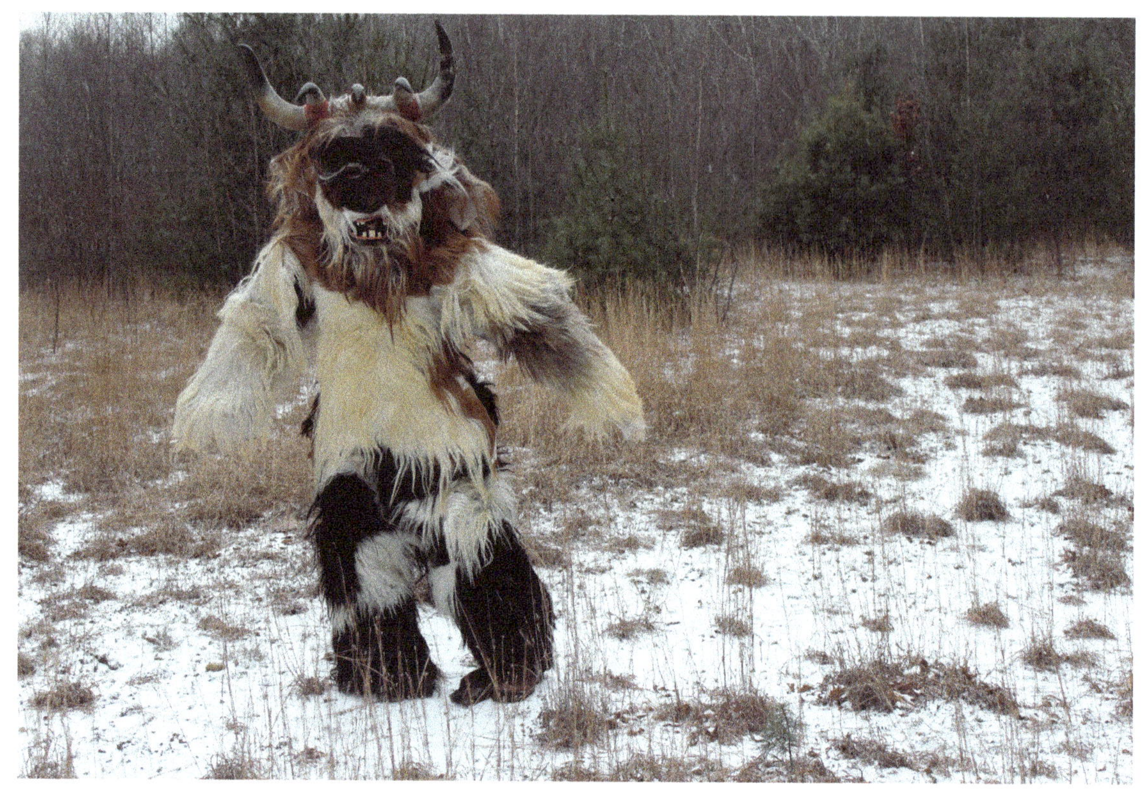

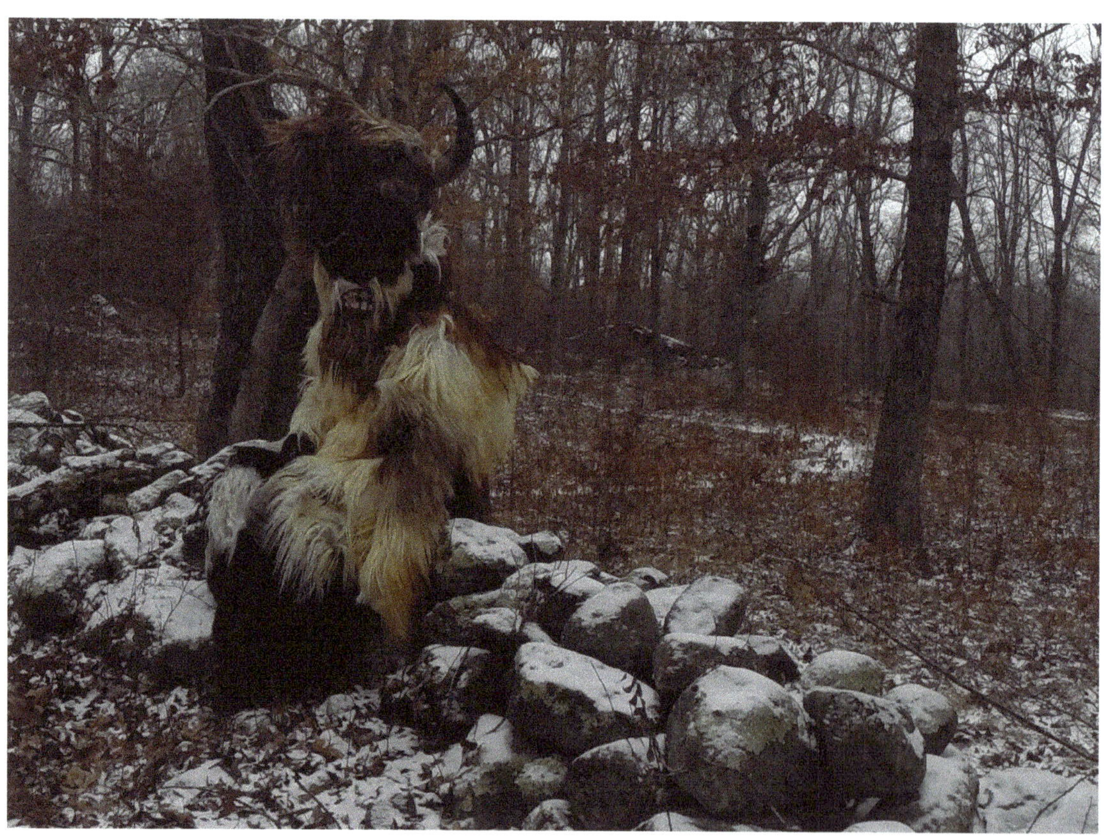

CHRISTOPHER ZHANG

ABOUT MY PAINTINGS

As a professional artist, I have received the most institutional education and substantial training of painting in both China and the US. In the last four decades, I have successfully developed my career and markets nationally and internationally through numerous exhibits and awards at home and abroad.

My subjective paintings are mainly of two themes: (1) the Chinese minority nationality and their social customs, (2) ballerinas. My style and techniques can best represent and express these two subjects in light of realism. My equal success in painting these two remarkably different subjects with highly different skills has in fact become the differentiation between me and other artists and has thus become a characteristic of my art. In addition to the subjective paintings, I paint portraits and landscapes。

Christopher Z. Y Zhang

cxyzhang@netzero.net www.chriszhangstudio.com

I was born in Shanghai, China, received BFA in 1984.
I came to UAS in 1990, received MFA in 1993.
I am the members of the following artist organizations:
-Master Signature Member of Oil Painters of America 2014
-Copley Master of Copley Society of Art, Boston, MA since 2005
-Artist member of Salmagundi Club, New York, NY since 2006
- Elected Artist member of Connecticut Academy of Fine Art since 1998 and board member from 2010 to 2013.
-Elected Artist Member of Lyme Art Association, Lyme, CT since 1999

-Member of the Board of the Trustees of The Griffis International Art center since 2002

Major awards (for limited space list only to 2005 and not includes the 2nd and 3rd prizes):

-Figurative Award of Excellence	OPA 23rd National Exhibition, 2014
-Figurative Award of Excellence	OPA Eastern Region Exhibition, 2014
-Outstanding Work Prize	Salmagundi Club 130th Annual Exhibition New York, NY 2014
-Best in Show	Academic Artists Association 62nd Annual Show, Springfield, MA 2012
-Outstanding Work Prize	Salmagundi Club 127th Annual Exhibition New York, NY 2010. The painting was selected as the permanent collection of the SCNY
-Outstanding Work Prize	Salmagundi Club Fall Exhibition New York, NY 2011
-Best of Show	Connecticut Academy of Fine Art 99th Annual Show, Mystic, CT 2010
-First Prize	Copley Society of Art Member Show Boston, MA 2009
-Best of Show	Connecticut Academy of Fine Art 94th Annual Show, Slate Museum, CT 2006
-First Prize	Copley Society of Art Member Show Boston, MA 2006
-First Jurors' Choice	Copley Society of Art Spring Show, Boston, MA 2005

Publication	Images of Tibet	2002
	Royal Bee	2000
	Moon Festival	1998

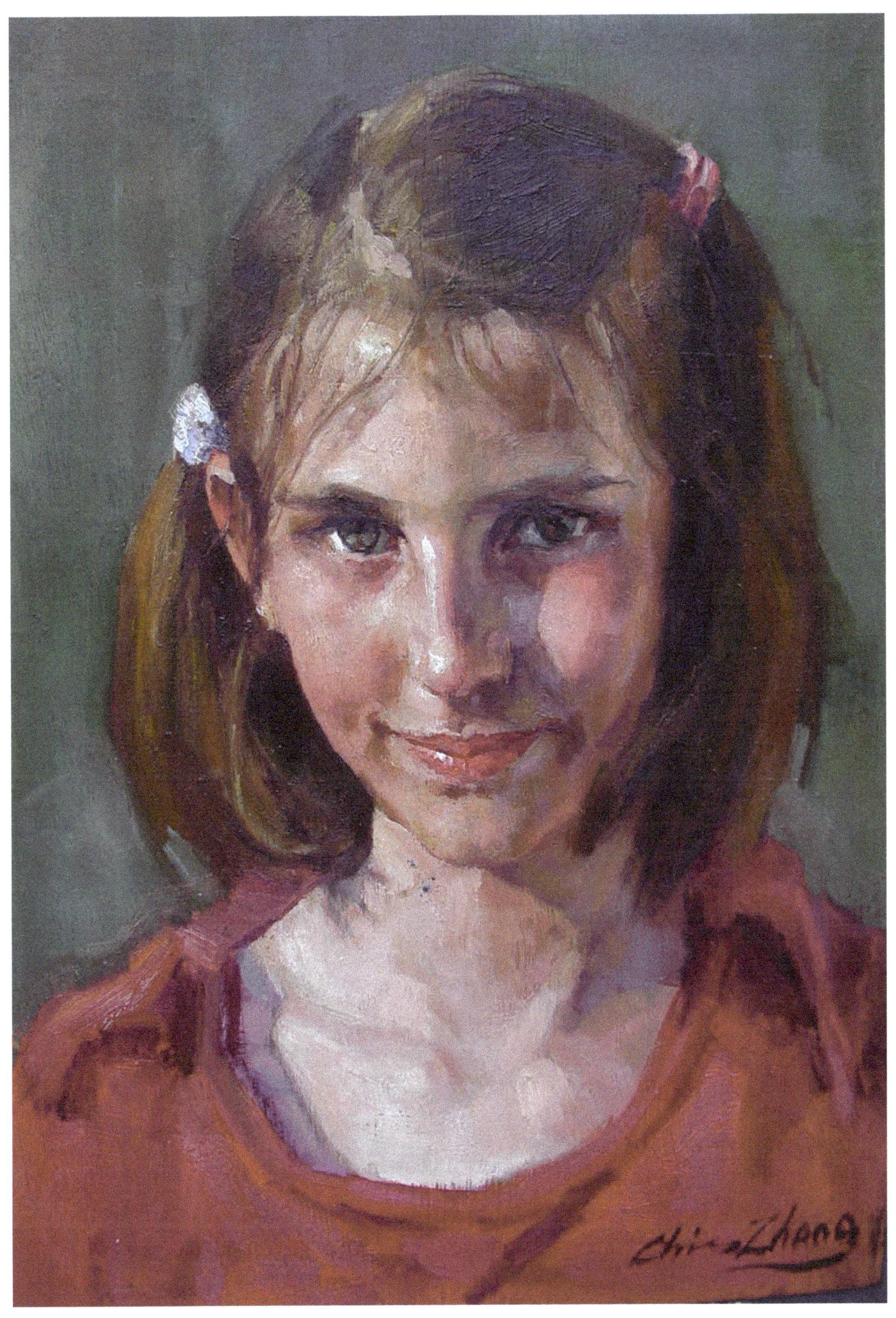

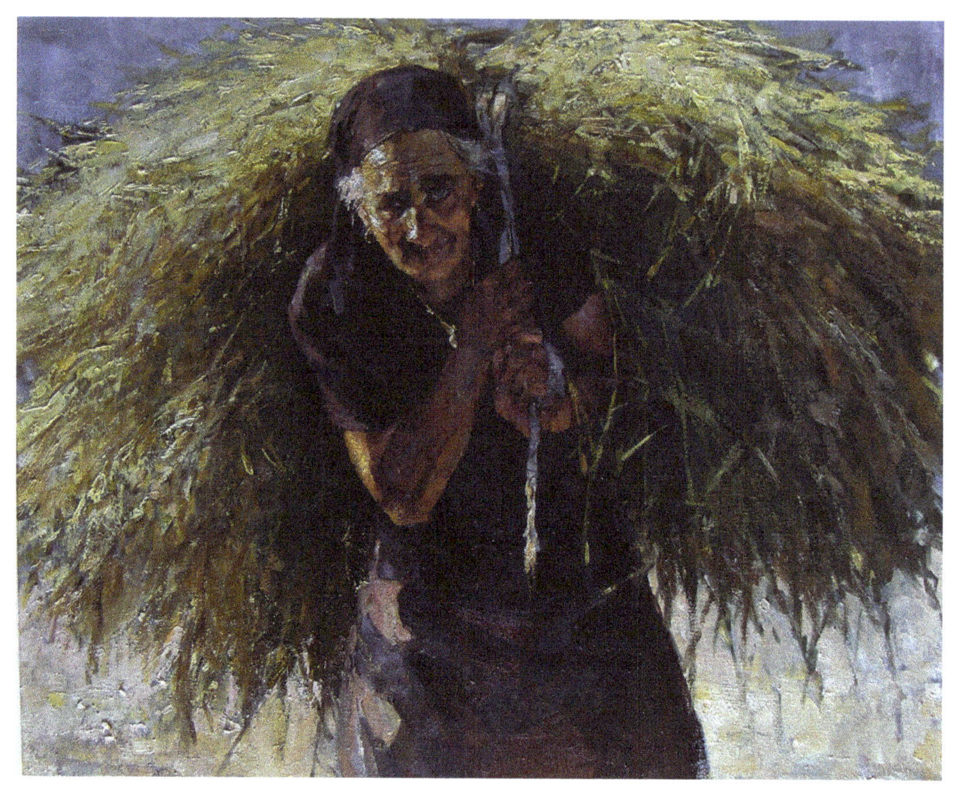

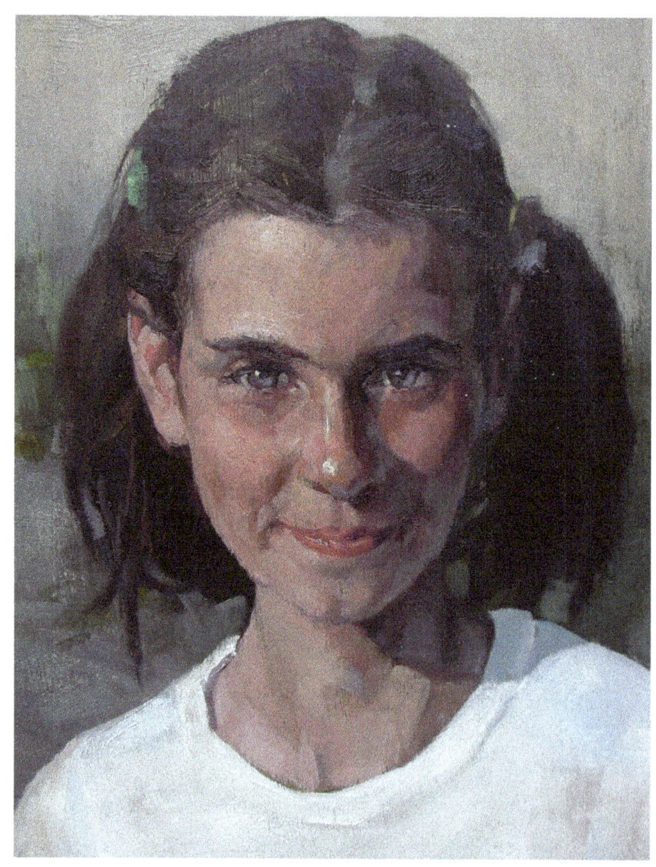

GREG BOWERMAN

E-mail: gbowerman@williamsschool.org

SELECTED EXIHIBITIONS:
December 2014 August 2014 March 2014 February 2014
January 2014
December 2013 Cooley Gallery Old Lyme, CT
Alexey von Schlipee Gallery of Art UCONN Avery Point Campus, Groton, CT
New Britain Museum of Art New Britain, CT
Slater Museum 70th Annual Connecticut Artists Exhibition
Mystic Arts Center Mystic, CT Honorable Mention
Mural Commission Private Collection New London, CT

AWARDS/ RESIDENCIES:
2009 Artist in Residence, Mellwood Art Center Louisville, KY
2006 Artist in Residence, Orpheus and Griffis Foundation, Polk Serivimova, Bulgaria
2004 Artist in Residence, six months, Scholarship Winner Open Studio Tour
Farmington Valley Arts Center, Avon, CT 1999 Student Exchange Program, Dublin, Ireland
1999 "100 sacred Visions" Juried exhibition with Ernst Fuchs Payersbach, Austria
Gregory P. Bowerman 14 Rogers Lake Trail Old Lyme, Connecticut 06371 Tel: 860-287-7412 E-mail: gbowerman@williamsschool.org
PROFESSIONAL EXPERIENCE:
2003-present 2007-present 2007-present Summer 2014

EDUCATION:
2001Art Instructor, The Williams School New London, CT
Gallery Manager, Cummings Art Center Connecticut College, New London, CT
Assistant Cross Country Coach, The Williams School New London
Production Assistant Provincetown, MA
BFA in Painting Lyme Academy College of Fine Arts Old Lyme, CT

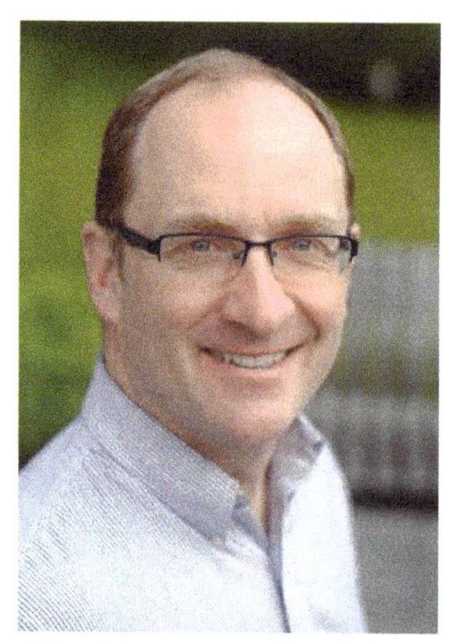

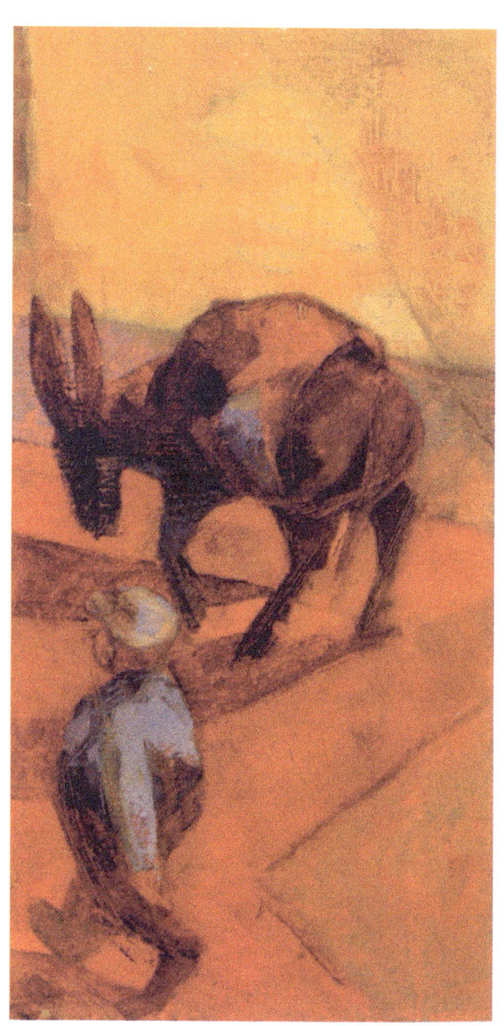

XINGXIN ZHANG

Xingxin Zhang is currently studying for her bachelor's degree at Columbia University and resides in New York.

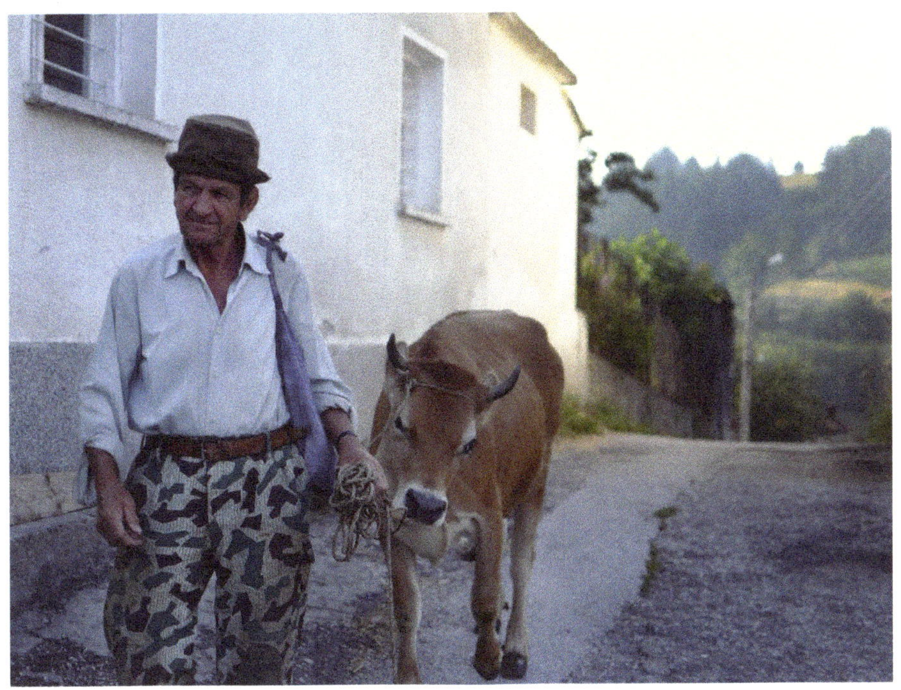

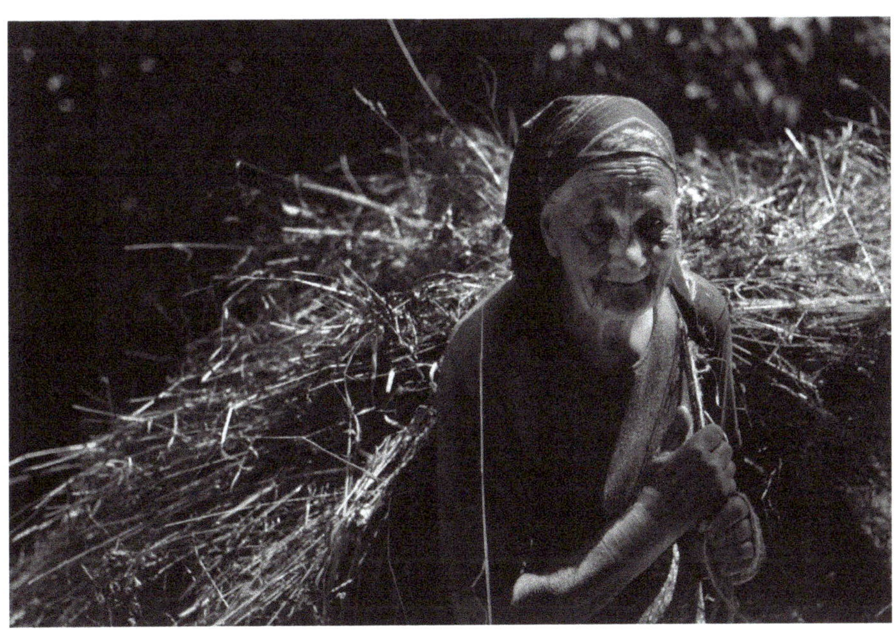

NANCYFRANKEL

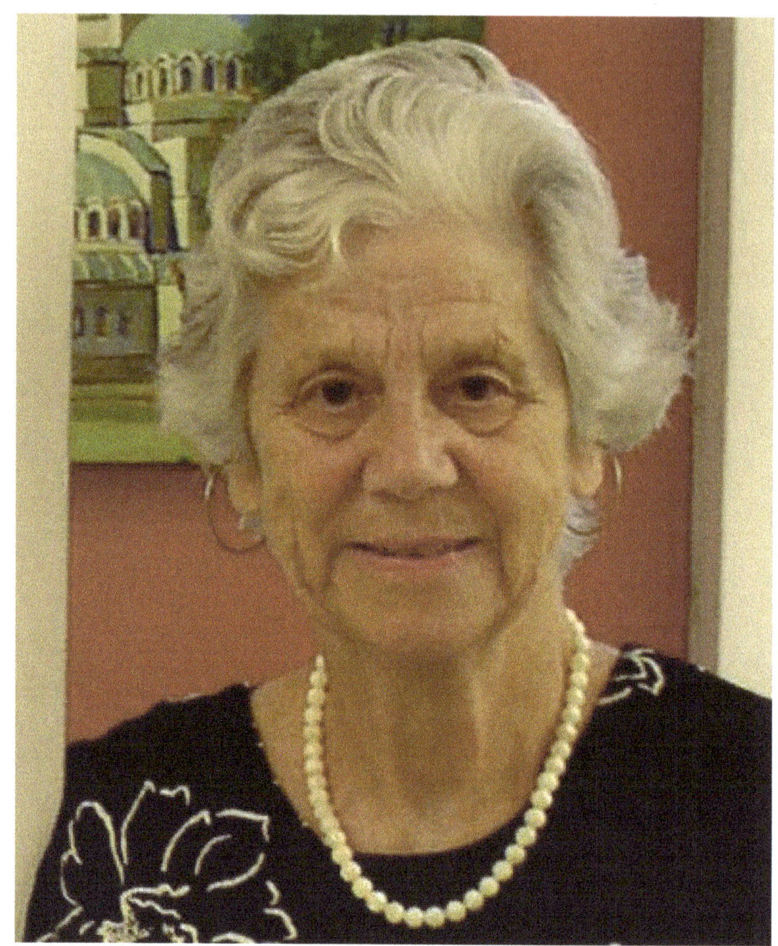

Nancy Frankel earned her BFA from Tyler School of Fine Arts, Temple Univ.,Philadelphia, PA; an MA in Art ED from Columbia University; and subsequently studied with Hans Hoffman in New York City and at the Art Academy in Munich, Germany. For many years she was an adjunct professor of sculpture at Montgomery College, Rockville, Md.

Frankel, a long time member of Studio Gallery in Washington DC, has shown widely in the area and beyond. She has had commissions in New Hampshire, Michigan and Ohio as well as locally, and her work can be found in public and private collections both here and abroad, including The National Academy of Sciences in Washington DC.

I

n I908, Frankel was invited, along with Russian and Bulgarian artists, to take part in an International Plein Air, dedicated to the 130th anniversary of the liberation of Bulgaria as a result of the Russian-Turkish War. The work created by the artists was exhibited in the in Sophia in September.

Nancy Frankel – Artist's Statement

I use "organic geometry" to give form to my love of nature and architecture. Space, either encapsulated or activated, a sense of balance, precarious yet centered, are integral to my work.

My sculptures range in size from small maquettes to tabletop interior works to large exterior pieces. The sundials and fountains, seamlessly merging form and function, reflect their environmental setting. The outdoor sculptures are made of design cast (a man-made stone), steel and bronze. These materials can be found in my interior works in addition to plexiglas, clay, plaster and wood.

I usually work in series, using the material a particular approach suggests. Recently I have been creating welded steel sculptures, both large and small.

Over the years I have done a lot of drawing and painting, mostly related to my sculpture. I explore forms in space, the subtleties and placement creating movement both in and out, back and forth. I find an exciting cross-fertilization between the two media. Some of my pictures have color as an important component.

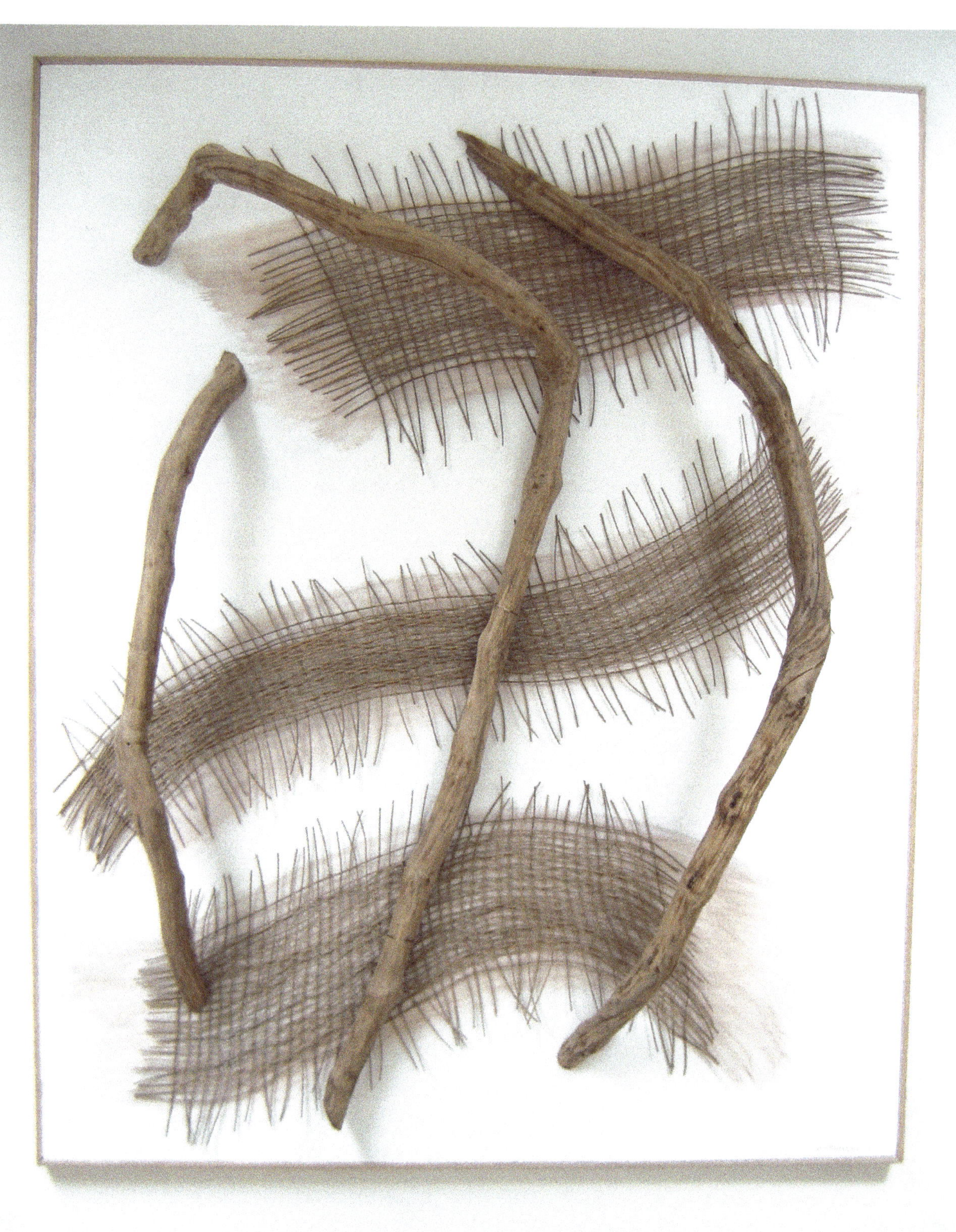

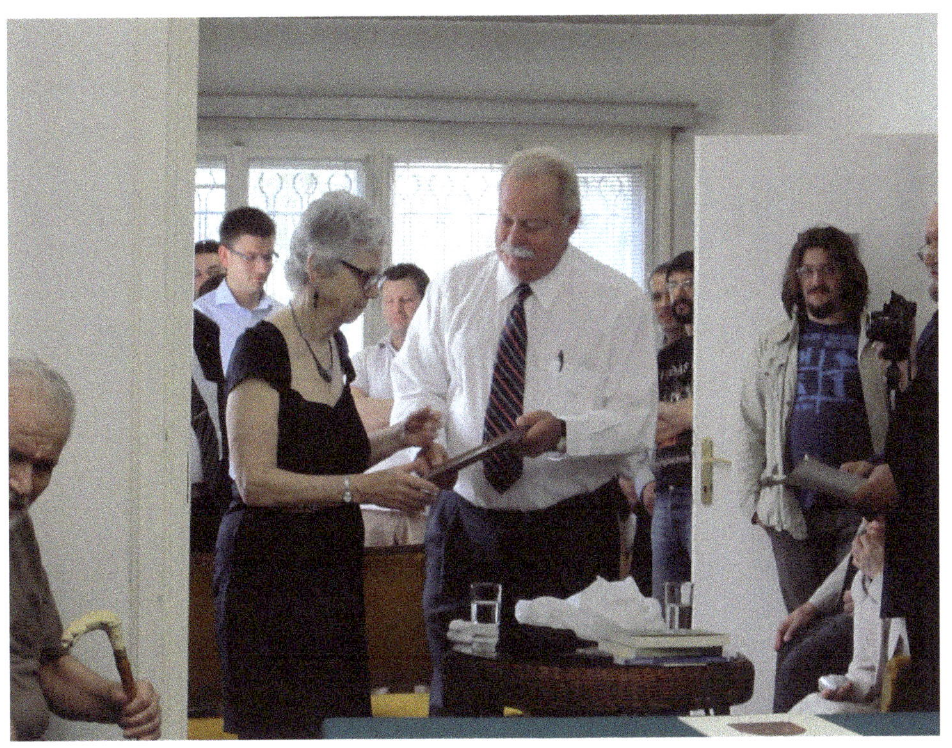

Nancy Frankel presents Meredith Award to Lyubomir Levhev in Sofia, 2013

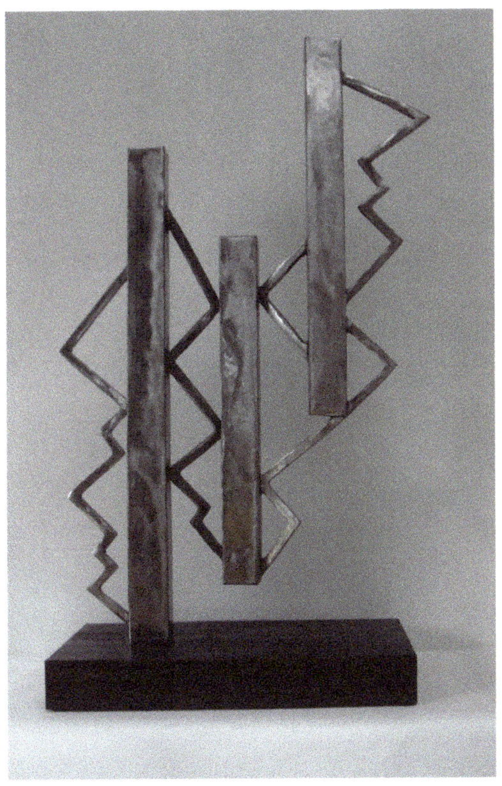

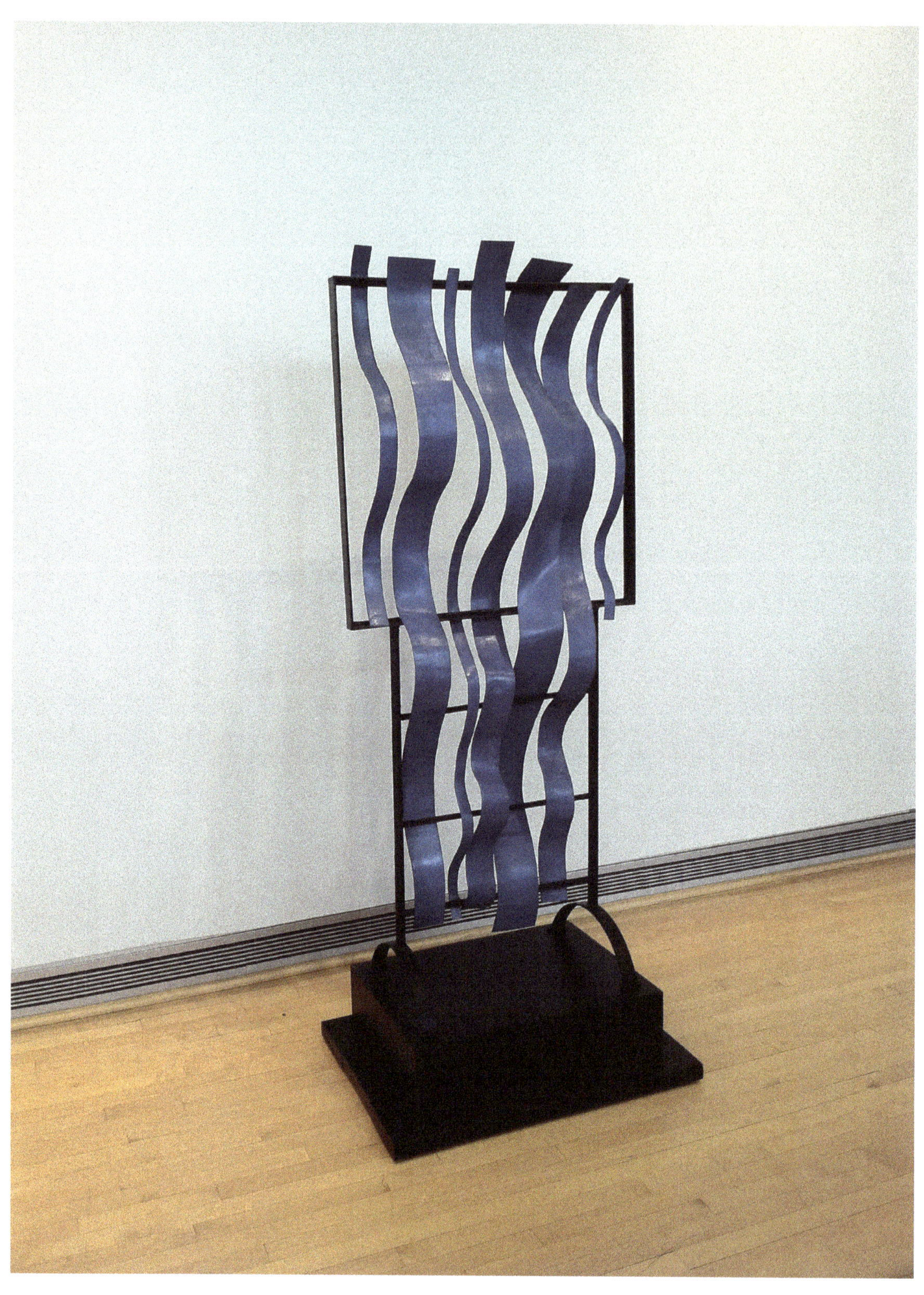

Watrerfall - Painted Steel, Six feet tall

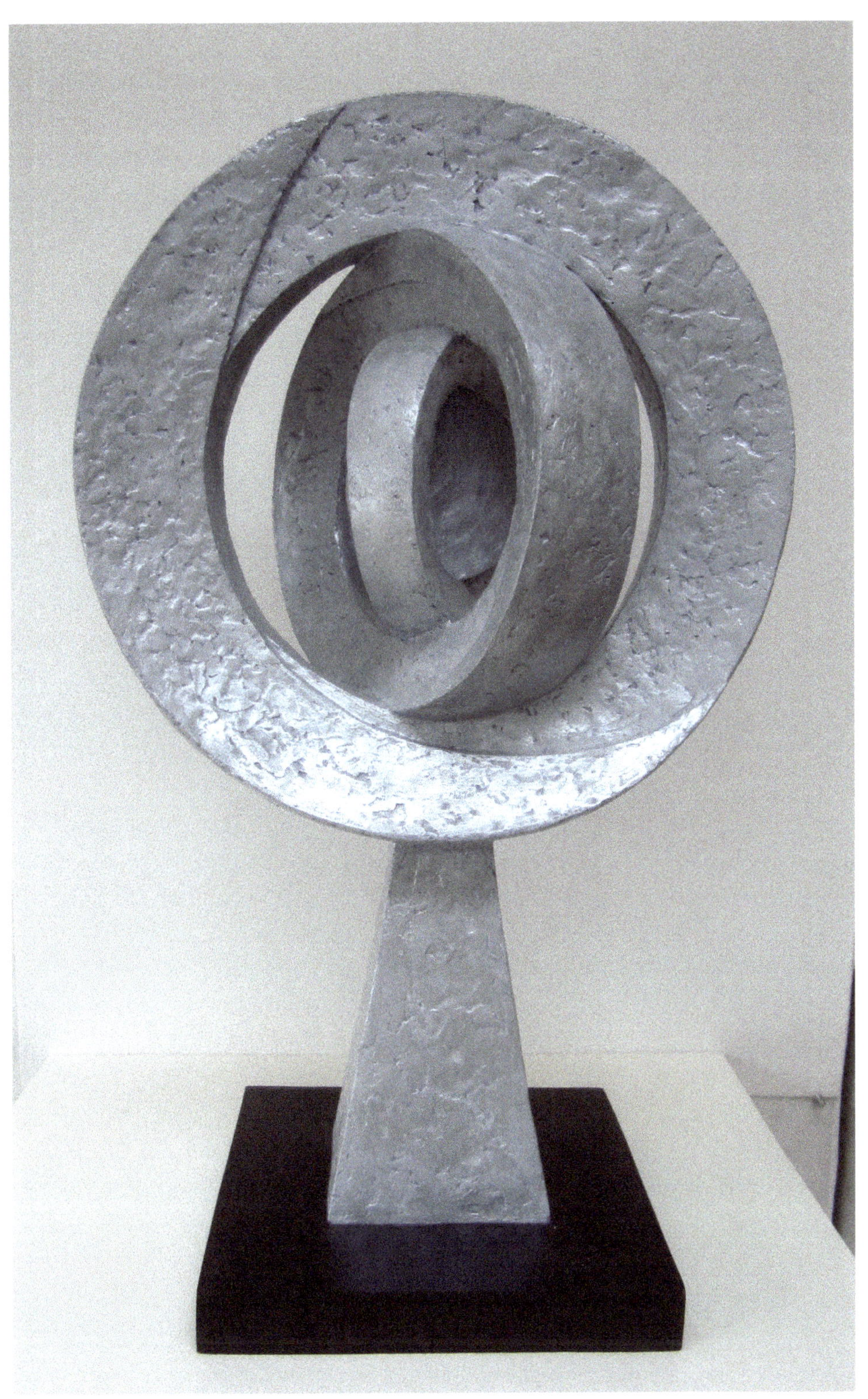

SHARON GRIFFIS

Sharon Griffis has given her account of the Griffis Foundation and a warm appreciation of the work of her colleague Lyubomir Levchev. Photos included depict various friends visiting the residence in Polkovnik Serafimavo and an early photo of the American Ambassador Ken Hill and wife Yvonne.

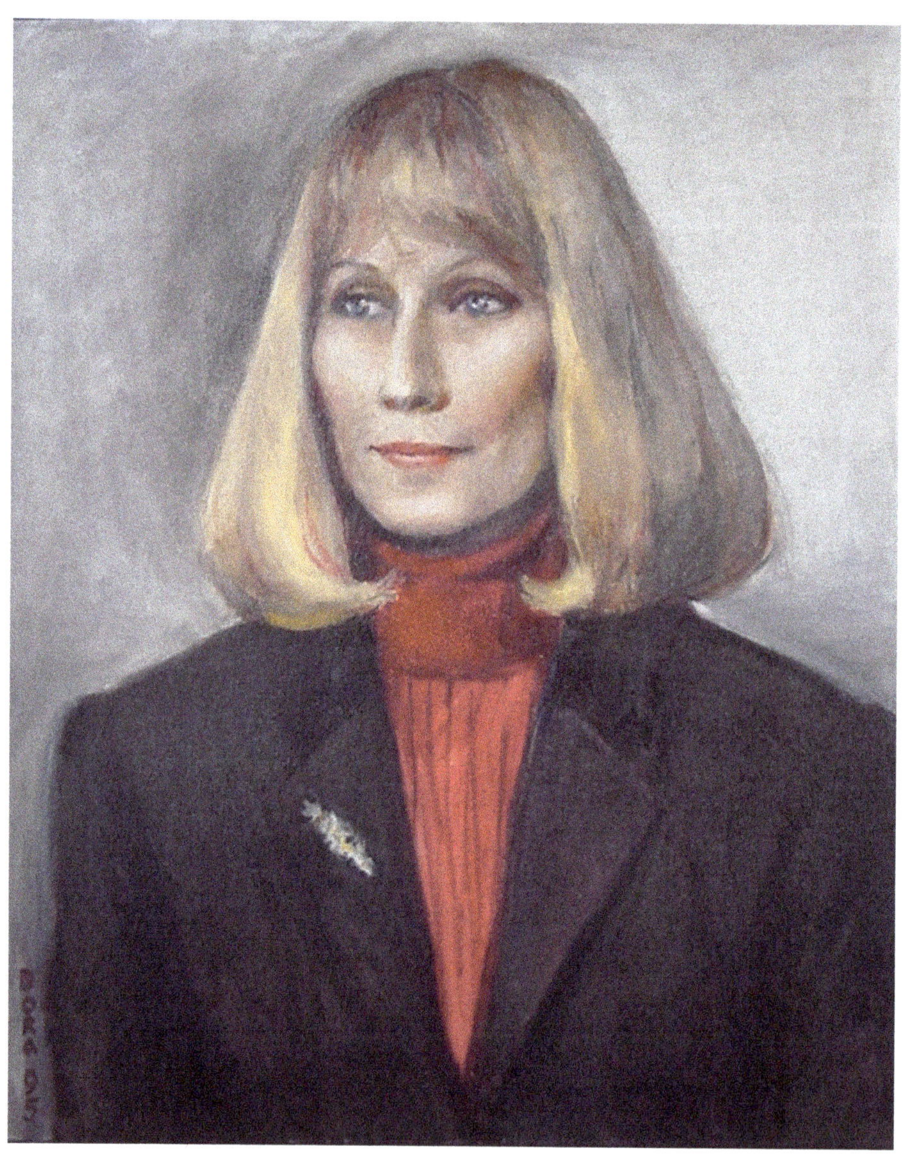

Portrait of Sharon Griffis by Dora Boneva

“Bridge of Light, Artistic Illuminations from the Balkans” ... what a wonderful title for a Bulgarian-American exhibition celebrating the cultural, artistic and spiritual exchanges that have blossomed, expanded and taken on a creative life of their own in our small part of the world.

As Director of the Griffis Art Center in New London, Connecticut, I have had the pleasure of creating Programs for over 40 Bulgarian artists, writers and musicians. And over the course of twenty years, it remains true that it is often the small things that can cement a relationship; brief moments that illuminate the soul and leave an indelible mark upon the heart.

In 1994, Dora Boneva was selected as The Griffis Art Center’s first Bulgarian Artist-in-Residence. She was referred by William Meredith and Richard Harteis, local poets who had traveled to Bulgaria and met Dora and her husband Lyubomir Levchev. Lyubomir joined Dora in New London shortly after she arrived. America was prosperous and complacent at this time, but Bulgaria was experiencing the difficult post-Communist transition to capitalism, and between 1992 and 1994 the privatization of land and industry.

At this time there was no e-mail, no desktop publishing, no Skype, nor Google Translation. Correspondence was long, difficult and often confusing. Plus, there was still fear about this former Eastern Bloc Country.

But as always with our visiting artists, people with an interest in the country or culture of our guests appear like magic to assist with language translations or with introductions and entertaining. In addition to William Meredith, Richard Harteis and the Griffis Art Center's Board of Trustees, several others were on hand to expand the network of friendship. The Honorable Kenneth Hill and his wife Yvonne Hill (Mr. Hill served as a U.S. Ambassador to Bulgaria during the 1991-1994 period) and Niles Bond and his wife Pamela Bond (Mr. Bond served as a U.S. Foreign Service officer 1929-1968 and was a poet, his wife Pamela was a writer and art critic.) I mention them in particular, because in the nine months of Dora's Residency, while she painted a visual story of New London, Lyubomir was writing a book of poetry titled Sky Break. The Hills and Bonds were instrumental in assisting with the subtle task of translating … shades of meaning and thought and truth into something simple … a true cultural and artistic exchange.

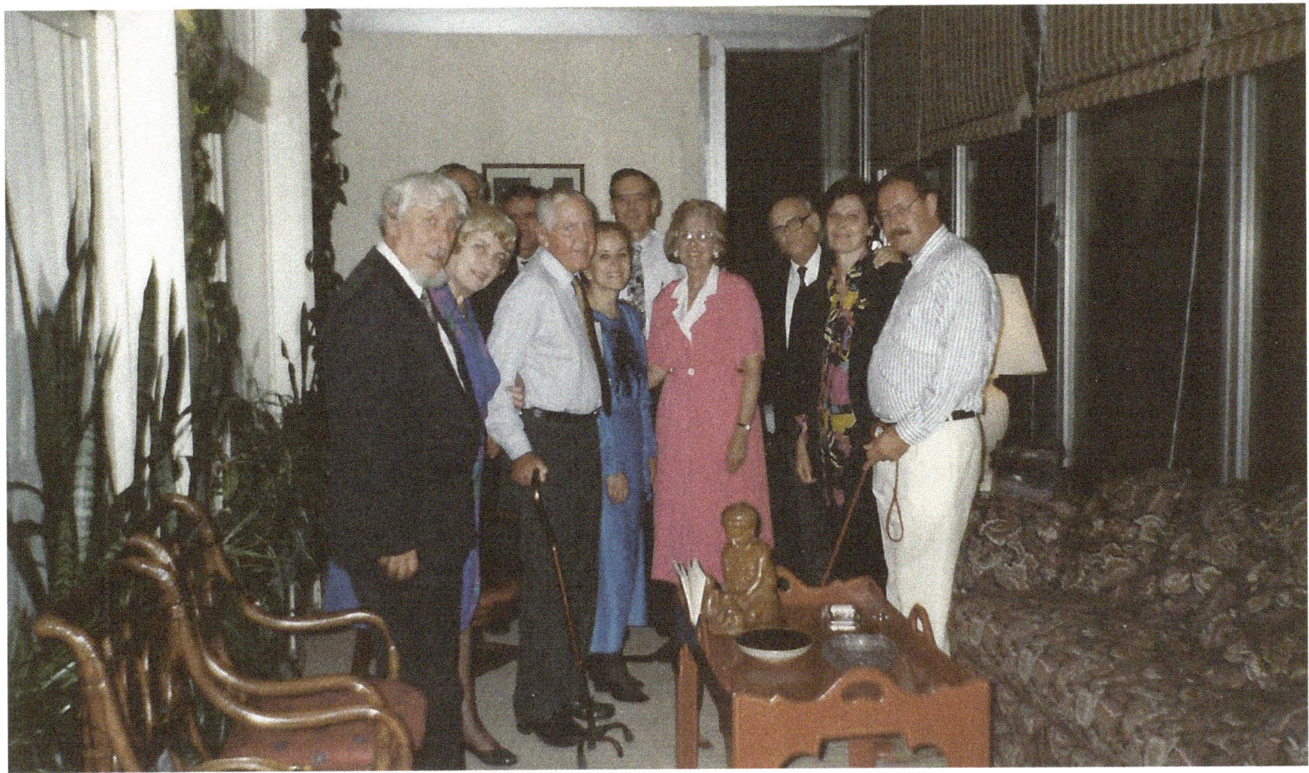

(Text for this photo by Richard Harteis: Radoi Ralin, Blaga Dimitrova, William Meredith, Lyubomir Levchev behind William, Ambassador Hill behind Dora Boneva in blue, Yvonne Hill in pink, Richard Harteis on the end holding one of the sweet dogs that lived at the embassy residence in the mid 1990's. Blocking on the names of the writer and his wife to the right of me.)

After that time, we have had the pleasure of several additional visits from Dora and Lyubomir – usually accompanied by the flurry of receptions, readings, lectures, exhibitions, formal dinners and exhaustive schedules. But what I still cherish most are the casual gatherings – relaxed and informal. This includes the day Lyubomir Levchev and Dora Boneva joined the Board of Trustees of the Griffis Art Center and we planted the Roger W. Dennis Impressionist Garden in memory of a well known local artist.

This is not the first time I had the pleasure of working side by side with these two extraordinary people; but in 1996, it is the first time that our hands were in the earth and we were planting the seeds of more than just a garden in New London, Connecticut. The seeds were planted for a Bulgarian-American exchange between the Orpheus Foundation (Bulgaria) and the Griffis Art Center (America.) And our beautiful garden is still inspiring artists from around the world.

I, in turn, along with so many other American artists and writers, have had the pleasure of traveling to Polkovnik Serafimovo, Bulgaria, where nestled in the mountains is the sister to The Griffis Art Center –

"The Sharon House." Hosted by The Orpheus Foundation, artists and writers enjoy the hospitality of Lyubomir and Dora, as they explore their souls in the mythical Rhodope Mountains. One can still feel the ancient Thracian myth and culture in these mountains, the wild, mountainous landscape where the great goddess hunts, the horse is sacred and the mysterious Thracian Horseman dispenses both life and death. And Orpheus ... the great singer, musician, healer and sorcerer, descends to the Underworld in search of his dead consort Eurydice, offering the promise of immortality and rebirth.

The journey between The Griffis Art Center and the Orpheus Foundation has now spanned twenty years. The Griffis Art Center has hosted over one hundred and eighty guests from forty-five countries, but it is only with Bulgaria that the Art Center has maintained such close ties. It is because of the bond with Lyubomir Levchev and Dora Boneva.

And truth-be-told, even after all these years, people still ask me "Why Bulgaria?" In this day of unlimited knowledge, available instantaneously, Bulgaria is not the unknown mystery it used to be.

I could respond that part of the answer is that it is through a series of serendipitous events, shared dreams and deep friendships.

But truly the answer is Lyubomir Levchev. He is the anchoring force on the other end of the bridge. He is a source of light and understanding. He is a man whose passionate belief in the arts is unwavering and all inclusive, and his commitment to beauty, truth, and human dignity never falters.

Sharon Tripp Griffis, April 2015

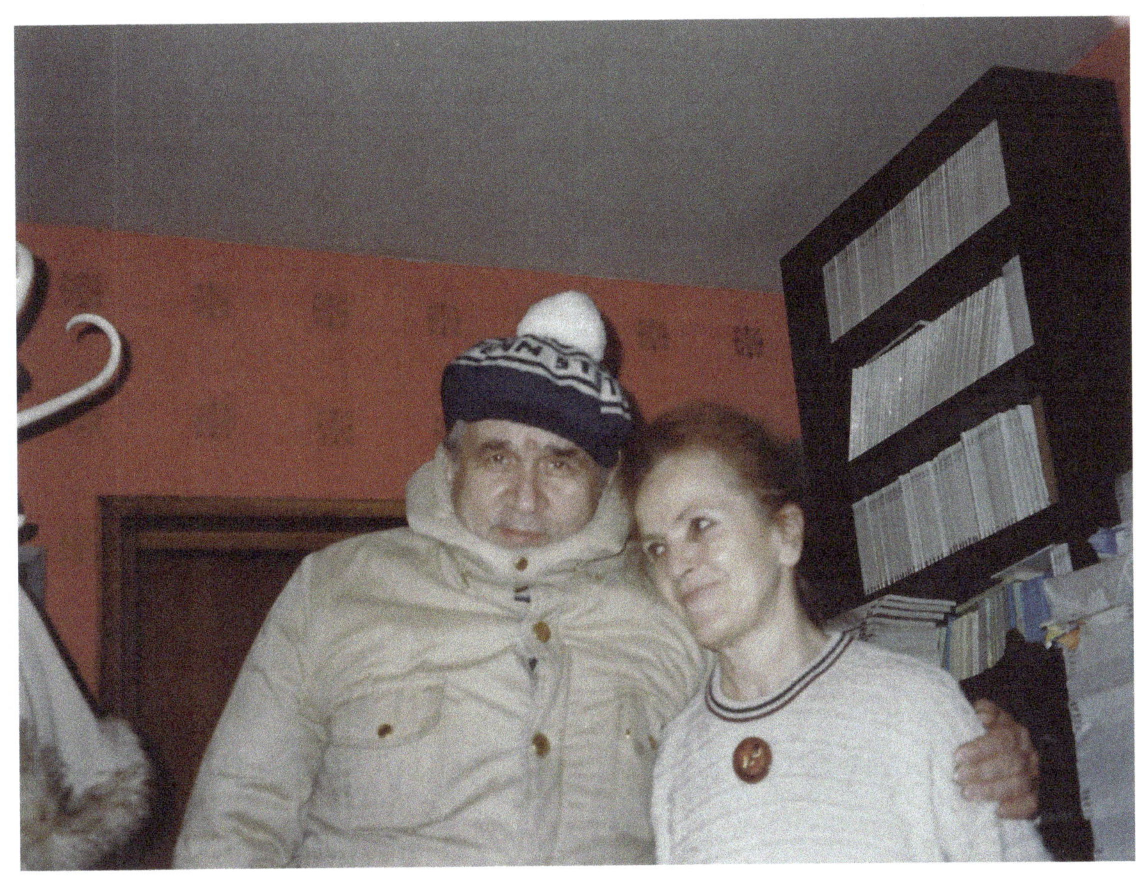

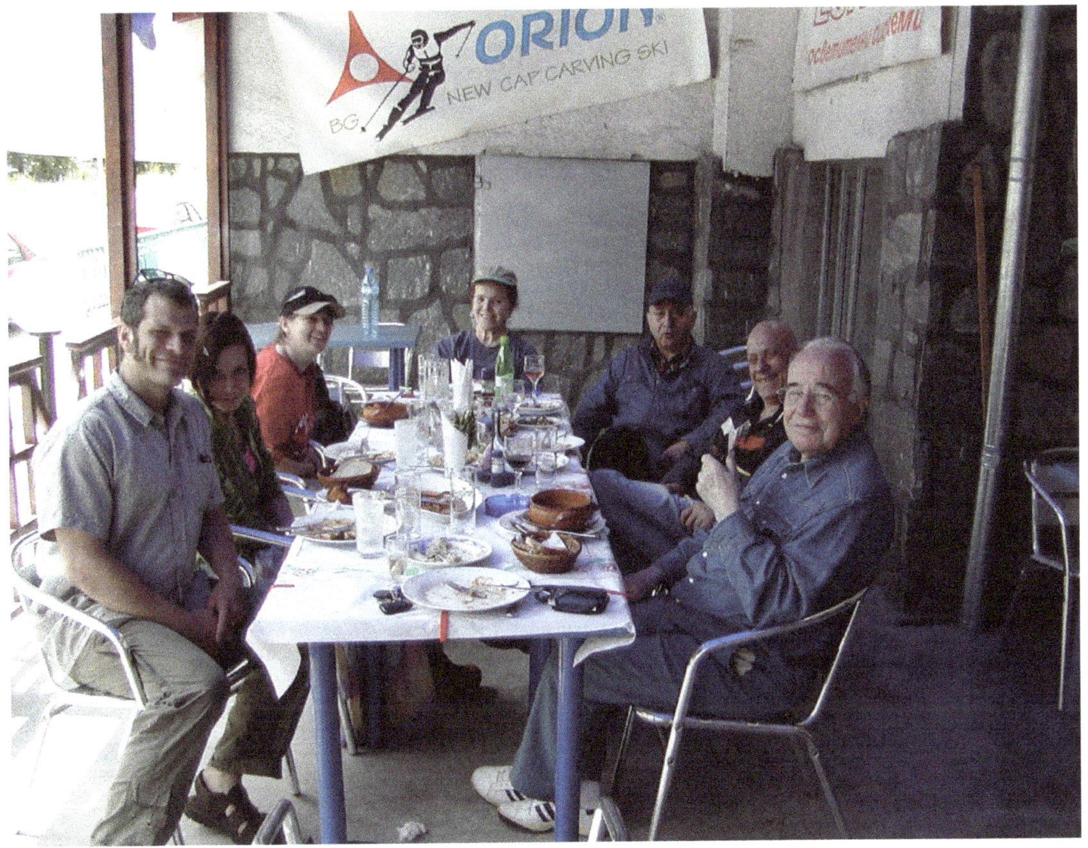
ORION
NEW CAP CARVING SKI
BG

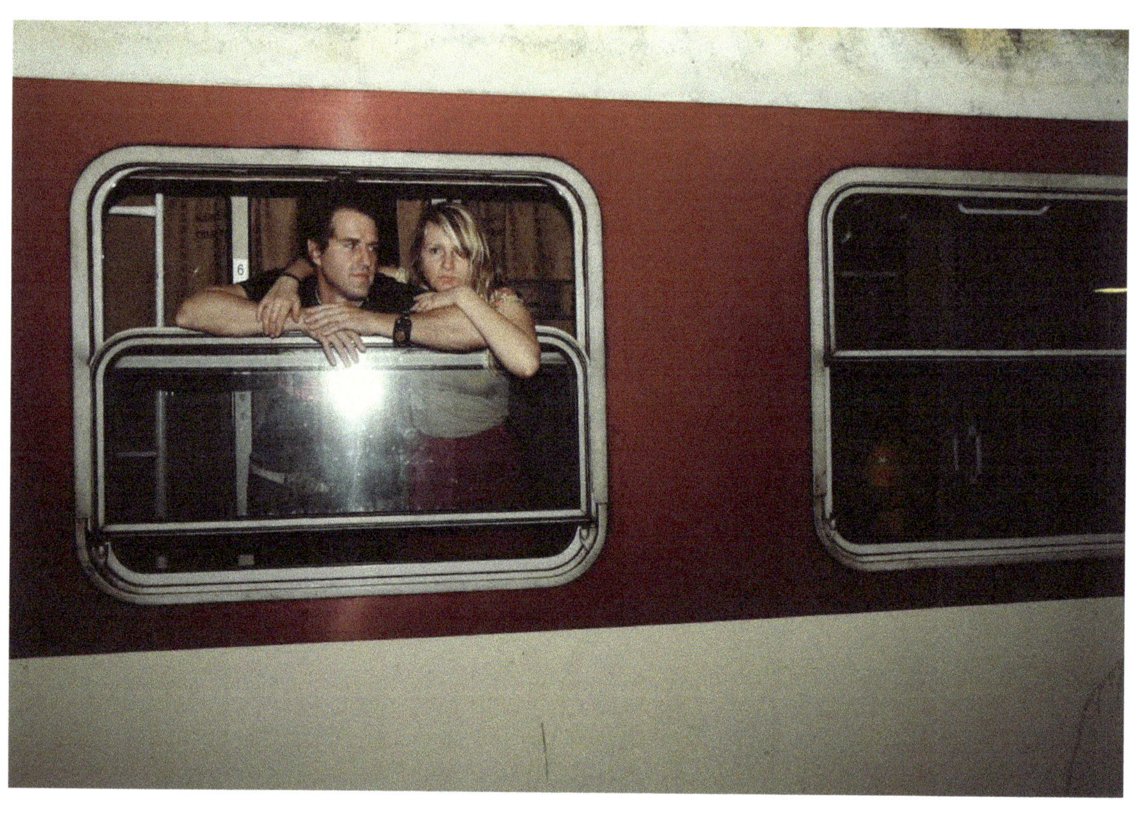

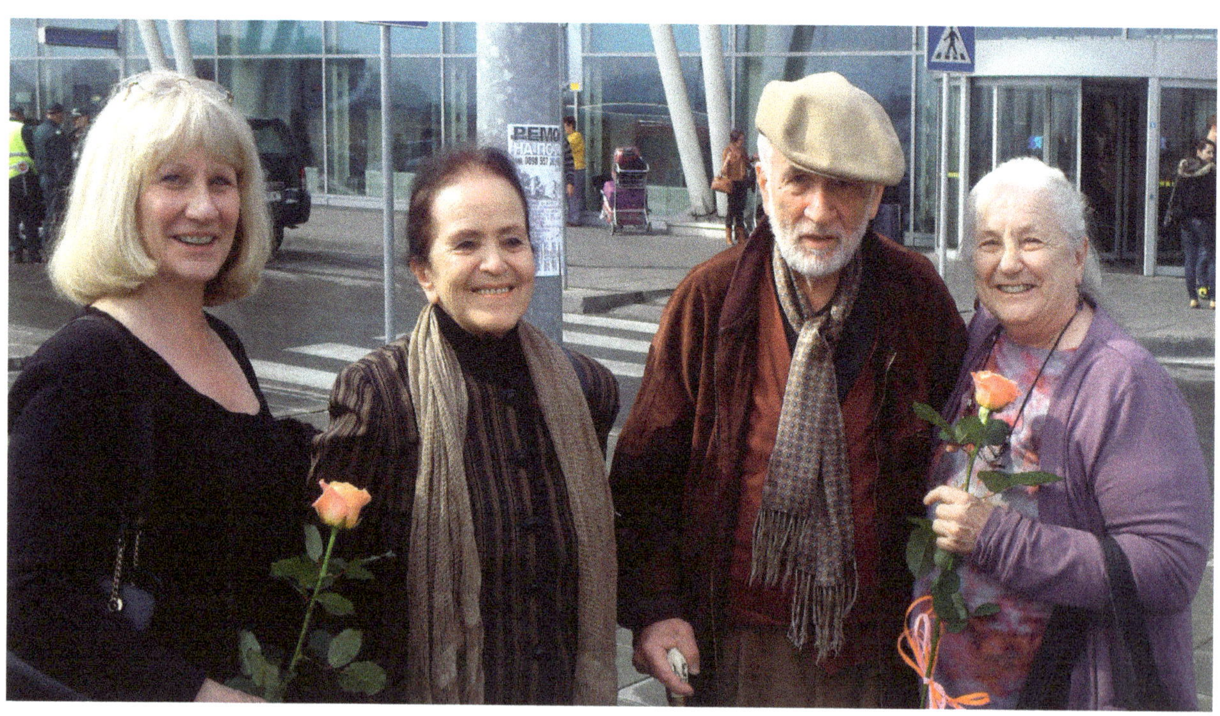

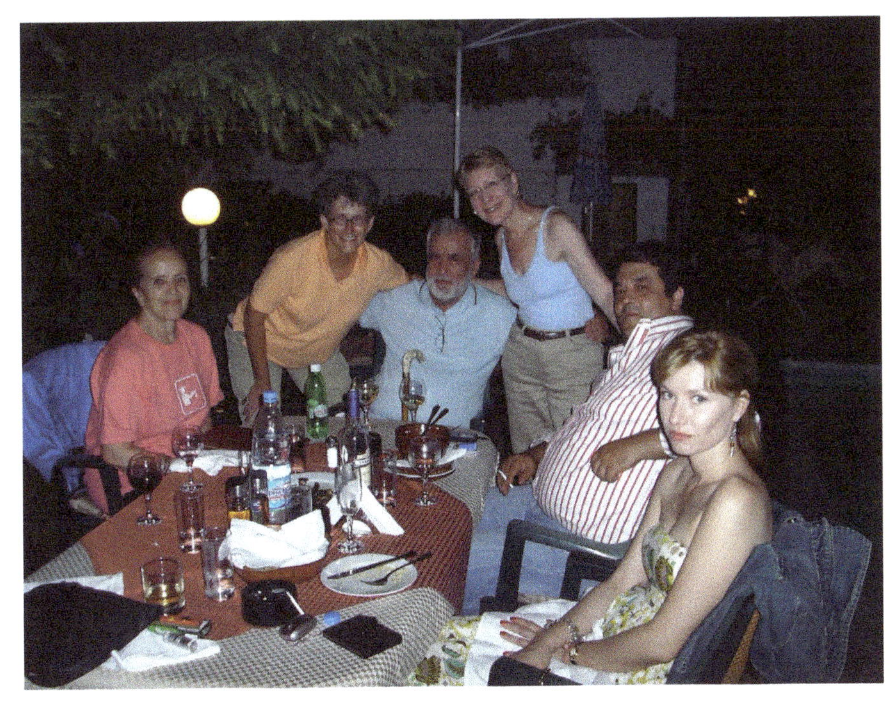

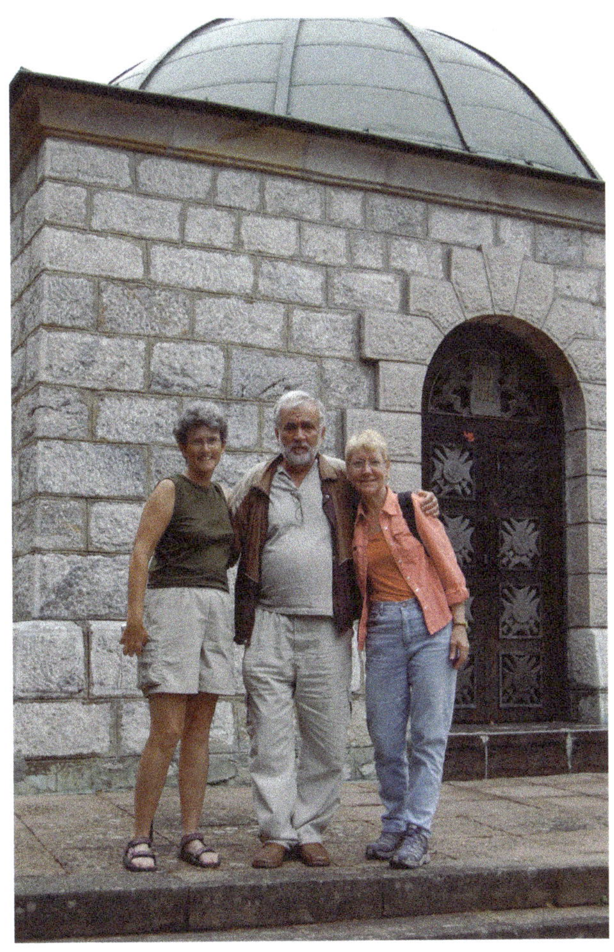

PHOTOS BY POLA ESTER OF HER TIME IN BULGARIA WITH BRIAN STEPHENS:

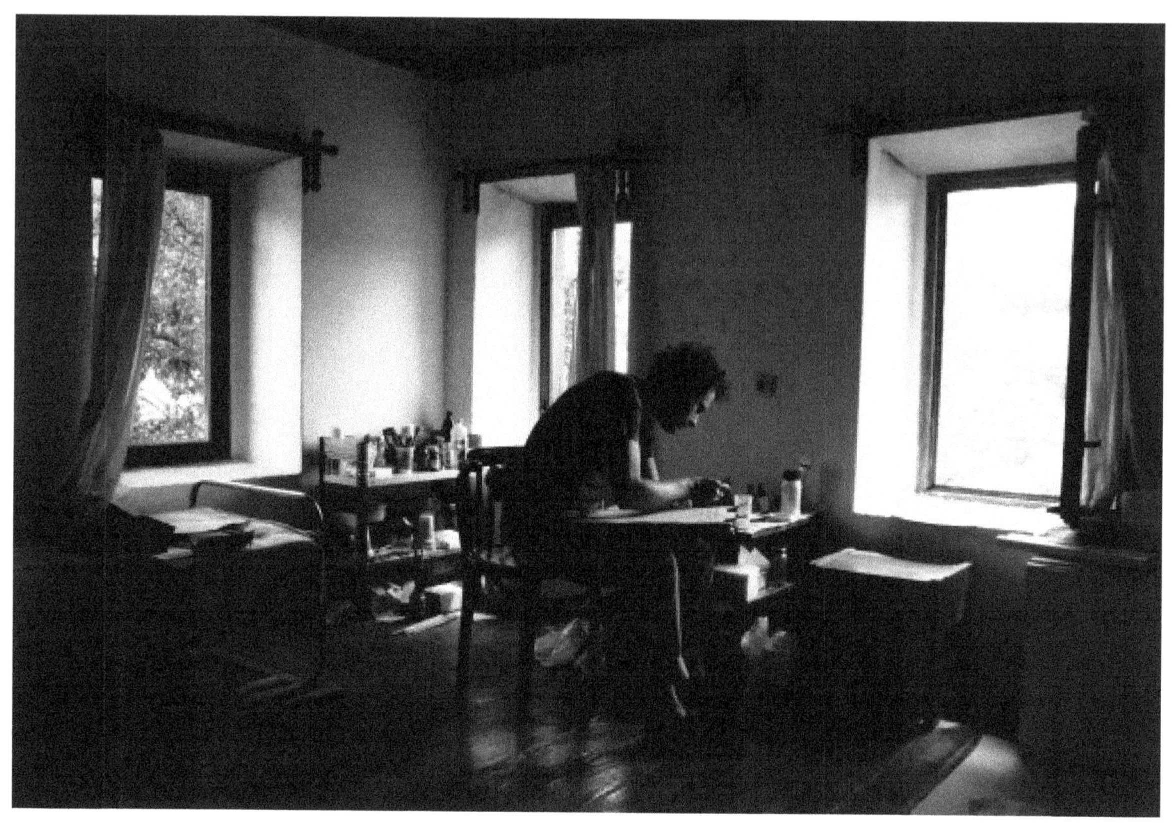

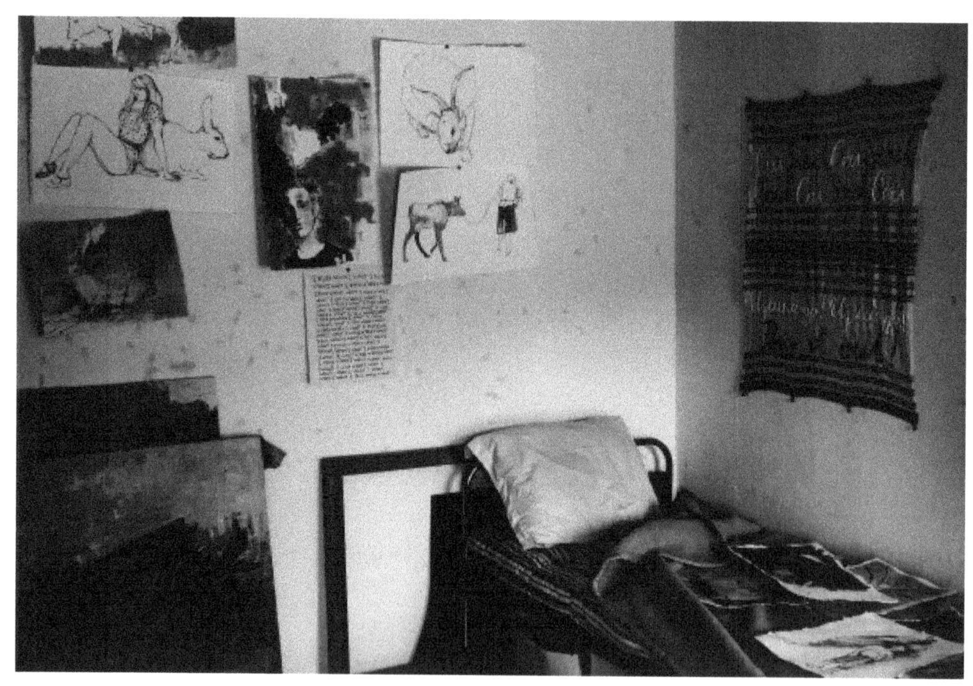

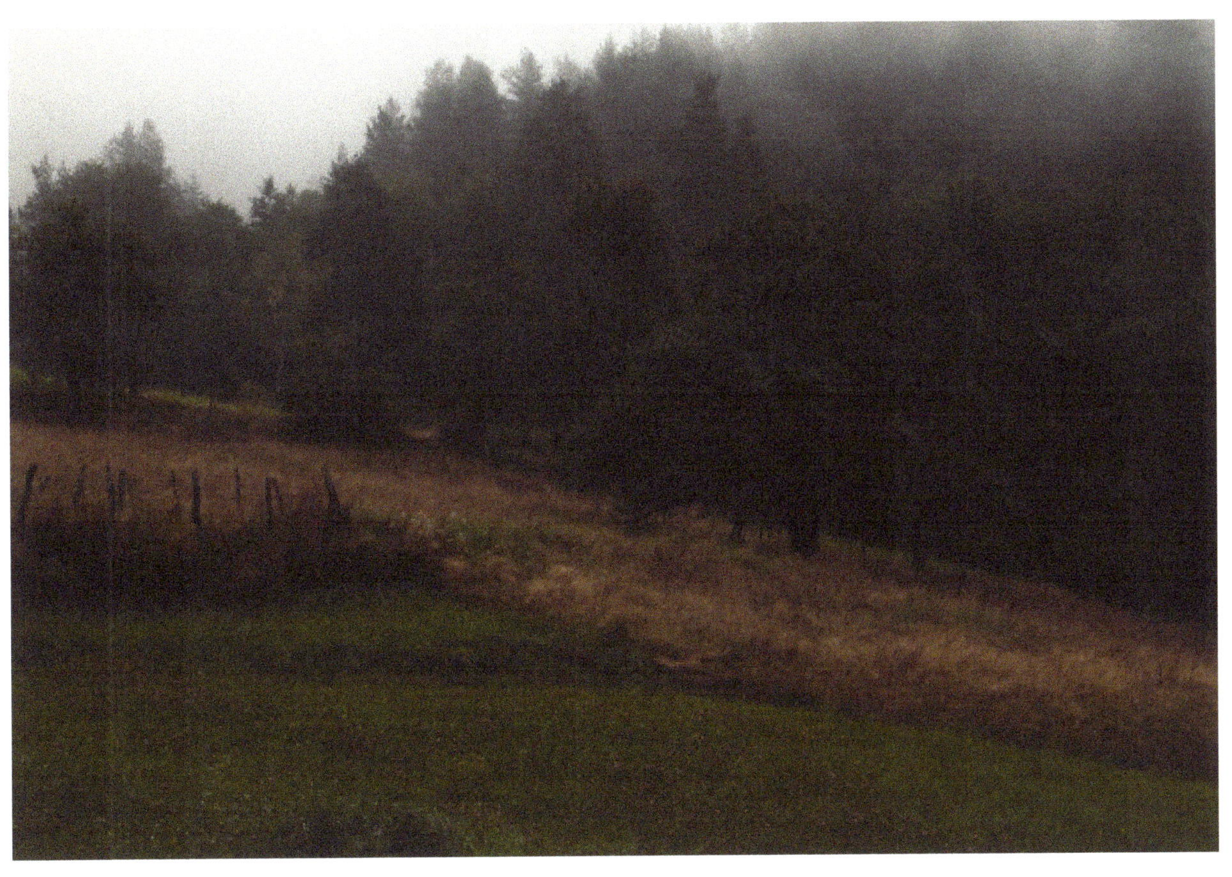

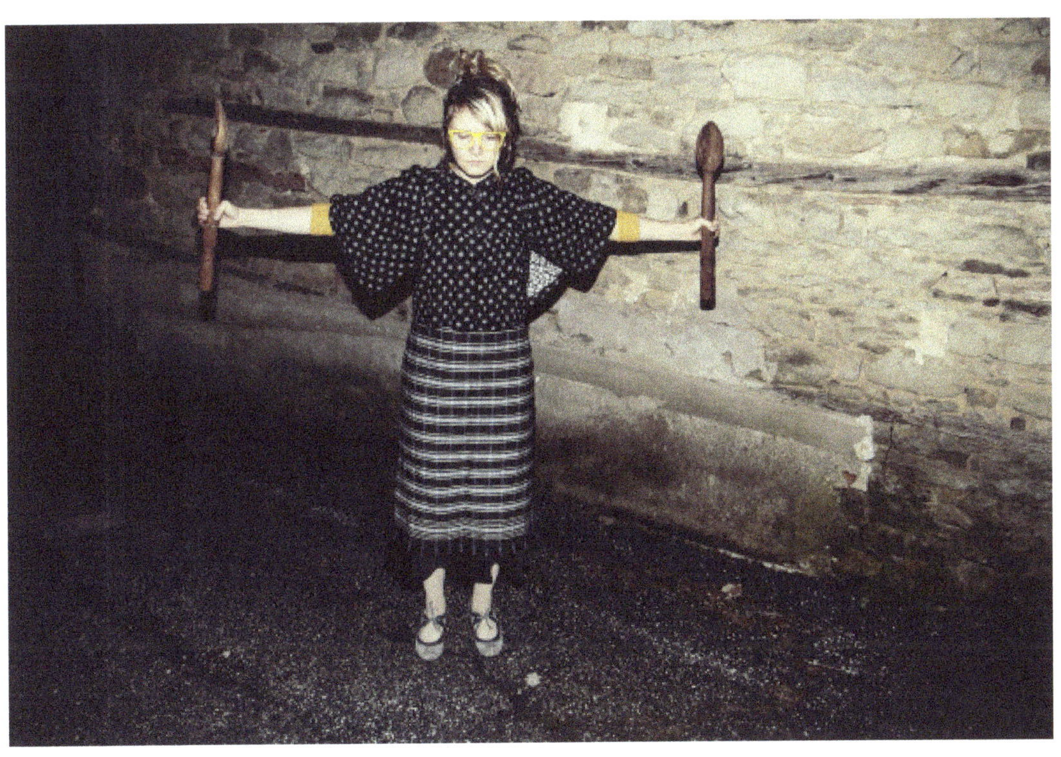

RICHARD HARTEIS

Family: Born August 18, 1946; became citizen of Bulgaria, 1996. Memberships: Union of Bulgarian Journalists. Addresses: Home: 337 Kitemaug Rd., Uncasville, CT 06382. Marathonfilm@gmail.com

Teacher and writer. Poet-in-residence, American University, Bulgaria, 1995-96. Worked as physician's assistant, health-care consultant, and radio producer.

Fulbright fellowship, 1995-96.

WRITINGS BY THE AUTHOR:

- *Fourteen Women* (poetry), Three Rivers Press (Pittsburgh, PA), 1979.
- *Morocco Journal: Love, Work, Play* (poetry), Carnegie-Mellon University Press (Pittsburgh, PA), 1981.
- (Editor and translator, with others) *Poets of Bulgaria,* Unicorn Press (Holland, PA), 1986.
- *Internal Geography* (poetry), Carnegie-Mellon University Press (Pittsburgh, PA), 1987.
- *Marathon: A Story of Endurance and Friendship* (nonfiction), Norton (New York, NY), 1989.
- (Editor, with William Meredith) *Window on the Black Sea: Bulgarian Poetry in Translation,* Carnegie-Mellon University Press (Pittsburgh, PA), 1992.
- *Keeping Heart* (poetry), Orpheus House (Paris, France), 1996.
- *Sapphire Dawn* (fiction), Vivisphere (Poughkeepsie, NY), 1999.
- *Provence,* Straw House (Poughkeepsie, NY), 2000.
- *The Revenant, Little Red Tree Publishing, 2008*
- *WMD, A Memoir, 2015 Poets' Choice Publishing*

Contributor to periodicals including *New Letters, Ploughshares, Seneca Review,* and *Virginia Review.Journalism: Washington Post, The Day, The Norwich Bulletin.*

"Sidelights"Richard Harteis is a versatile writer whose publications include poetry, fiction, and nonfiction. Harteis produced his first verse volume, *Fourteen Women,* in 1979, and in the ensuing years he followed that book with further collections, including *Internal Geography* and *Keeping Heart.* Harteis also served as an editor and translator of *Poets of Bulgaria,* and he collaborated with William Meredith in editing *Window on the Black Sea: Bulgarian Poetry in Translation.* The latter volume features poems by a range of writers including Gypsies and ethnic Turks.

In *Marathon: A Story of Endurance and Friendship,* Harteis writes of his training for the 1987 New York marathon and his relationship with longtime companion William Meredith, a celebrated writer who received the Pulitzer Prize for poetry in 1988, only a few years after suffering a debilitating stroke. Elizabeth Kastor, who wrote in the *Washington Post*that Meredith's stroke left him "paralyzed on the right side and stripped of language," described *Marathon* as "the story of Harteis's life with Meredith, the frustrations and triumphs forced upon them by Meredith's stroke." Another reviewer, Russell T. Clement, wrote in *Library Journal* that Harteis's book constitutes an "open and honest account," and a critic in *Publishers Weekly* praised *Marathon* as "uncommonly moving."

In 1996 Harteis received Bulgarian citizenship and joined Meredith in the Union of Bulgarian Journalists. "What a way to end the year," he once told *CA.* "Like the parasailors drifting over the Black Sea outside my window, I am filled with a sense of elation and a certain valedictory nostalgia as well."

FURTHER READINGS ABOUT THE AUTHOR:PERIODICALS

- *Library Journal,* November 1, 1989, Russell T. Clement, review of *Marathon: A Story of Endurance and Friendship,* pp. 88-89.
- *Publishers Weekly,* May 15, 1989, review of *Marathon: A Story of Endurance and Friendship,* p. 107.
- *Washington Post,* January 2, 1990, Elizabeth Kastor, "The Poet and His Brave New Journey, " pp. C1, C8-9.*

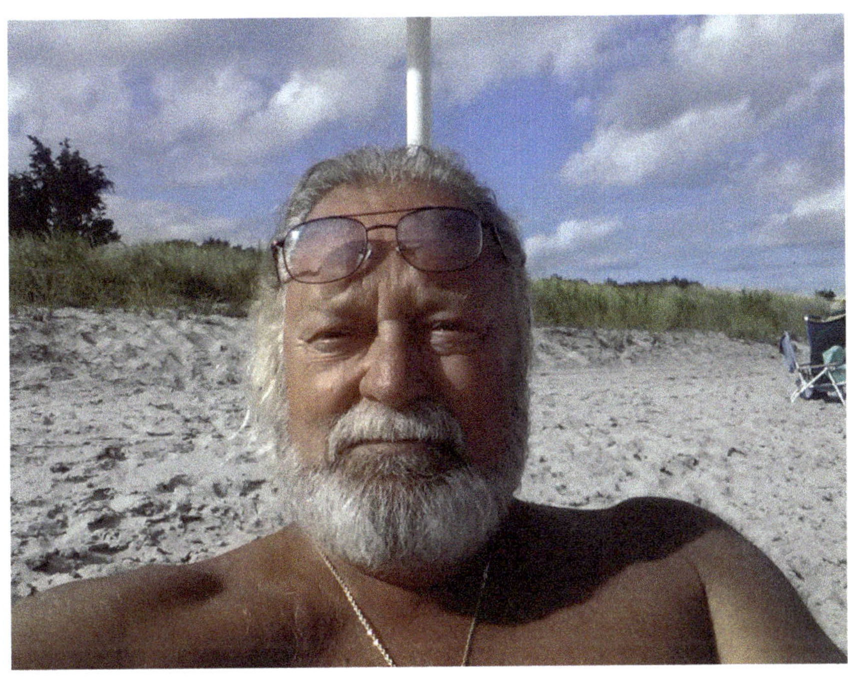

Memorial Minute: William Meredith

by Janet Gezari

William Morris Meredith was born in New York City on January 9, 1919 and died on May 30, 2007 at Lawrence & Memorial Hospital after an illness of some weeks. He received a Pulitzer Prize in 1988 for Partial Accounts: New and Selected Poems, a National Book Award in 1997 for Effort at Speech: New and Selected Poems, and many other awards, including fellowships and grants from the National Endowment for the Arts and the Guggenheim, Ford, and Rockefeller Foundations. He was a chancellor of the Academy of American Poets and served as Consultant in Poetry to the Library of Congress, a position re-titled Poet Laureate in 1985. He published nine volumes of poetry as well as Shelley: Selected Poems, Poets of Bulgaria, and Alcools, poems by Guillaume Apollinaire that he translated.

William earned his BA at Princeton University in 1940, where he followed his father and grandfather. He wrote his senior thesis on Robert Frost, who was a lasting influence on his poems and, later, a friend. Our library has a copy of the senior thesis, An Analysis of the Poetic Method of Robert Frost, inscribed by Frost, with gratitude, in 1940. The inscription suggests that Frost hadn't read the thesis and also says why: "I am assured on the best authority his results are very good. No man is supposed to look at himself in the glass except to shave." This was a view with which William would have concurred: "Study something deeper than yourselves" is how he puts it in one of his own poems.

After Princeton, William worked briefly for The New York Times (some of the obituaries said as a reporter, but I always understood he was a copy boy) before enlisting in the U. S. Army, and then the Navy, where he served as a pilot, making night landings on the decks of carriers. He re-enlisted for the Korean War, achieved the rank of Lieutenant Commander, and was awarded two Air Medals. His formally precocious first book of poems, Love Letter from an Impossible Land was selected by Archibald MacLeish for the Yale Series of Younger Poets and published in 1944. Between active service in the Pacific and Korea, he did graduate work and taught English as a Woodrow Wilson fellow at Princeton and at the University of Hawaii. At Princeton, he met and became close friends with Charles Shain, who was also doing graduate work in English there. Much later, when Rosemary Park was due to retire here, William lured Charlie to Connecticut College, where he served as President from 1962 to 1974.

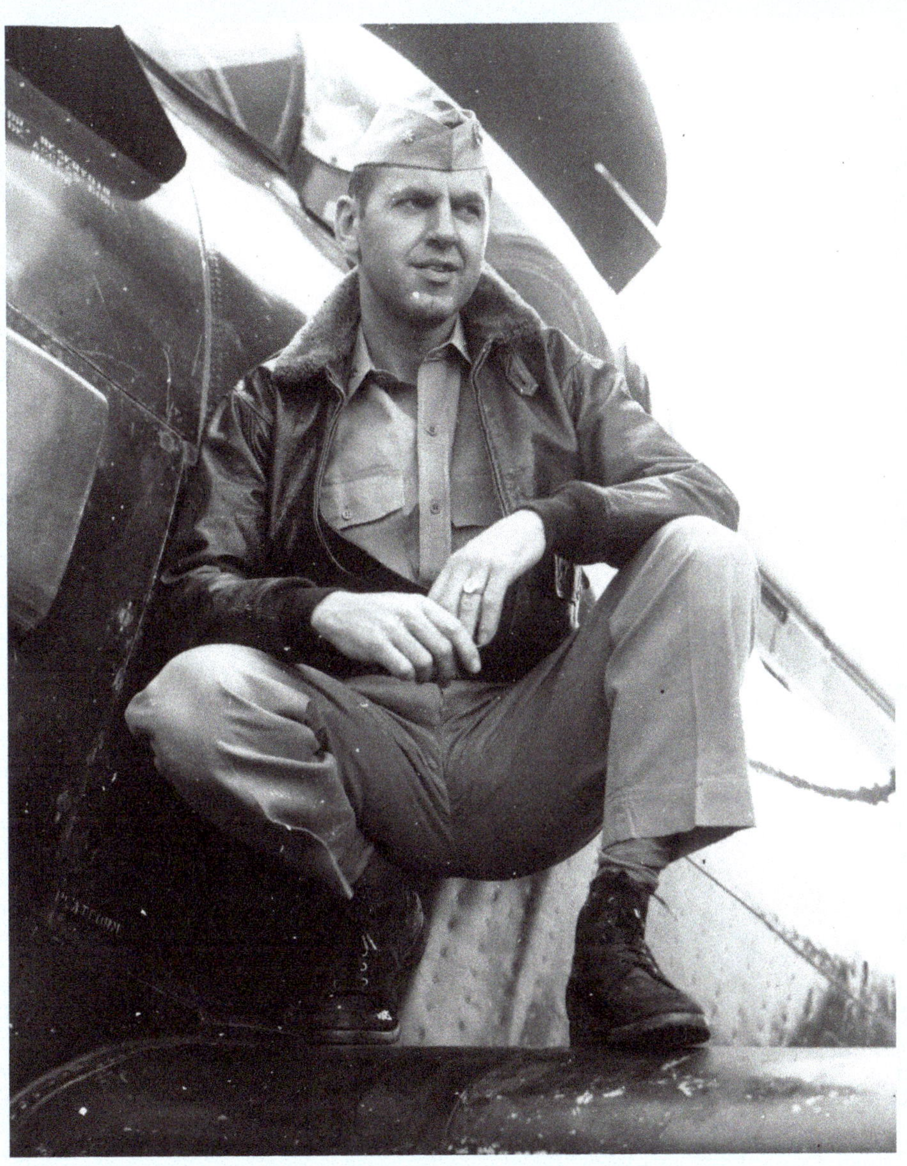

William on the wing of his plane in WWII

William began teaching at Connecticut College in 1955. In the mid 1960s, when Upward Bound programs were a fresh idea, he founded and taught in the college's first enrichment program for low-income inner city high school students. He taught until his retirement in 1983, after a stroke that immobilized him for two years and left him with lasting expressive aphasia. It was difficult for those of us who knew him well to fix the boundaries between what he understood and what he could say, although it often appeared that his apprehension of the world remained full and satisfying, and that only his capacity to articulate it was affected. I can remember afternoons in Uncasville, in the early years after the stroke, when I and several of my colleagues took turns reading poetry to William and helping him with the exercises in the speech manuals provided for his rehabilitation. If I missed a word in a poem or put the stress in the wrong place, he would stop me; meanwhile, the manuals had him reciting simple commands using the smallest number of linguistic units. The irony of his situation did not escape his notice, but it never diminished his resolve. Those who knew him after the stroke will remember his courage in the face of obstacles and his optimism about his progress. During this time and until his death, William was loved and cared for by his partner, the poet and fiction writer Richard Harteis.

Only those who knew William before the stroke know the magnitude of his loss, and ours. William was consummately articulate, and his conversation was one of the highest pleasures of his company. His letters, typed on his old manual machine if he was at home or handwritten if he was traveling, spoke about cadged meals, boozy evenings with friends, and the cornus alternifolia (or alternate-leafed dogwood) he thought you ought to have in your garden. He told wonderful stories and liked elaborate jokes. He was effortlessly and often savagely witty. His judgment of language was impeccable and accounts in part for his centrality to what was then the world of American poetry. William knew all the poets, and several of his more celebrated contemporaries—Robert Penn Warren, John Berryman, and Robert Lowell—relied on his responses to their poems and drafts of poems.

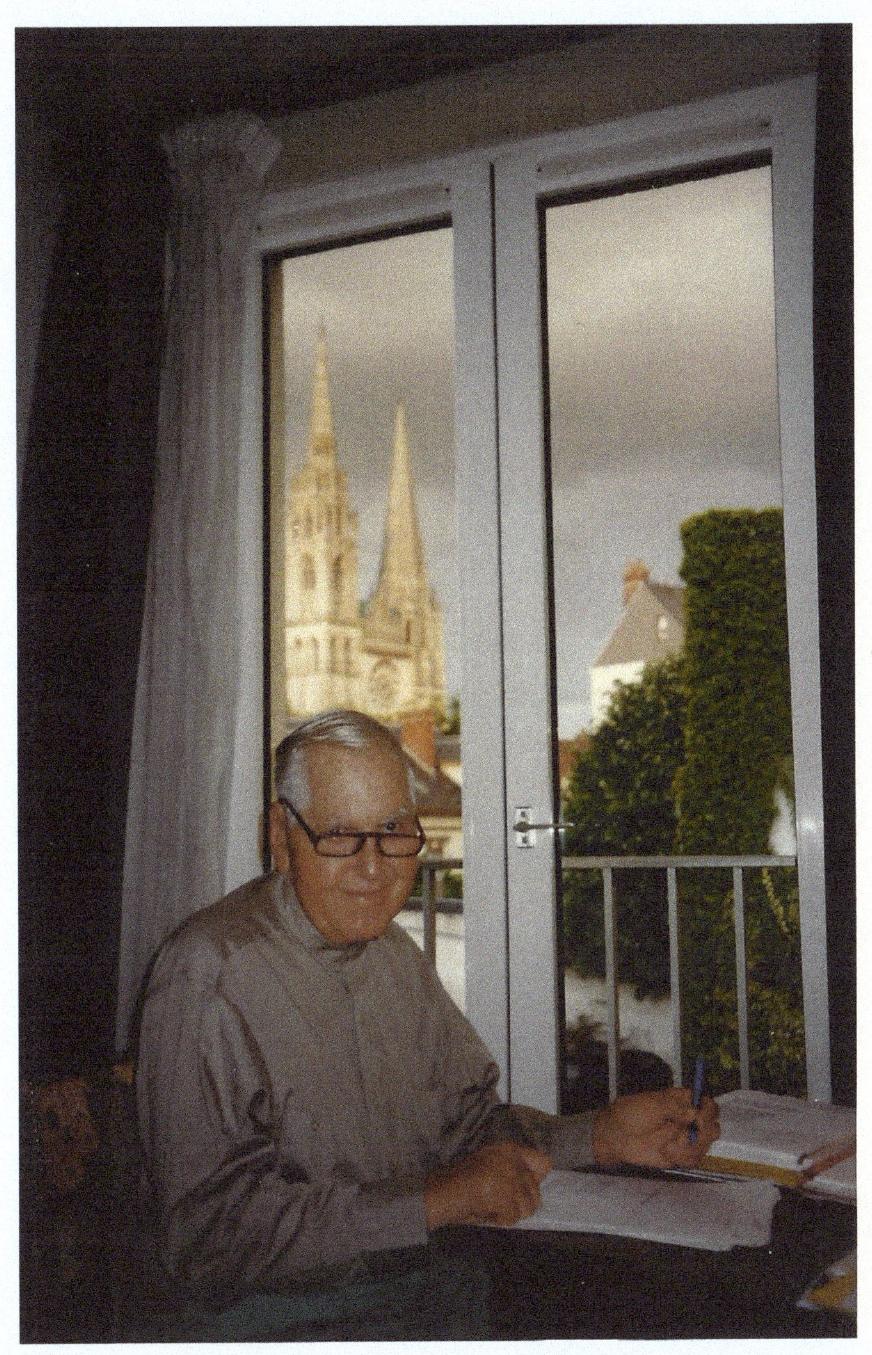

William with Notre Dame de Chartres in background

While he was here, William saw to it that poetry was a part of life at Connecticut College. In addition to the writers I've just mentioned, Derek Walcott, Thom Gunn, Muriel Rukeyser, Eudora Welty, Maxine Kumin, Richard Wilbur, and Robert Frost all came to New London to give readings. Afterwards, there were long dinners in Uncasville where conversation flowed as generously as the drinks did. William was most his own strange self when he was hosting one of these dinners. He believed that food was meant to be served, and served with love. He wasn't particular about what we ate but he was very particular about how we did it. Stacking the dishes when you helped to clear the table was never permitted. During the thirteen years I was William's colleague, I don't remember his taking a sabbatical, but when he did take time away to teach at Carnegie Mellon or to perform his duties at the Library of Congress, he would produce his substitute. I remember all of these replacements well because they made extraordinary contributions to the life of the English department and the college. Blanche Boyd was one; the others were a former student and widely published writer of historical fiction, Cecilia Holland; the distinguished poet Robert Hayden, who had been the first black poet to serve as Poetry Consultant at the Library of Congress; the playwright Romulus Linney; and the Pulitzer Prize winning short story writer, James Alan MacPherson.

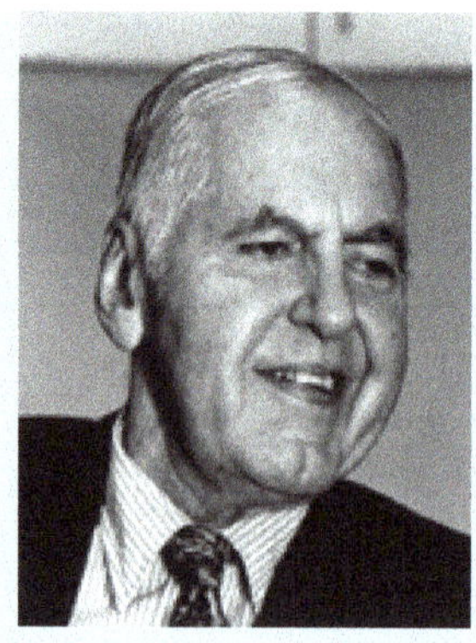

It was a mark of William's humility that his own poetry readings always combined a few of his poems with a larger number of poems written by other poets. He had no truck with grade inflation, and he used a teacher's shorthand when he described himself as a B+ poet who had written a few A plus poems. In the eulogy he gave at William's funeral, Michael Collier, William's former student and now a poet and teacher of poetry at the University of Maryland, reminded us that William used to say that he was proud of only three things: his knowledge of prosody, his knowledge of trees, and his immunity to poison ivy. His knowledge of prosody and trees was immense, as was his knowledge of many other things human and natural. He knew, for example, a lot about music, and had been opera critic for the Hudson Review, but he wore his knowledge lightly. He was always more interested in what you could tell him than in what he could tell you.

No one could have fought harder against death than William did, and this was entirely consistent with the life he had led and the poems he had written. He felt himself bound to continue, whether he was flying a mission for the Navy or composing a sestina. He feared cowardice more than other terrors, but he also felt grateful for the beauty of the universe and never stopped being conscious of its particular kindness to him. A poem titled "John and Anne" takes John Berryman's words about Anne Frank as its epigraph: "the hardest challenge, let's say, that a person can face without defeat is the best for him." Just outside the door to William's house in Uncasville, there was a tamarack tree that had been savagely cropped by an oil truck. He liked to point out that the accident had made the tree thrive as it never could have otherwise.

William Meredith was the least suicidal poet of his generation. His last book of new poems, published a few years before his stroke, was titled The Cheer, an improbable title for any poet but William. The first poem in the book, a kind of envoi, goes like this:

Frankly, I'd like to make you smile
Words addressing evil won't turn evil back
but they can give us heart.
The cheer is hidden in right words.

By cheer William means morale or confidence or, better still, courage, with its etymological connections to heart. He wanted us to be heartened, even though—or perhaps because—we live in "a culture in late imperial decline." The Cheer, written during the Vietnam war, includes a poem in which the poet presents himself as a "mild-spoken citizen" and respectfully accuses his country's president of "criminal folly." "A man's mistakes," the poem slyly notes, "his worst acts,/ aren't out of character, as he'd like to think." The Cheer includes several elegies, wry and celebratory poems written in memory of Lowell, Hemingway, Plath, and Berryman. All of them except Lowell, who tried to kill himself more than once, succeeded in ending their own lives. William dreamed and imagined death over and over. The elegy had been an important kind of poem for him since "The Wreck of the Thresher," which he wrote to commemorate "a squad of brave men" who died at sea in 1963. If his career as a wartime pilot, someone who faced death down daily, provides one important context for his struggle to survive after his stroke, the too short lives of the poets he loved, past and present, provide the other.

In "Talking Back (To W. H. Auden)," William rejects Auden's idea (in his elegy for W. B. Yeats) that "poetry makes nothing happen." "What it makes happen is small things," his poem says. William's highest aspiration as a poet was always spiritual, but he was never solemn. He agreed with Frost that "all the fun's in how you say a thing." His most memorable poems enable us to see the most forgettable things newly and to be changed by what we've seen. In one of Tom Stoppard's plays, there's a sentence honoring the effort at speech that defined William's life: "If you get the right [words] in the right order, you can nudge the world a little or make a poem which children will speak for you when You're dead."

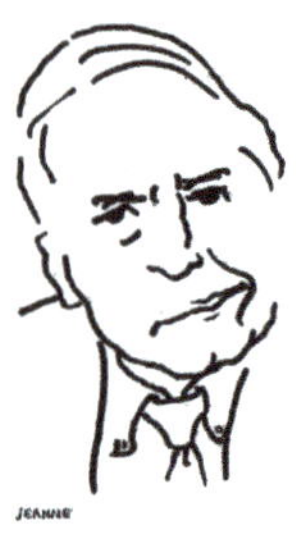

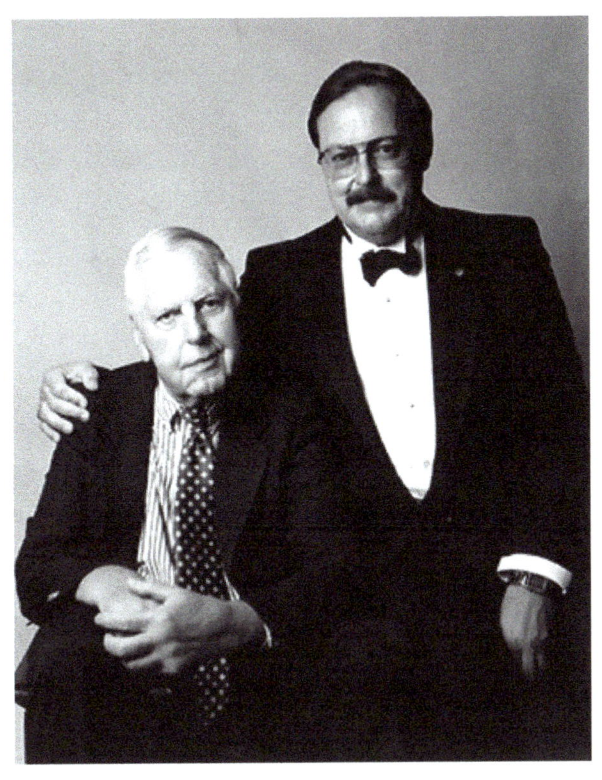

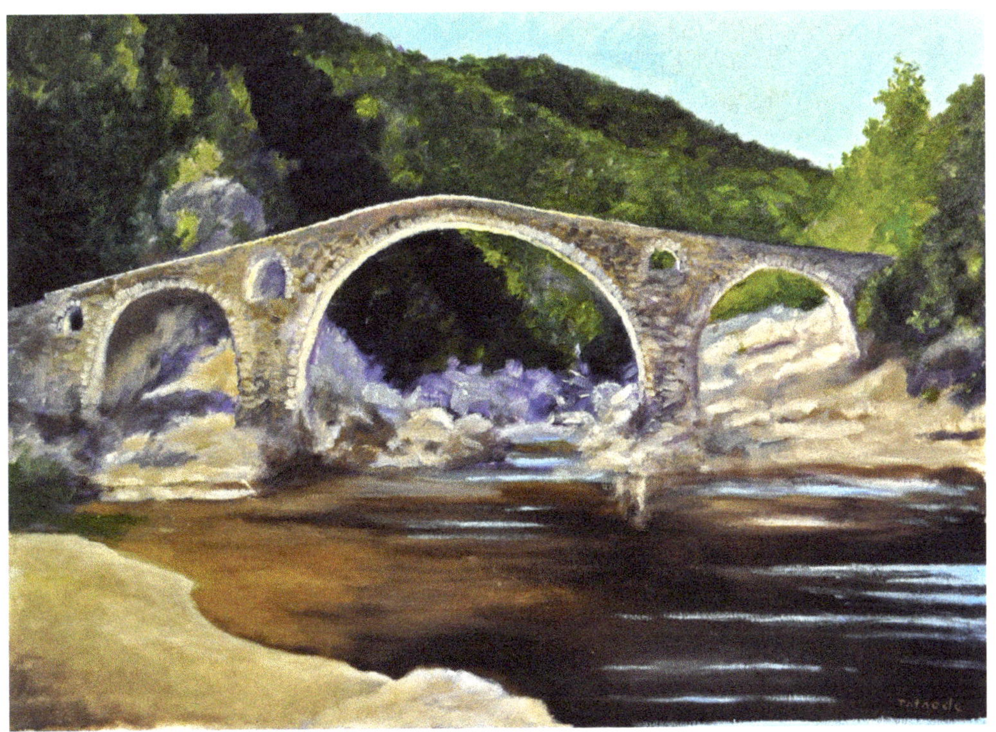

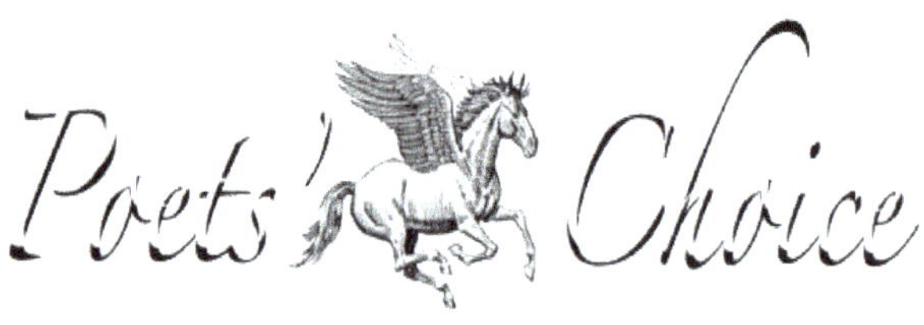

Poets' Choice Publishing
337 Kitemaug Road
Uncasville, Ct. 06382

MarathonFilm@gmail.com

www.Poets-Choice.com

www.ingramcontent.com/pod-product-compliance
Ingram Content Group UK Ltd.
Pitfield, Milton Keynes, MK11 3LW, UK
UKHW062000290726
14090UKWH00021B/1312